eCULT

eCULT

▼

A Sister's Memoir

Betty J. R. Chavez

Writer's Showcase
San Jose New York Lincoln Shanghai

eCULT
A Sister's Memoir

Writer's Showcase
an imprint of iUniverse.com, Inc.

For information address:
iUniverse.com, Inc.
5220 S 16th, Ste. 200
Lincoln, NE 68512
www.iuniverse.com

This memoir represents the author's perception and opinion of persons, characters,
places, and events. Although some names have been changed, the people and
events are real. The events and dialogue portrayed in this book are based on the
recollections of Betty J. R. Chavez and some of the people portrayed in this book.
Some scenes have been dramatically re-created, and in a few instances the sequence
of events has been compressed or slightly rearranged to enhance clarity.

ISBN: 0-595-17039-0

Printed in the United States of America

In loving memory of my father and sisters Carol, baby Nancy, and Jan . . .

This book is dedicated to my mother, the epitome of selfless giving, And my brothers Larry and Lenn . . . may our hearts always feel unconditional love.

PREFACE

▼

The Concerned Christians were perhaps one of the first alleged doomsday cults to sustain a cohesive bond through an electronic medium. Whether in Denver, Israel, Greece, or New York, the cult leader of the Concerned Christians effectively controlled 50 to 80 members of the "heavenly kingdom church" through email correspondence.

Possibly driven by self-serving greed or dementia, the Concerned Christian cult leader created a god with unreasonable demands that changed the victim's lives. Society accused the victims of being weak minded. Few people recognized the intelligent victims as strong willed individuals who acted on their commitment to live by their doctrine.

In the beginning, many of the unsuspecting victims only wanted to nurture their souls with the word of the Lord. Instead the cult leader threatened them with venomous words demanding faithful service and poisoned them into believing that the rest of the world was evil as he turned his victim's hearts and souls to stone, away from the world they once knew. The unsuspecting victims were deprogrammed from their happy and abundant lives, convinced that they had to prove that they did not worship their money, material possessions, and family members. The victim's lives mirrored the cult leader's idea of dutiful Christians. To prove their faith and love to the Lord they gave everything they owned to the Concerned Christian ministry.

Since my sister, Jan disappeared from Denver in October 1998, I have tried to reach her through email, the media, the United States Courts of Justice, and when given the opportunity…in person. My goal was to touch Jan's heart, mind, and soul and to persuade her to leave the cult. I wanted to stop Jan from destroying her life and breaking the hearts of everyone she left behind. Once Jan responded to my email messages, I was filled with the hope that I could somehow rescue Jan and her husband, John. But the Concerned Christians had another agenda. The Concerned Christian's apparent strategy was aimed at persuading me to join the cult and to use my assets to help perpetuate their faith.

Email correspondence with my sister and other members in the cult resulted in a cyberspace battle filled with threats, abuse, persecution, denial, and rejection. Even though the email exchange was distressing in many ways, I was thankful that email also provided an opportunity to tell Jan and John that I loved them and that their family wanted them both to come back home. Then, one email message dared me to show the Concerned Christians what was wrong with their theology. I started to document all the major events in both my sister's life and my life in an effort to compare our chosen paths. I attempted to find answers as to why Jan made the decision to leave everyone and the majority of her worldly possessions to join the Concerned Christians. I realized, that I didn't recognize the warning signs. If only I could have seen the clues and sought the help of professionals to intervene early enough to rescue Jan and John from the cult…then maybe both Jan and John would be with their families and fully enjoying the wonderful blessings that the good Lord gave them.

This story is a medium to try to reach Jan and John and to persuade them both to come back home and to let Jan and John know that their family and friends will always love them regardless of what happens. Our arms are open and ready to accept them when they return back into our lives. We love Jan and John unconditionally.

PART I

▼

CONCERNED CHRISTIANS VANISH

CHAPTER ONE

▼

ARVADA, COLORADO– OCTOBER 1998

She was visibly shaken. I watched the dear seventy-five year old woman hasten down the stairs after she was abruptly torn away from making krautburgers for supper. She clutched the handrail with dough covered hands as she hobbled frantically down the stairs by placing both feet on each stair before moving to the next. Her knees seemed to ache at each landing. Her disheveled white hair punctuated the questions on her mind. With antagonizing anticipation she finally reached the couch and slowly sat on the edge next to me. We both stared in disbelief as we watched the 6:00 Evening News. Tears swelled in the elderly woman's tired eyes and streamed down the crevices of her wrinkled face. I looked over at her and shook my head in disgust as I thought…she has had enough pain in her life, she didn't need this too.

I wanted to hold her to absorb her pain and to make everything perfect for her for the very first time in her life. But I too, felt weak and confused.

Unaccustomed to openly displaying affection, I managed to reach over and softly pat her left hand, "Oh Mom…I'm sure everything will be okay, it's probably a mistake."

I touched her crooked index finger, and remembered she had been denied the luxury of medical attention as a child, when her finger was nearly cut off while topping beets and was held together by a few tendons and a strip of skin. She worked in the fields to help her German immigrant mother and American father feed their family of thirteen.

Suddenly Mom gasped. The empty shell of an all too familiar Boulder, Colorado home filled the television screen. A home once rich with childhood laughter was now without a soul and stripped of life.

The film crew panned through each room like crime detectives recording the remains of the life of the affluent and now infamous. Walls were empty and precious artwork and family heirlooms were mysteriously missing. Ghostly shadows of valuable antiques and fine furnishings not visible to the unfamiliar eye were haunting the screen where they were once lovingly placed.

Something looked odd…*Red* carpet. In a day and age when most people were placing off-white, pastel, or earth tone colors in their homes, it seemed strange to see *red* carpet. Something in the back of my mind gnawed at me. Then I wondered if the *red* carpet was left behind, as an eerie cryptic message.

In my peripheral vision I could see Mom place her right hand over her heart. I turned and gave her my complete attention, as she closed her eyes tightly. Worried, I slowly moved my hand up to quietly check her pulse. "Are you okay, Mom?"

"Why? Why did she leave like this? She has a beautiful daughter. You know she wanted nothing more than to have that baby…we all love her…why?"

Not knowing what else I could say, I just whispered, "Mom, I don't know, I just don't know, but you can't take the blame. You've been a perfect mother."

She shook her head in dismay and said, "I'm so tired, Betty. We have so much sickness in the family, and now...now *this*."

My attention turned to the news and my quiet anger grew. I resented that our mother had to learn about Jan's disappearance in such a cold, inhuman manner. Ordinarily, authorities notify immediate family members before releasing devastating stories to the media. The stabbing message was delivered in my home, with cold excitement of a news-breaking story. Hundreds of innocent people's hearts broke as they learned the news of their loved ones disappearance through the media.

My mind filled with questions, as I tried to sort out the events of my sister's past. Could I have prevented Jan from joining the cult?

Ironically, I started to become angry because Jan didn't invite me to the mass exodus. Did Jan judge me as being unworthy of being a member of the Concerned Christians? By not including the rest of Jan's family, I wondered if the Concerned Christians intended on sentencing us all to Hell. Did the Concerned Christians determine that the remaining family and friends were unworthy of belonging to God's higher court?

My head filled with questions about the mass exodus and why fifty to eighty people would leave Denver, their loved-ones, homes, and jobs in the middle of the night. I wanted to answer some of these questions for my family and myself. There were too many broken hearts and too many promises of more heartache to come.

Mom stood up and wiped the tears from her eyes. "Betty, I'm going to bed. I have a pounding headache."

"Okay, Good-night, Mom, I hope you feel better. Let me know if I can do anything for you."

Mom slowly turned and said, "Good-night, Betty. Oh, there is something you can do for me, when the oven buzzer goes off, please take the krautburgers out of the oven. I just don't feel like staying up any longer."

I watched as Mom slowly walked up the stairs with drooped shoulders. Her head hung low as she painfully stepped up each stair. For a moment, Mom seemed older and frailer than ever before. Saddened by her pain, I sat in front of the flickering light of the television in the darkened room and searched for answers.

I knew that Jan's decision to leave Denver didn't happen overnight. In fact, the events leading to her disappearance took years…but how many years, I wondered. I began reliving the fleeting moments that I spent with Jan during the past forty years in hopes that I could understand Jan's disappearance. I wanted to gain knowledge to help convey what I learned to other distraught family members. Maybe I could find a hint of destiny in our childhood, a glimpse of our future hidden in our childhood laughter and pain. So I began a comfortable journey back to the past, to a time when Jan and I could be together again. I needed to see if I could put together the puzzle, to find the clues that would have pointed to Jan leaving and deserting her only daughter, her family, and a very comfortable life.

PART II

CHILDHOOD MEMORIES

CHAPTER TWO

▼

EVANS, COLORADO-1958

My earliest memory of Jan was in October 1958, when changing leaves created the distinctive colors of autumn and carving pumpkins was just an excuse to celebrate one of the four seasons that God gave us. Soon, it would be dark and the sparse-toothed pumpkins with illuminated smiles would sit on the porch of our small white clapboard house in Evans, Colorado.

It was difficult being five years old. Too young to go to school, I fought off boredom by practicing to write cursive by scribbling in a neat line on grown-up Red Chief tablets like the one that Jan used. But not today, I enjoyed music from the Big Bopper, Buddy Holly, and Patsy Cline. One by one I listened to each '33 and '45 record as I covered by big sisters, Carol and Jan's bedspread with albums and sang off key at the top of my voice. I contently waited for ten-year old Jan and seven-year old Larry to return home from elementary school so we could carve pumpkins.

In the kitchen, Mom scooped the stringy pulp out of the pumpkins to make German pumpkin and pepper pies. She was more interested in baking than carving pumpkins for Halloween, but Mom knew the importance of building memories with family tradition and had the three pumpkins lined up on the table with their scalped tops neatly in place.

"Its 3:45, Betty," Mom said loudly so that I could hear her above the records.

I scrambled off the tall bed and ran past mom, slamming the screen door behind me, I knew I had to hurry. I opened the door of the shed, climbed on my horse Blackie, and rushed to meet the big yellow bus. I arrived just in time to hear the bus brakes squeak to a stop. I watched the folding doors pop open and waited for Jan and Larry to hop out of the bus. As soon as Larry climbed down the stairs I slapped my backside and galloped up to him. I huffed between breaths, "Guess what? We're gonna make jack-o-lanterns!"

Larry looked at me in excitement and we both raced into the house. Minutes later, Jan walked in with schoolbooks cradled in her arms. "Come on Janet, let's make our pumpkins!" I shouted.

Jan smiled and put her books down to join Larry and I in carving faces in our pumpkins. "Know what I'm gonna be for Halloween?" I asked as I poked holes in a miniature pumpkin. "Cinderella! Mommy and I went shopping and I saw a mask at Woolworth's Five and Dime Store. The mask comes with a sparkly dress that slips over my head and ties in the back."

Larry and Jan ignored me as they continued to carve the eyes and nose of their pumpkins. Jan's carved a sweet toothless smile into her jack-o-lantern while Larry beamed as he knifed a frightful grin into his pumpkin.

After we finished carving our pumpkins, Jan helped Mom clean up the mess in the kitchen like Mommy's *little lady* always did. I could hear Mom as Larry and I ran outside. She praised Jan for being such a good helper. Thankful that Jan liked to help in the house, I preferred to be outside everyday playing with my brother. Larry and I placed the newly carved jack-o-lanterns on display at the edge of the porch and waited for Daddy to drive in the driveway to see the smiling faces of our artwork.

Mom opened the screen door and yelled, "Larry…Betty, come here a minute."

At the sound of the door slamming shut, Jan walked into the kitchen. Her hands were placed stiffly on her hips and her eyebrows furrowed, "I told you not to get into my records." Jan turned to Mom and said, "Betty has my records spread all over my bed. Does she have to mess up my room like that?"

"Oh Janet, Betty gets bored during the day. She isn't hurting anything." Mom shook her crooked finger at me, "Now Betty, you go pick up those records and when you're done we'll go see Carol at work."

"Okay," I pouted as I walked away. I liked to listen to the records because it made me feel like a big girl…like my sister, Carol. But, it saddened me that my fun made Jan mad. Anxious to see Carol, I haphazardly threw the records on the shelf and hurried back to the kitchen.

Mom smiled and said, "Are we ready? Let's get in the car. I'll buy you each a small root beer, hamburger, and fries. Daddy won't be home for a while and I have supper for him in the oven."

We arrived at the drive-in diner called the *Frost Top* and sat patiently until one of the carhops recognized Mom and nudged Carol to come out to our car to take our food order. I enjoyed watching our seventeen-year old sister, Carol in her new job. The local "Sweet Heart Queen" of Evans didn't seem to be aware of her beauty. Carol's blonde ponytail bounced and her change belt clinked as she walked up to our car and said, "Yes madam, may I take your order?"

Mom responded in her best business voice, "Yes miss, we would like four small root beers, four hamburgers, and four french-fries please."

"Will that be all, madam?"

"Yes, thank you."

In a short while, Carol returned with our food on a tray. "Mom, you need to roll up the window about three inches."

"Like this?" Mom asked.

"That's good," Carol said as she hooked the tray snugly on the window next to the driver's seat. "I'll be back later to pick up your tray."

I watched Carol in admiration as she went to the next car to take their order. "Someday, Mom, I want to be just like Carol."

"That's nice, Betty. Finish your hamburger so we can go back home and light the jack-o-lanterns!"

Mom left an extra quarter on the tray and told us she was giving Carol a tip. Carol came to the window to pick up the tray and smiled at Mom. "Thanks Mom, I'll see you in about an hour!"

Okay, be careful driving home." Mom said as she backed up the car.

When we got home, Jan, Larry, and I got out of the car and stood a few feet from the porch, to admire our masterpieces, while Mom walked into the house to get matches to light the candles in the pumpkins.

"Hey Betty, yours looks a little funny." Jan laughed.

"My name's Jackie." I scolded.

"Where's your horse, J-a-c-k-i-e? Larry joined in.

"Blackie's in the shed. That's where he lives," I said matter-of-factly.

Jan and Larry both laughed and sneered at me, "Why don't you go ride your horse, J-a-c-k-i-e?"

I didn't understand, I thought having a horse was the greatest thing in the world. When relatives came by our house for a visit, I couldn't wait to show them my horse. I gave Jan and Larry a puzzled look as they snorted with laughter.

Mom walked around the corner of the house with a flashlight in her hand. She stood and listened to our conversation. "Betty, I want to show you something, we need to go out to the shed."

I darted in front of Mom and opened the door and smiled with excitement. Mom caught up with me and stopped in front of the door of the shed and illuminated the interior of the shed with the flashlight. We both peered inside and then Mom pointed and said, "Betty, look in there, there's no horse."

My eyes widened in disbelief as I looked at Mom. She stared at me shaking her head no.

"There's no horse?" I asked.

"No, Betty, Blackie is not real, he's imaginary."

"Imaginary?" My bottom lip puffed out so far that I could see it. I turned and slowly walked back into the house with Mom. As I entered the kitchen door, Jan saw the expression on my face and snickered, "You're going to step on your lip, Betty."

Mom scolded, "Okay, we've had enough teasing. No more understand? Listen, I'm worried about your Daddy, he should be home by now."

By 8:30 in the evening, Daddy was still not home from work. Mom paced back and forth impatiently pausing to look out the window at the vacant driveway. Our young eyes watched as Mom sat down on the edge of a wooden chair then she walked over to the telephone and pleaded with her eyes for it to ring. Before long Mom was back sitting on the edge of the chair. She looked at us and apparently realized that her uneasiness was disturbing us and in an effort to explain, said, "Your Daddy's never this late. I just wish he would call."

Mom had a habit of folding her hands and making her thumbs go round and round, over and over. The more impatient Mom got, the faster her thumbs went, first one direction, then the next. She was staring out the window when the telephone rang. Mom ran to the telephone and picked up the receiver. Her face looked pale. Mom's voice cracked, "Hello?" We looked up at her trying to read her expression. We knew that something was wrong.

Mom gasped and said, "Okay, I'll be right there." She slammed down the telephone and with a wild look on her face, frantically searched the room. Mom regained her composure for a moment and picked up her purse. With an unsuccessful attempted to eliminate the alarm in her voice, she rapidly blurted out the words, "They-took-Daddy-to-the-hospital, don't-worry, I'm-leaving-to-go-see-him. He's-in-a-hospital-near-Fort-Morgan…and…and…I'm sorry-they-won't-let-children-visit. I'll-have-to-call-you-when-I-get-there." She grabbed her coat and ran out the door and with a louder sing-song voice said, "Carol will stay with you until I get back. Everything's going to be okay now, I'll call you soon."

By the time Mom reached the car, Jan, Larry, and I stood with our noses pressed against the picture window. We watched as Mom drove away. Our stair step nose prints remained as we slowly walked away in silence. We were worried about the disturbing telephone call. We just wanted our Daddy home.

We fell asleep waiting to hear about Daddy. It was hard to believe that our father was sick. I heard people comment on how healthy he looked. Daddy's strong six-foot-one, 200-pound frame, dark hair, and tanned skin were apparently deceiving. Daddy was not well; and to complicate matters, he smoked a pack of cigarettes a day.

Mom knew we were too young to understand that Daddy had a massive heart attack. Mom called the next morning and told us that Daddy had to stay in the hospital because of something called a massive heart attack. A few long weeks passed by and Daddy was still confined to his hospital bed. Restless, he told the nurse, "I want to go to the Greeley hospital, and I need to be close to my children."

The nurse stopped adjusting the heart monitor "I'm sorry sir, but the doctor has given us strict orders. We'll do everything that we can to make you comfortable right here."

"I have five children at home and they need their father."

"I understand sir, we'll have to talk to the doctor about it."

Mom said that eventually the doctor realized that Daddy needed to see his children before he could get well and allowed Jan, Larry, and I to visit him. I remember the three of us walking in the room and seeing my Daddy covered in sheets with a clear plastic tent over him. The sight of tubes coming from Daddy's arm and nose made me cringe. We didn't stay long before Mom ushered us out of the room to a solemn waiting room. I prayed to God that He would make Daddy well. Jan, Larry, and I were accustomed to praying to God in Sunday school and before we ate our meals or went to bed, but this was the first time that I remember praying to God when I really wanted Him to hear me.

Finally, Daddy arrived home from the hospital. Mom made his bed on the couch in the living room so Daddy could be with the family. Jan, Larry, and I were on our best behavior and thankful that we finally had our Daddy back. Each day we watched as he struggled to take one more step than the day before. Slowly Daddy got his strength back.

I heard Daddy tell Mom, "You know I'm living on borrowed time, that heart attack could have killed me. I'm worried about you and the kids. There's so much that the kids need to learn. I need to spend more time with Larry so that he can take care of the family."

"Don't talk like that. You're going to out live me, we'll just make sure you eat right…skim milk, no egg yolks, cut-out the fat…we'll keep you healthy, and we'll pray to God that you'll get stronger everyday…and stay strong."

For the next few weeks we all pitched in to help Daddy recover. I watched Jan perform small acts of kindness for Daddy to make him comfortable. Even at her young age, Jan's strong maternal instincts were undeniably present.

Daddy eventually gained his strength back and went back to work. Our lives adjusted to a healthier diet but there was a new sense of urgency that we learn to be more independent. The rest of us knew that we desperately needed to hone our praying skills and ask God to please take care of our Daddy. Many nights I fell asleep talking to God, pleading to Him to keep Daddy alive and well.

CHAPTER THREE

▼

QUALITY OF LIFE

Daddy always wanted to live on a farm. Worried that his dream may never be fulfilled, we moved from Evans to a small ten-acre farm outside Windsor, Colorado. By 1962 Carol was married and living on her own. The move was difficult for Jan and Larry. Both of them had established strong friendships at school. I was entering second grade and was anxious to meet new friends.

Daddy called me into the kitchen. I leaned on one of Daddy's knees as he asked, "Betty, what do you think about us getting you a horse? We're going to have room for a horse at the new house."

My eyes grew big as I said excitedly, "Really Daddy? Oh boy!"

"It's always been my dream to have a small farm where I can raise cattle, pigs, rabbits, and a few egg-laying chickens. If you want a horse to ride, we'll start looking for one."

A few months later, Daddy and Mom went to the auction and picked out my new horse. I remember seeing Mom and Daddy driving up the long driveway past the house and to the stable. I ran back to the barn to see my new horse and as I rounded the corner I abruptly stopped. This has to be a joke, I thought, Mom and Daddy were trying to trick me. I blurted, "That's not a horse! That's a donkey!"

"You can ride it like a horse," Mom said hoping to convince me.

"I don't want to ride a donkey."

Mom and Daddy tried hard to get me to like the donkey and tried demonstrating how much fun a person could have, by climbing on the mount and riding around the corral. I laughed hysterically at the sight of Mom riding the galloping donkey around the inside of the stable. As entertaining as it was to watch everybody acting like they were having fun, I refused to ride the donkey myself. The big animal scared me.

I walked back to the house and got an all too familiar reception. Jan and Larry relentlessly teased me about Blackie. Now that I had a "jack-ass" for a horse, Jan and Larry couldn't stop tormenting me about my beautiful "horse." Fortunately, their badgering was short-lived. Mom walked in the house and pulled Jan and Larry aside and told them not to mention the donkey again.

Within a month Daddy took the donkey back to the auction and came back home with an Indian pony named Paint. I said to myself, now that's a horse! I ran up to daddy and gave him a big hug. He reached in the back of the truck and surprised me with a beautiful black leather saddle and bridle, trimmed with silver studded rivets. My eyes filled with tears of joy. I had a real live horse and a beautiful saddle to call my own!

While I was outside riding my horse, Jan prepared to go to her first dance. She spent the day in curlers primping and polishing her manicured nails. By evening, I came into the house just in time to see Jan in all her splendor. Her blue eyes sparkled as she paraded in her new sequined red spaghetti strapped dress. The full-skirted dress, accented Jan's small waist as she spun around on her tiptoes in her red high heels. "Wow! Do you have two can-can's under that dress?"

"Actually three."

"That dress is pretty, Janet," I said wistfully as I sat on the floor.

Jan looked down at me and smiled, as we heard a knock on the door. Jan answered the door, a young boy with light brown hair stepped into our living room. He looked at Jan with admiring eyes and greeted the family by nodding his head repeatedly. Jan said, "Well, you ready to go?"

The boy nodded his head at Jan and they both turned to the family and said good-bye as they walked out the door.

For the first time I imagined myself in nylons and a party dress. I want a dress just like Jan's, I thought.

That night I missed Jan. I had nightmares. When Jan finally got home, I felt relieved to have her lying in bed next to me.

Summer break began the next week. The muddy waters of the irrigation ditch looked inviting in the hot afternoon. Larry and I agreed that we would disregard previous warnings about swimming in the ditch and decided to tell Mom and Daddy that we fell in the water, that way we could swim and we wouldn't get in trouble. We enjoyed the refreshing two-foot of water, until I suddenly saw a snake swimming downstream. I screamed as my feet slid on the muddy embankment in attempt to exit the water. My lack of traction in the muddy ooze narrowed the distance between the approaching snake and my bare feet. As I frantically scrambled through a treadmill of mud, the snake swam past me in the slow moving current.

"Gads, Larry!" I gasped, "That about gave me a heart attack! Let's look for another swimming place, one without snakes!"

"I know a great place to swim, free from critters, Betty. Follow me."

Larry showed me the new swimming place and I wanted to share the fun with Jan, so I ran as fast as I could into the house. With short breaths between each word I blurted out, "Hey Jan, we found a new place to swim, want to come and learn how to swim in the cow trough?"

"Are you crazy? I'm not swimming in that thing. There's cow cud and bugs floating around in there!"

"Yeah, but there are no snakes! It's really fun! I know how to do a face float, Jan. I can swim all the way to the other side."

"Great Betty, that's just great. And when you come up do you have anything on your face?"

"I don't think so. I just turn around and go back to the other side of the tank. If you want I'll show you."

"That's okay, I'm not interested. I don't like to stick my head under water anyway. You go have fun…go ahead…scoot!"

I ran out the door and up the hill to the barn just as Larry swam across the tank. "Larry, I don't think Jan wants to get her hair wet. I think she's afraid to go swimming. She's missing all the fun."

"Maybe…Jan never wants to have any fun, Betty. Come on, let's swim!"

When Larry and I finished swimming we both walked in to the house. I guess we didn't do an adequate job drying ourselves off. We tracked mud through the kitchen and by the time we got to the living room Jan screamed at us, "You guys get out of here, you're making a big mess! I just mopped the floor! Get out!"

"Oops," Larry and I stopped. We knew if we went any further there would be a terrible war. But we needed to change clothes. We stood there wondering what to do next.

In our old fashioned family, there was a definite distinction between women's work and men's work on the farm. The women of the house made beds and did the dishes while the men worked in the fields. I kind of straddled the fence and got to do both. The whole "women's work" routine was unsettling to both Jan and I and we developed an attitude about being our brother's servant. But today, I joined Larry and became part of the problem, still I empathized with Jan. I regretted making a mess on her clean floor.

Jan glared at Larry as he stood in the middle of the floor with a smirk on his face. "I can tell by the way you're standing there that you're not even sorry that you made that mess. Isn't that right?"

"Actually, you're right." He continued to walk toward his bedroom. "I'm not sorry. *You* Jan, may wash my dishes tonight, *woman*!"

"You're disgusting." Jan stormed over to the mop to wipe the mud off the floor." We laughed and imitated her as she chased us out of the house, but not before she dug her long sharply manicured fingernails into the meaty flesh of our upper arms.

By the time Mom arrived home, Jan was fuming. "Mom, Larry and Betty went swimming in the ditch today."

Mom turned and quickly faced Larry and I with a frown, "Didn't I tell you two not to swim in the ditch? Wait till your Daddy comes home!"

I dreaded when Daddy came home that night, I knew that we were going to get a whipping. I thought for a moment and it occurred to me that I didn't remember Jan ever getting a whipping. I knew what was in store for me. One swift lash with a belt and it was all over but the crying. When Daddy came home, I was the only one who got spanked that night. Larry had medical problems, so he didn't get punished.

When everything settled down again, Mom asked Jan, "Would your please curl Betty's hair for her, I want her to look nice for pictures tomorrow."

"Why can't Betty learn to curl her own hair? I used to curl my hair at her age."

"I know, Jan, she just doesn't know how. Would you just please curl Betty's hair for me? Do it for me, Jan, okay?"

Jan frowned and said, "Well, okay."

I looked at mom with dreaded anticipation. This was going to be a painful experience. I liked it so much better when Mom curled my hair.

"Betty, get me the curlers and come here and sit down."

I got all the hair supplies and cringed as I sat on the floor in front of Jan. I tried unsuccessfully to get Jan in a better mood. She dug the rat-tail comb into my scalp as she parted my hair. She quickly combed through the parted hair with a jerk and rolled the curler as tight as she could. The bobby pin pressed hard against my skin. I guess she was going to make it so unpleasant for me that I would eventually learn to curl my own hair. But, I didn't care if I ever learned how to curl my own hair.

Carol called and talked to Mom and asked her why I was making such a fuss. Within a week, Carol surprised me with a doll hair salon to encourage me to learn to curl hair as I played with the doll. Compassionate and wise, Carol's strategy worked and Jan and I moved on to other battles

Bedtime was the time to sleep with the enemy. The double sized bed that Jan and I slept in was the only bed in the house with an imaginary line drawn down the middle.

"You stay on your own side, and I mean it!" Jan warned.

I scooted to the edge of the bed and hugged the slightly raised side so that I wouldn't slide toward the middle of the bed.

Jan had me well trained. I only crossed the imaginary line on occasion, involuntarily. I always wondered if Jan got any sleep, she seemed to be in the combat ready position at all times. Any indication that I was moving toward "the line" Jan was ready with her trademark long fingernails in the claw position. There were too many nights that Jan dug her long fingernails into the flesh of my little butt cheek. I spent countless hours and many nights hugging the wall, afraid to fall asleep and of accidentally breaching our temporary truce.

Chapter Four

▼

The Sabbath

The next year I hardly rode my horse, Paint. At the end of the workweek, the family drove into the Rocky Mountains to work on our cabin. After Daddy's heart attack, it was impossible for Daddy to finish the cabin. Mom, Larry, and I helped lay stones for the foundation while Jan watched our little brother, Lenn. When Daddy finally realized that he needed to spend more quality-time with his family, he purchased a completed cabin with a dark rustic bark exterior.

I loved the new cabin. Jan and I had a room with a balcony overlooking the town of Red Feather Lakes. Hidden deep in the dark corners of a storage area in our room, Jan and I found a treasure of books left by the cabin's previous owners. Excited Jan and I reached into the cache and pulled each book out into the lighted room to read the titles and the antique copyright dates. There were many books about the old west, Central City, and Cripple Creek. We each selected our favorites and climbed into our big brass bed. I snuggled under the homemade quilt. Together, Jan and I read our books. It was the earliest memory that I had spending quality time with Jan. Her domestic girly nature and my tomboy energy rarely interacted. Finally, we were sharing something that we both enjoyed...reading. I accidentally touched her foot under the covers. I immediately flinched as I prepared myself to feel the pain caused by her claws. But Jan didn't pinch me, in fact she didn't do anything. Jan continued to enjoy her book. I smiled and thought how wonderful it was to finally have a sister for a friend.

The next day was Sunday. Since our weekends were spent either going to the cabin or working on the farm, we seldom went to Sunday school, besides we lived miles from church. The fact that our family did not attend church regularly seemed to bother Jan more than anyone else in our family. Jan rarely asked for anything, self-sufficient, Jan worked to earn money to buy anything that she wanted. Jan told me that money couldn't buy what she wanted. More than anything in the world, Jan wanted her whole family to go to church...every Sunday.

The following weekend we didn't go to the mountains so Jan asked Mom if we could all go to church. Mom said she didn't think Daddy would go. She said that although Daddy loved the Lord Jesus, Daddy didn't believe in organized religion. I listened and realized that I didn't remember Daddy ever going to church.

I ran outside into the alfalfa field. Larry and Daddy were sitting in the sun preparing to start the hay baler when I asked, "Daddy, will you go to church with us Sunday?"

Daddy continued to fiddle with the piece of farm equipment. "I have to take care of the alfalfa," Daddy stopped momentarily and said, "but I want you kids to go to Sunday school and learn about the Lord Jesus. Don't worry about me, I can talk to him right here in the field. I don't need anyone to talk to God for me, I can do it all by myself. God and I have a personal relationship. Besides, there are too many hypocrites in churches anyway."

I was relieved to hear that Daddy had a relationship with the Lord. I thought it was wonderful that Daddy could talk to the Lord in the most beautiful environment of all, a field nourished with rich soil, a field that fed animals that ultimately nourished us. A field that God created. I understood that Daddy was at peace with the Lord and I was happy as I turned to walk away, "Okay Daddy. We will all go to church and learn about Jesus. I will say a prayer for you too."

After Daddy told me that God was everywhere, I found myself thinking about God in the strangest places. God was in the barn when we watched Daddy take the cow udder and squirt the barn kittens in the mouth with fresh milk. God was on my horse with me. God was with me everywhere I went and I talked to Him anytime I wanted. I began to see the beauty in everything around me. I noticed that it was God that made everything beautiful. I was thankful that Daddy opened my eyes about how I viewed Jesus.

The following Sunday, Mom dropped Jan, Larry, and I off at Sunday school and then joined Grandma in church. When Sunday school was over, the preacher ordered the doors locked to teach the parents a lesson. There were too many parents dropping their children off at church and not attending church themselves. I remember sitting behind the large closed door and not understanding why I couldn't leave the building. Angry parents began beating on the door. When the door was finally opened several angry parents grabbed the arms of their children and walked briskly away from the church.

Mom was angry at the church. When we arrived at home, Mom and Daddy decided that we would never return to Grandma's church. It was a decision that probably disturbed Jan more than the rest of us and it would be years before Jan and I walked into another church together.

CHAPTER FIVE

▼

HOUSE BY THE DITCH

With the possibility of running out of valuable time, coupled by the growing demands of the farm, Daddy decided to sell the ten acre farm and purchase a smaller parcel of land so he could enjoy his family more and still reap the benefits of raising a few farm animals. After a careful search, Daddy found a small farm close to the hospital.

Daddy was a private man and made it clear to everyone that he didn't like people asking him personal questions. Nosey people were idiots, who didn't deserve the dignity of an answer when they asked personal questions. Unfortunately, our new neighbors across the ditch proved to have every character flaw known to man.

It was a warm day in early June 1965 and Daddy and I were outside. While he admired the new calf that he bought at the livestock auction, I swept the dirt floor of the clubhouse. I heard our neighbor, Mr. Weiden yell something over the ditch. I peeked outside the window and listened to the conversation. It was apparent that Mr. Weiden obviously noticed the auction tag on the new calf's ear. "Hey! You didn't actually pay for that calf, did you? You were robbed!"

Daddy took his foot off the bottom fence rail and turned around in a snap, "Are you talking to me?"

Mr. Weiden yelled again across the ditch, "They should have paid you to take that scrawny little calf."

Daddy narrowed his pointed eyes in anger and shook his head in disgust. He started to walk to the house, "I really don't think what I buy and what I do, is any of your business."

Mr. Weiden put his hands on his hips and cocked back his head as he boasted, "Well, you know, I have horses. I have enough money to buy my beef from the grocery store, I don't have to buy livestock to eat."

Without saying another word to him, Daddy continued walking. As he passed by the clubhouse he motioned for me to follow him. Worried and confused, I hurried and walked along next to Daddy taking two steps to his one.

Mr. Weiden's voice was filled with rage and sarcasm as he bellowed, "Hey! I'm talking to you!"

Mr. Weiden's thirty-five year old daughter, Virginia stepped out of the house and noticed the conflict. She walked over to the edge of the ditch and stuck her tongue out at Daddy as he neared the house.

We reached the house and Daddy told me to go play in the living room. Daddy sat at the kitchen table and told mom that he was going to put up a privacy fence, so we wouldn't have to look at the neighbors anymore.

By the end of the month, Daddy started to build the fence on our side of the ditch. Tragedy struck the family that day, as we learned that my aunt committed suicide. Daddy was noticeably disturbed about her death as he worked on the fence. Daddy put up about twelve feet of fence when Virginia came out of the house. She walked to the edge of the ditch and bent down, grabbing a couple of rocks and threw them in the water close enough to splash Daddy.

Daddy kept working and ignored Virginia the best he could, under the circumstances, knowing the only way to stop the harassment, was to have the fence up as a barrier between them. Virginia seemed determined to irritate Daddy, I watched as the grown woman placed her hands on her large hips and distorted her face into some immature contortions and screamed obscenities at him. Determined to give his family sanctuary from the dysfunctional family next door, he kept working on the fence.

Jan, Larry, and I overheard Daddy talking to Mom at the dinner table that night. We could hear the stress in Daddy's voice as he relived the anguish he experienced earlier that day. Jan, Larry, Lenn, and I sat in the front room quietly, worried that any outburst of emotion from us would add to Daddy's anxiety.

That night I crawled into bed next to Jan, my face wet with tears. Daddy's words played over and over in my head like a distress signal…I had a strong feeling of impending doom and terrified that Daddy was going to die. I turned facing the wall and prayed to the Lord to watch over Daddy and keep him safe. I found comfort talking to the Lord and ended up praying until early in the morning, sleep wasn't important to me. All I knew was that I needed to pray and the Lord needed to hear me.

CHAPTER SIX

▼

INDEPENDENCE DAY-1965

It was that time of year again. I looked forward to a full week of fun beginning with the Greeley Independence Day parade, rodeo and carnival and ending with my birthday party on the ninth of July. Today we were going to go to the Parade and then to the carnival filled with excitement in the air.

I wanted to get ready to go to the Parade but I couldn't, I had to wait. I watched as Jan left in her red and white '56 Ford. Finally, I could dabble in Jan's face paint. As an amateur makeup artist, I couldn't draw a straight line and thought that bright pink cheeks looked healthy. Jan hated when I got into her makeup and she didn't mind letting me know. But it was safe, Jan was gone for the day.

I didn't notice Jan's car pull back into the driveway.

Jan burst into our room unexpectedly. Startled, the frosted pink lipstick slid across my jaw as I jumped at the sound of a screeching voice, "Mom! Betty's into my make up again! Would you tell her to stop?"

"Betty, stop getting into Jan's makeup," Mom said in a monotone voice.

"Okay Mom." I said as I turned and snarled at Jan.

I washed the lipstick off my jaw while Jan tucked her makeup neatly in their designated places. Like many sixteen-year old girls, appearance was everything and she worked hard to pay for her car and clothes. As soon as Jan straightened up the dresser, she grabbed her forgotten billfold and ran out the door and into her car anxious to meet her boyfriend Derry.

When we returned from the Independence Day Parade, the telephone rang, I heard Mom thank Carol before she hung up the telephone. "Betty, Carol offered to take you, Larry, and Lennie to the carnival tonight. Daddy and I would rather not go. We'll just relax at home. Better get ready, Carol will be her in a few minutes."

Larry, Lennie, and I hurried around the house and waited patiently on the front porch with our allowance in hand until Carol came. We saved our allowance to spend on arcade games, cotton candy, sno-cones, and carnival rides. "I can't wait to throw darts at the balloons. I never had a stuffed animal and I'm going to win one this year, Larry."

"If I win, I'll give a stuffed animal to you, Betty."

"That would be neat!"

Carol always spoiled us by taking us places that we wouldn't normally go and treating us with snacks that we rarely had at home. Carol and her family pulled in the driveway and motioned for us to hurry into the car.

When we arrived at the carnival, Larry and I ran up to the dart-throwing booth. I tried three times but the balloons moved every time the dart rubbed by them. Then I heard someone in the booth next to me win a stuffed animal by throwing a ball at bottles. "Heck Larry, bottles don't move like balloons, I can knock those bottles down."

I paid my money and threw three balls at the bottles positioned like bowling pins on the shelf. I totally missed the bottles with my first two throws. On the last throw, I hit the bottles, but they didn't fall. "Hey, what are those bottles made of? Let's go Larry." Frustrated with the arcade games, Larry and I walked over to see what Carol was doing.

Carol and Jack let us ride the adult rides while they were busy with the five children in Kiddy Land. Lennie was having a great time with Carol,

Jack, and their four children. Carol's oldest son was particularly excited since his birthday was the next day.

Larry and I gravitated to one of our favorite rides called the Octopus. We anxiously took our place in line. Our smiles widened as we watched the people on the ride laughing and screaming at each rapid turn.

"You are stupid little kids." A voice from behind us growled.

Larry and I turned around to see who was speaking. It was our dreadful neighbor, Virginia and two other hefty females. Larry and I looked at them in amazement. We had never encountered anyone like them. Our mouths dropped as we observed three crazy women sticking their tongues out of their mouths like imbeciles and taunting us by saying childish remarks.

Larry told them, "Leave us alone!"

The youngest of the three suddenly immerged from behind and slapped Larry across the face then quickly darted behind Virginia.

Virginia laughed as she turned to walk away. "You're both little creeps," Virginia said in between her snorts of laughter. After the youngest woman was safely by her mother's side, they looked back with a smug look on their faces, then disappeared into the crowd.

I could tell that Larry was really fighting the urge to get even but he was taught to never hit girls. He was in a no-win situation. The girl that slapped Larry was at least five years older then me and I wasn't aggressive enough to take matters into my own hands. Larry and I were left with our anger building but managed to restrain our tempers. We heard the three of them cackling in the distance. Stunned, we stood in line speechless for a few minutes. Finally, I broke the silence, "Can you believe that? Those people are crazy! They are imbeciles!"

Larry shuffled his feet, still fuming mad, "They're lucky I didn't beat the heck out of that ugly beast! If she wasn't a girl…how are you supposed to respect something like that?"

All Larry and I could think about was revenge. We lost our desire to ride any more rides and just wanted to go home.

"You can't. Let's forget about this ride and tell Carol and Jack that Virginia is harassing us."

CHAPTER SEVEN

▼

UNLUCKY 5%

Losing a parent is difficult at any age. I once heard that 5% of the American population loses a parent while under the age of 20 years old. Now my family had this unfortunate distinction. I wished that I could have appreciated the years that I spent with both parents. We had a model family, one that could be compared to the popular television sitcoms of the 60's. At least we had the opportunity to experience a wonderful family life, even though it ended prematurely. At eleven years old I realized how short life really was and how foolish it was to waste time on unimportant matters.

The day Daddy died, July 5, 1965, we were on the grass in front of our house enjoying the beautiful sunny day. In the distance a woman was riding down the road on a horse. As she rode closer to the house we all realized it was Virginia. She stopped directly in front of our house. Cackling with delight, she said, "How did you like your son getting slapped in the face last night?"

I watched as Daddy stood up from his lawn chair and said, "That girl had no right hitting my son."

The words no sooner left his mouth when four angry men carrying rocks and sticks in their hands appeared at the end of our driveway taunting Daddy and demanding that he come and fight them. Daddy walked to the edge of the lawn and said, "I have a weak heart, I'm not interested in fighting. Leave my yard now."

In a tone that was meant to impress his visiting relatives, Mr. Weiden yelled, "Well, I have a bad heart too and I can still fight. You're just a coward, a yellow bellied chicken."

Daddy turned and slowly walked into the house as Mr. Weiden continued to verbally reduce his manhood, "Come on coward, you chicken shit, come on and fight like a man!"

Mom was scurrying around trying to gather all of us into the house. Once safely in the house, she slammed the front door and locked it. Scared and breathing heavily, I watched as Mom nervously fumbled around the telephone to find a pen. With her hands shaking Mom dialed the local police while searching for a random piece of paper from the desk. She gave the police dispatcher our address and Mr. Weiden's address. The police said that they would be right over to get a full report.

Daddy appeared calm as he slowly walked in his bedroom and came back out wearing a fresh shirt. He walked up and gave us each an all too rare hug. All my fears that I prayed wouldn't come to pass surfaced. When I realized that Daddy was leaving to go to the hospital, my own chest hurt with a heavy pain. Daddy turned to Jan and said, "Mom's going to have to wait for the police, and I need you to take me to the emergency room, get the keys to your car." Jan ran to her bedroom without saying a word. She quickly grabbed her keys. I watched as they walked out the door, entered the car, and sped out the driveway toward the hospital.

The room was silent as we waited for the police to arrive. Our pain was just beginning. When the police arrived they went to Mr. Weiden's house first. We waited. Finally, the police came to our house and listened to the story. The policemen shook their heads and said, "I'm sorry, your neighbors haven't broken any laws. There is nothing we can do about the harassment.

All we can do is fill out this report and if it continues, then we can possibly do something about it. But, we don't have enough to go on right now."

When Jan and Daddy arrived at the hospital, Jan waited while Daddy was admitted in the emergency room. I remember Jan telling Carol what happened. Daddy was in the next room but Jan could still hear what was going on. Jan said that she could hear Daddy's pleading with the nurse to give him an electrocardiogram. His pleadings turned into screams, "Give me an electrocardiogram! I have a bad heart. I need an electrocardiogram now! Don't make me wait! Check my heart! Where's the doctor anyway?"

A female voice said half laughing, "Oh, you don't need an electrocardiogram, your fine, just relax and sit down, we'll be with you in a minute."

The next thing Jan heard was the loud crash as if a cart had tipped over. And in a split second she heard another man's voice yelling, "We need a doctor quick, get this man a doctor, he's having a heart attack!"

There was a lot of shuffling of feet, moving of equipment and furniture and then someone yelled, "Stand back! Oh no! His heart is in fibrillation! What are his vitals? We have to open him up, **now!**"

The emergency room came alive. Mom arrived at the hospital and immediately ran into the emergency room just in time to see them make the incision from his chest to his naval. She watched blood splatter all over Daddy's clothes and around his body. With his clothes intact, they opened Daddy's chest up and manually massaged his heart.

But it was too late. There was nothing more they could do.

Daddy was gone.

Mom was in shock and said that she couldn't remember driving home. I often wondered if Jan felt the same devastation, I wondered if Jan saw Daddy die.

Carol came over to the house as soon as she heard the news. She was celebrating her son's birthday and was unaware of the problem at home. Jan asked Carol to come into our bedroom so Jan could talk to her. I was lying face down on the bed smothering my tears with my pillow when I overheard

Jan say, "I think the nurse in the emergency room was Mr. Weiden's relative. You know who I'm talking about, the neighbor, Mr. Weiden. The nurse laughed at Daddy when he asked for an electrocardiogram."

Carol said, "There is already too much turmoil and anger surrounding this incident, don't ever mention anything about the nurse again."

About a week later, I asked Jan whether the nurse was related to Mr. Weiden. Jan refused to talk about it. For years, I've played the day that Daddy died in my mind over and over in my mind. I wondered if the nurse was mocking Daddy or if the nurse was making an ill attempt to calm Daddy down. I wondered if Jan knew that Larry and I would revenge our father's tormentors, if we knew the real truth.

Chapter Eight

▼

One Mans Grief, Another Mans Party

July 8, 1965 was the day of Daddy's funeral and a day before my twelfth birthday. Mom was getting seven-year old Lennie ready for the funeral when Lennie pleaded, "Mommy, do I have to go?"

Mom stopped adjusting Lennie's suit jacket and touched his little face, "No, honey you don't have to go if you don't want to. You can stay at the babysitters with Carol's children."

I didn't remember the trip to the funeral parlor. In a zombie like trance, I walked through the special entrance and toward the five rows of padded chairs behind the curtain. The sobbing and sniffling of the people in the adjacent area permeated the room. I mimicked the motions of my brother and sisters as my mind tried to erase the reason why I was sitting in the room filled with sadness. I sat down in the front row, the tears swelled in my eyes as I bowed my head and prayed. I prayed that someone would wake me up and tell me that I was having a terrible nightmare.

I opened my eyes and saw Mom's brother, Uncle Richard sitting next to Mom with his arm around her. It was less than three weeks since Uncle Richard attended his wife's funeral. Together Mom and Uncle Richard held hands and tried to comfort each other. I felt another wave of sadness with the thought that both of their life mates were gone, forever.

For a moment, I felt each one of my brothers and sister's pain. I loved them and I didn't want them to feel the pain that I was feeling, I knew that their hearts were shattered like mine and there was nothing anyone could do. We sat and listened to the eulogy and feeling the worse pain of our lives.

After the words stopped, I panicked. I was afraid as I watched the rows of guests empty systematically. I watched the guests walked up to the casket, some paused, some of the guests walked quickly by the casket, barely looking inside. As the last row paid their respects, a man at the end of the pew bent down sympathetically and motioned for us to stand. My heart raced as my rapid breathing choked me. I stood up with Jan, Larry, Carol, and Jack. I felt a hand on my arm as Uncle Richard lovingly guided me toward the satin lining. My feet were moving forward but my mind was telling me to go the other way. As I got closer to the casket I could see him. I felt strange, I really didn't know what I was expecting but I didn't expect to see my Daddy lying in the coffin. *My* Daddy always had a tan from working outdoors. But the man lying in the casket was gray and puffy. The truth was undeniable and I was frightened. Daddy was really *dead*. My Uncle Richard grabbed my hand and gently guided it towards my father's body so that I could touch my Daddy for the last time. I screamed and jerked back my hand and ran out of the church crying uncontrollably. Daddy was really dead.

Outside, I found myself standing in an unfamiliar crowd of relatives and friends. I felt a warm hand on my shoulder and as I turned to see my Uncle Elmer standing by my side I turned toward him and buried my face into his shoulder and cried. Uncle Elmer walked me over to the long black limousine and I quietly climb in behind Jan and Larry.

I sat in the middle of the leathery seat and silently reminisced about Daddy. Then, I remembered that Daddy could fix anything, from tractors to broken hearts. I tried to think of happier times. But the happier times made me sad too. There would be no more happy times with Daddy. I would miss him sitting at the table in his sleeveless undershirt with his tan well defined muscles bulging…making me laugh as I watch his biceps dance. Those were good memories, I thought, I need to hang on to the good memories.

We arrived at the gravesite, Mom, Carol, Jan, Larry, and I again sat in the front row facing the casket. Daddy's eternal bed was now closed forever and I realized that I wanted to touch him one more time, but it was too late. I wished I could talk to Daddy but he couldn't hear me, so I silently prayed and asked God to tell Daddy that I love him and that I will miss him very much.

The gravesite minister said words that I didn't hear. I stared at the flowers on top of the coffin as people at the gravesite filed in front of us like they did in front of Daddy's casket. With sad expressions, they bent down and touched my hand and whispered unintelligible words. I watched their mouths move and heads nod in affirmation of their compassionate feelings. As the line in front of me dispersed, a strange, loud voice broke the gentle hum of the crowd, inviting the despondent friends and family to a memorial potluck held at our Greeley home.

The limousine drove past Mr. Weiden's house and we noticed that Mr. Weiden and Virginia were having a party on their front lawn. As I stepped out of the limousine, I heard several people at our neighbor's house shout and laugh, proclaiming victory over our misfortune. I didn't understand how anyone could be so insensitive, so cruel. Our guests realized the pain that the neighbors were causing our grieving family, and tried to distract us and to keep our mind off the antagonists. Still, we heard an occasional cheer.

Jan, Larry, and I walked into the house to join some of the elderly relatives who traveled from distant places to show their respect for Daddy. I walked over to the desk and leaned against the chair just as the telephone rang. I quickly turned around and picked up the receiver. The room hushed and everyone's eyes were on me as I said, "Hello?" Stupefied, I listened with tears streaming down my cheeks as I held the telephone to my ear.

Alarmed and angry, Mom grabbed the telephone from me and listened. She heard a dial tone. "Who was it? What did they say?"

"I don't know who it was." I choked on the words, "They asked for Daddy…they ask for him by his full name and then they starting laughing."

"I can't believe it," Mom said disgustedly. "I don't want any of you kids answering the telephone again. You let me or your uncles answer the phone, you hear?"

I said weeping, "Okay."

The same telephone prank was played off and on over the next week. Uncle Richard stayed with us for a while to try to protect us from suffering needless pain at the hands of the heartless neighbors.

CHAPTER NINE

▼

FAMILY BOND

Jan's focus on the family changed and she offered to do more things with me. Three weeks after Daddy died Jan said, "Hey Betty, do you want to go to the drive-in movies with me and my boyfriend on Saturday?"

"Yeah sure. That would be fun!"

When we arrived at the movies Jan and Derry took me in the snack bar and told me that I could have anything I wanted, "Don't worry, Betty, I'm buying," Jan reassured me.

I've never been told that I could buy anything and everything I wanted before at a snack bar. I walked out of the concession stand with a big smile on my face. Jan watched me struggle with my loot as I carried the largest size tub of buttered popcorn, a large coke, large bag of plain M&Ms, and taffy. She laughed as me and said, "There you go Betty, you are in hog heaven now!"

I enjoyed the movie and stuffed my face until I thought that I was going to burst. When I got home I didn't feel well. My stomach hurt so bad I thought that I was going to die. I hated to wake up Mom…but I had to. I quietly stood outside her bedroom and said, "Mom, I don't feel good."

"What's wrong with you, Betty?"

"I've got a really bad stomach ache. It hurts so bad Mom, I can hardly stand up straight."

"Oh Betty, you're probably just going to start your period. It's something that all women have to go through once a month. Just lay down and try to get some sleep."

"Oh great!" I said as I walked back to the couch bent over clutching my side. I layed down on the couch and tried to sleep but the pain was excruciating. I curled a pillow around my belly to minimize the pain and softly prayed to God out loud. "Dear Jesus, I don't think I can take this pain every month, please help the pain go away."

It seemed like an eternity but finally daybreak came. The torturing pain had long gotten the best of me. Mom came in the front room and touched my forehead. "You still feeling bad?"

I looked up with tears in my eyes, "Yeah Mom, my stomach hurts so bad."

"Well, that doesn't sound right, there must be something else wrong with you. We better take you into the doctor."

Mom called the doctor's office and hung up the telephone. "The doctor wants us to come in right a way."

I didn't bother changing clothes. When we arrived at the doctor's office we were immediately sent to the examination room. The nurse watched as the doctor pressed lightly on my stomach until he located the area that made me scream the loudest.

In childhood innocence I blurted, "I hate doctors."

The doctor paused a moment and looked at Mom in surprise. "Umm, I'm afraid that we are going to have to admit her in the hospital right a way. Your daughter is suffering from an acute appendicitis attack. We can't wait, we'll have to do an emergency appendectomy as soon as possible."

The doctor turned towards me and patted my hand and said, "We'll take your appendix out and you'll be as good as new. You won't feel a thing. The nurse will get you ready for surgery."

The nurse smiled and introduced herself quickly as she started to poke and prod my body as if I was an alien. My eyes pleaded to Mom to save me from becoming the next medical experimentation casualty. "Oh Momma! That hurts!" I cried as the nurse inserted the catheter.

Finally, it was over…I thought…I watched as the nurse walked around my bed and picked up my right hand and started probing in the bend of my elbow. "I'm going to have to start an IV in your arm here, you're just going to feel a little prick of a needle."

Just as the needle broke my skin, it occurred to me that I shouldn't have told the doctor that I hated doctors. Mom sympathetically touched my hand and reassured me that everything would be fine. The last thing I remembered was talking to God, as the room became hazy and the edges of my view fuzzy…

After surgery, I woke up and to see a big stuffed tiger sitting next to me on my food tray. The tiger had a ribbon around its neck and a card that read, "*To a sweet sister, get well real soon. Love Janet and Derry.*" Pain free, I was so happy to finally have a stuffed animal to call my own and even happier about my relationship with Jan. As I lay on the hospital bed in drug-induced ecstasy, I realized that life at that very moment was wonderful. I felt Jan's loving kindness and I realized how much I always wanted Jan and I to have a good relationship. I smiled. Our sibling barriers were gone.

Days went by before I was allowed to go home from the hospital. When I returned home, the house had a coldness that I couldn't explain. The house wasn't home anymore. Our family routine had changed, and I was in denial about Daddy's death. Every day at 5:00, I would look out the window and expect to see a big black GM pickup pull into driveway. Everyday, the disappointment renewed itself. Mom worked with a realtor to sell the house and remove us from the horrible neighbors and the terrible memories. Mom watched as I slowly sank into a deep depression.

Mom decided it would help if I got away for a while, so she sent me to visit my cousin Rene in South Dakota for the remainder of the summer. I found comfort through prayer and the distance from the recent turmoil at home helped my heart heal.

I often wondered how my brothers and sisters were able to overcome their grief after Daddy died. I wondered how Mom, Jan, Larry, and Lenn were able to live in that house and with the terrible memories of the last days. It was a struggle that each of us had to deal with…alone. As for myself, I was thankful that Mom had the foresight to send me away.

When I returned from South Dakota, Mom had sold the home and purchased a home in town.

Chapter Ten

▼

"When it's Gone, it's Gone!"

When it's gone, it's gone" was Mom's way of saying that there is *no more and to enjoy it while you have it.* It applied to many things but especially *time.*

Mom married a man named Luke the summer of 1968. We readily accepted Luke because he was Daddy's friend during World War II. Mom, Lenn and I moved to Boulder, Colorado to live with Luke and his youngest daughter, leaving Larry in Greeley to live with relatives to finish high school.

Jan was working for a large insurance company. She was detail oriented and organized and had no problem advancing in her new job. Jan became increasingly independent and adventurous and eventually transferred to California. I guess Jan missed us as much as we missed her. The physical distance separating Jan and the rest of the family brought us closer together and hugs became a regular routine when we saw each other. It was nonexistent before.

I became aware of Jan's giving heart the first year that we lived in Boulder. The only person I knew my age in Boulder was my step-cousin

Gail. It was nice to know someone that was tall like me. Gail was a beautiful brunette who appeared to have everything. I was impressed when I met Gail, she told me that she was a cheerleader at Baseline Junior High School. I was anxious to see her cheerleading uniform but Gail always said that her uniform was at the cleaners.

One day Gail walked over to my house as said, "Hey Betty, you want to go with me to a modeling job? You can help me get my clothes ready for the next shoot. I would really appreciate it if you could help me. I'm so busy between "takes" that I have a tough time, you know, with my hair and makeup and looking "together."

"Wow Gail, You're kidding! That would really be fun! I always wanted to model. I would love to have an opportunity to see what goes on behind the scenes."

Gail theatrically placed her hand on her cheek and sighed in dismay, "But we don't have a ride, do you think your mom can take us?"

"We can ask her. Let me go and see."

I walked quickly into the garden and stood by Mom as she moved the irrigation hose. "Mom, can you take Gail and I to the *Hill* in Boulder? Gail has a modeling job and she asked me if I wanted to help her."

For years, Mom told me that she wished that she could send me to modeling school, but classes were too expensive. Seeing an economical way to satisfy me, Mom quickly responded, "Okay Betty, just give me a few minutes."

Gail and I climbed in the car and waited for mom. Mom walked into the house and washed her hands and grabbed her purse. We pulled out of the driveway and Mom asked, "Gail, so where is it you need to go?"

"Well, we need to go to the *Hill,* just west of most of the university buildings."

Mom drove to the Colorado University campus. "Well," Mom said, "where do you need to go from here?"

Gail pointed to one of the shops, "Oh this is good, just let us out here."

Gail and I slid out of the car. I leaned through the passenger side window and said, "We'll call you after we're done Mom. Thank you for taking us."

Gail bent down and peeked through the window next to me, "It should only take us a couple of hours. We'll be done about 4:30."

We turned and walked down the sidewalk as Mom drove off. Twenty minutes later, it occurred to me that we were aimlessly walking up and down the sidewalk. "Well? Where's your modeling job?"

"Gee, I can't seem to find it. Let's just sit here on the park bench for a while."

Moments after Gail and I climbed on the backrest of the park bench with our feet resting on the bench seat, a convertible with four young college guys screeched to a stop in front of us. One of the guys yelled over to us, "Hey cuties, you mind if we take your picture? It's for the campus newspaper?"

"Go ahead." Gail responded as she flashed a bright white smile.

After taking the picture the guys yelled, "Thanks!" and sped away.

"That was weird," I said, "Oh look, it's almost four o'clock. We better call Mom."

We walked over to the pay phone on the corner, "Mom, do you want to come and get us now? We are at the park across the street from where you dropped us off."

"I'll be right there, Betty."

A short time later, Mom pulled up in her car, "Did you guys have fun?"

Trying not to show my disappointment, I said, "Yeah, it was fun, Mom."

On the way home I didn't say much. I was thankful that Mom didn't quiz us any further. I didn't understand why Gail arranged such a stupid outing but I was glad it was over. As we pulled into the driveway Gail said, "Hey, I've got to go home so I can't stay. Thank you for the ride."

After Gail left, I told Mom that we never found the modeling job. Mom looked at me in surprise and then slowly shook her head as if to say, "Humph, so that's the way Gail is."

CHAPTER ELEVEN

▼

HERE! TAKE THESE!

It was September 1968 and I avoided thinking about the incident on the *Hill*. School was starting in three weeks and Mom and I combed through the Boulder stores to find just the right school clothes. I walked out of each shop disappointed, unable to find fashionable clothes to accommodate my 5'10" frame. It was hard being a tall fifteen-year-old during a time when fashionable bell-bottom pants swept the dirt behind Jesus sandals. All the pants that I tried on looked like they were pre-shrunk. Even the long sleeved blouses fastened two inches above my wrist. Fashionable short skirts were shorter on me than the average sized girl and made me look like a spectacle to conservative parents. My enthusiasm for new school clothes soon turned to frustration as I finally settled with five short, but cute, dresses.

Within a week, Gail came over to see my new clothes. Gail had an eye for identifying gullible people and I must have radiated a distinct aura of naiveté. One week before school, Gail came over to my house to borrow clothes for a modeling job. I opened up my closet and told her she could use anything she wanted. She pulled each article out of the closet, examined them, and selected her favorites and promised that she would return them right away.

One week passed by and Gail had not returned my clothes. School was starting on Monday. I walked over to Gail's house and knocked on the door.

Her mom answered the door and said, "Gail isn't home."

"That's okay, I just came by to pick up the clothes that Gail borrowed from me."

"Gail got those clothes for babysitting." Gail's mom shook her head, "You can't have them. Gail said she got those clothes for babysitting."

"What? No, Gail borrowed those clothes from me. Gail has a little white dress with navy piping, a short navy dress that buttons in the back, some navy culottes, a red shell sweater and skirt set, a green jumper and a white long sleeved turtleneck sweater…. They're my new school clothes."

Gail's mom continued to shake her head and looked at her watch. "No, Gail told me that she got those clothes for babysitting. I'm cooking supper right now and I have to go before our supper burns on the stove."

"Oh, okay." I slowly walked back home afraid to tell mom how stupid I was to loan Gail anything after the whole modeling fiasco. I needed to get creative. Besides, I was going to a new school, no one would know that the clothes I wore were last year's school clothes.

On Monday, Gail didn't waste any time telling everyone in school that she and I modeled together on the *Hill* in Boulder. Half the school was under the impression that Gail and I were professional models before I realized what was going on. Embarrassed to be part of a lie, I tried to repair the damage but it was too late.

I was still without school clothes. I called Jan in Los Angeles and told her what happened. Although Jan was shorter than I was, we wore the same size clothes. Jan had a plethora of "hip" clothes and she quickly offered to send me half of her wardrobe and promised to exchange them with other clothes every month. I was happy that Jan understood how important clothes were to a young high school girl.

Within a week, Jan sent me the first suitcase of clothes. I walked proudly through the halls in school. I was rarely seen in the same clothes twice. Each day was a reminder of how giving my sister Jan was. I missed seeing her and thanked God for her kind heart. My senior year school clothes budget was spent on a variety of red and black cheerleading uniforms. We continued exchanging clothes for the next two years.

Jan took an active role in my life. I wished that my family could come to watch me cheer at one of the games, but we lived several miles away in a neighboring town and unfortunately, there were much bigger problems in our home. In spite of the miles between us, Jan was the only one in my family to watch me lead cheers at any sporting event. She arranged to fly back to Colorado for the homecoming game because she wanted to support me. Although I couldn't hear the three voices in the crowd above the overwhelming groan of disappointment that radiated from the locals in the grand stands, I knew that Jan and my future in-laws were cheering for the unknown girl who was crowned Queen. That night, I smiled happily as I looked toward their seats in the stands, and hoped that someday I could repay them for their support.

CHAPTER TWELVE

▼

ALCOHOLIC STEPFATHER

Jan met and married a man while she was living in California. The young couple struggled to get ahead by balancing their personal lives, work, and school. She continued to work in a small insurance office while her husband studied to become a Certified Public Accountant. Like our father, Jan was very private about her life and did not share the details of her deteriorating marriage. She seemed to have everything, a beautiful home in Thousand Oaks, a loving husband, and a respectable career, but her marriage soured.

While Jan quietly struggled in her private life, she knew that life at home in Colorado was equally bleak. I could feel Jan's frustration mounting when I told her what was happening at home. No one suspected the Daddy's war buddy harbored secrets that not only threatened Mom's marriage but also threatened our lives.

I first realized that something was wrong as I searched in the hamper for my favorite pair of jeans when I discovered a false bottom in the hamper. As I looked harder, I noticed a half-full bottle of whisky lying next to a pistol. I quickly placed it back where I found it and walked out to the kitchen where Mom was peeling potatoes, "Mom, why is there a bottle of whiskey and gun in the hamper?"

"What? Let me see." Mom dropped the potato peeler and dried her hands as she hurried to the bathroom to see what I was talking about. "Well! I'll be…just leave it there I'll take care of it."

I walked into my bedroom and yelled through the door as I hopped on one leg to pull up my hip-hugger jeans, "Mom, I won't be here for supper. I'm going to the movies and I'll be back around midnight."

"Okay, Betty. I can't sleep when you are not home so don't be late."

"Okay, Mom. Don't worry about me."

When I returned home at midnight I looked down the hall toward our only bathroom. I stopped short startled at what lie before my eyes. Luke was sprawled on the floor face down in our very small bathroom. I was sure he was dead. I stormed into my Mother's bedroom and screamed, "Mom! I think Luke's dead! He's on the floor in the bathroom!"

"Oh just leave him alone and go to bed, Betty."

"What?"

"Go to bed!"

Dumbfounded, I slowly walked to my room, it was so uncharacteristic of Mom to respond the way she did. How could she just leave Luke? I shook my head, worried and not understanding. What happened while I was gone?

I didn't know what else to do, so I crawled into my bed and tried to go to sleep. All I could think of was Luke lying on the floor, dead or dying and Mom didn't care. I tossed and turned, one o'clock, three o'clock. I must have fallen asleep. Finally at six o'clock I heard Mom in the kitchen making coffee. I walked out of my bedroom and glanced at the bare floor where I saw Luke lying just hours before, "Mom, what happened last night?"

It was obvious that Mom was thoroughly unhappy with her husband as she slammed every drawer and door in kitchen to make sure that the noise sent a painful message to the party boy. She responded disgustedly, "He had too much whiskey and passed out."

"He did?" I could tell that Mom didn't want to talk about it anymore.

The events heightened my awareness and I began to notice more odd behavior. His drinking problem became increasingly apparent. Liquor bottles that were once cleverly hidden were predictably found around the house, yard, and automobiles. I envisioned a Dr. Jekyll, Mr. Hyde persona as I watched a hard working sober man with an uncanny ability to fix anything mechanical, transform into a mysteriously troubled soul. The idiosyncrasies connected to Luke's drinking startled Mom, Lenn, and I. Luke seemed to be sinking into an abyss. After drinking, Luke had a fascination with guns and chose to fool around with his pistols and rifles while intoxicated. Finally, the day came when our fears almost became a reality. Lenn was playing outside and he noticed Luke sitting on the grass with the butt of the gun on the ground and the gun barrel placed snuggly under his chin. Without hesitation, Lenn ran over and kicked the gun out from under Luke and ran in to tell Mom.

Afraid for Luke's safety and the safety of the family, Mom secretly threw away all the bullets she could find in the house. Afterwards, she methodically gathered all the guns and wrapped them together with ropes, belts, and wire, then hid them, hoping that the tangled mess would slow Luke down in a heated rage or at the very least buy a few extra minutes of time to escape. It was apparent that Luke was suicidal but unknown if he was homicidal.

That following Sunday afternoon, my boyfriend, Nick, came over to talk to me about going out with my girlfriends the night before. Nick noticed the whiskey bottle on the porch as he walked past Luke and a visitor. I don't know if it was jealously or just part of the Latino culture, but Nick expected me to stay home and wait for him as he enjoyed running around with his friends. My girlfriends convinced me that I should go out and have a good time with them.

Engrossed in our conversation, Nick and I didn't notice that Luke was standing over us eavesdropping. We were startled when Luke demanded loudly, "Nick, do not raise your voice in my house."

Nick responded, "I'm not raising my voice." Suddenly, Luke punched Nick in the mouth.

I knew right then that it was going to get real ugly. Nick, was a no-nonsense weightlifter and Nick didn't take any static from anyone. I cringed as I remembered the fight that I saw Nick in just a month earlier when he broke poor old Sam's arm for simply asking me directions to a local party. Most of the Louisville guys in school respected Nick and knew better than to talk to me, but Sam was from Erie…he didn't know any better.

A second later, Nick instinctively retaliated by knocking Luke on the ground, slugging him all the way to the floor and knocking him out with the first punch. I stood up and moved out of the way. Luke's brother hid in the shadows as Nick turned toward the door. He told me that he loved me and cautiously walked out of the house, ready for another fight if necessary. I slowly followed him across the room and stopped at the door. I watched through the window as Nick climbed in his Corvette and sped away.

I turned around and Luke was still on the floor and in a stupor. Luke was bleeding, his false teeth broken and protruding from his mouth. He slowly got up and walked over to the telephone and called the sheriff. When the sheriff arrived, Luke started to give a bogus account of what transpired. I couldn't stand listening to Luke's version of the incident, so I interrupted the conversation. "Luke started the fight. He provoked my boyfriend by hitting him in the face. It was a real cheap shot! Luke was drunk and stupid and didn't have any business interfering in our conversation."

The sheriff turned to Luke and said, "Is that true? Did you hit the guy first?"

The look in Luke's eyes sent a chill to the core of my soul. I knew that Nick could never come around the house again. Luke nodded and said, "I'm not going to press charges."

I often wondered if Luke would shoot Nick if given the chance. With Luke's suicidal tendencies, I wondered if Luke would ever consider murder. Mom was obviously concerned too. She told me to ask Nick not to come around the house anymore and said that she was afraid that Luke would try to kill him.

For days I worried about Nick. I waited, he didn't call and he wasn't home. Just when I thought I couldn't stand the suspense any more, Nick called from San Francisco, "Betty, I just needed time to think. I'll be home in a couple of weeks."

"Good Nick, I've been worried about you. You know that you can't come around here any more. Luke didn't press charges but I know he is harboring a tremendous amount of anger. I wish the whole thing wouldn't have happened."

"I know Betty. But Luke hit me. I lost it. I just lost it. He just should not have hit me."

"Well, it's done and there's nothing we can do about it. Just call me and let me know that you are okay once in a while, Nick. I'll be waiting for you when you get home."

"I'll call you. Just remember that I love you and I miss you, Betty."

"I love you–be careful. I hope to see you soon."

I hung up the telephone with a sigh of relief. Nick was safe and he still loved me.

CHAPTER THIRTEEN

▼

TIME TO MOVE

I don't know how long he had been standing outside my window, just staring at me like a depraved predator. Sheer curtains were inexpensive and they were plentiful in our house. My stepsister and I shared a bedroom. The window in the bedroom was directly above the cellar, a place where a person could find a thousand excuses to visit. I cringed, thinking about what was going on in his mind. It occurred to me, that the bathroom had short opaque curtains that gapped open in the middle and at the bottom. I imagined that it would be easy for someone standing outside the window to look into the bathtub below the curtain. The bathroom backed up to a big hill where we had a few livestock sheds. There was little reason to believe that anyone would be in the backyard since we did not own any livestock. But after seeing Luke lurking in the window at me that day I was careful to place a heavy towel over the window before I took a bath and cover the bedroom window when I changed clothes.

I told my stepsister that I suspected her dad was a peeping tom. My stepsister was not surprised and said that she was very happy that my

Mom married her dad. Before my Mom, brother, and I moved in the house, she said that Luke sometimes came into her bedroom while she was sleeping and stood at the foot of her bed. My stepsister said she was too afraid to do anything but keep her eyes closed and pray that he would leave. She didn't know why he was there but she was uncomfortable. Maybe Luke was just admiring his beautiful young daughter like so many fathers do, but then again…maybe not.

A month later, I was sitting in the front room with Mom. Our sofa had a distinct dent molded to fit the average size butt. Anyone who sat on the sofa would naturally sit in the dented area instead of sitting on the awkward hump. Mom was sitting on the other side of the room and I was sitting in the sofa dent talking when I noticed that Luke went into the bathroom. The bathroom door did not fit very well which resulted in a large crack where the hinges met the door jam. I don't know what made me look, but for the first time, I noticed a figure of a man through the crack in the bathroom door. Surprised, I said to Mom, "Luke's standing in the bathroom looking at me!"

Shocked by the unsuspected news, she responded, "What?"

I immediately moved out of view and explained to Mom what I suspected to be true. Mom sat there in disbelief and shook her head with a thoughtful pause.

Later, I called Jan and told her that I was very uncomfortable living in Luke's house. I wished that there were some way that I could leave. Jan suggested that I fly out to see her for a few days. When I arrived in California, Jan gave me a whirlwind tour of Los Angeles and introduced me to her friends. For the first time in my life I tasted barbecued shrimp, saw the ocean, and shared a few moments of carefree living in Southern California. I began to realize that my sisters were my only true friends. Jan was there when I needed her and I knew that Carol would be too. Unfortunately, I couldn't stay with Jan.

I had to eventually return back to Boulder. Mom picked me up at Stapleton Airport and as we drove home she said, "Luke got in trouble with the law for drunken driving and was forced to submit to a mental evaluation at Ft. Logan Hospital. The hospital suggested that I accompany Luke to class to help him recover. You know, Betty, something's not right with that man. The last time Luke and I attended a session the Psychologist asked everyone to draw a picture of whatever we had on our mind. I drew a picture of flowers and of a bright and cheery home. Luke's picture was black with only a little bit of yellow in the corner."

"That's weird, Mom," I shook my head as I felt the burden of my life at home erase the healing that I received at Jan's house. "I don't know what's wrong with Luke but he makes me very uncomfortable."

It wasn't long before Luke terrified us. I was sleeping soundly in my bed when Mom ran into my bedroom and yelled, "Luke's got the gun!"

I immediately woke from a deep sleep and ran out my bedroom in my baby-doll pajamas. I met Luke as he was coming out of the camper holding a 22-caliber rifle. Awaken by the commotion, Lenn ran next door to get help from our neighbor. Mom grabbed the gun barrel while Luke held the butt of the gun. I grabbed the opposite side of the gun opposing both of their forces trying to get the gun away from Luke. The three of us tugged and pulled trying to get the gun away from each other. I thought to myself, this is really stupid, the objective is to get the gun away from Luke. I'm pulling on one end while Mom and Luke's combined forces were resisting me. It seemed like an eternity past by and none of us gained in the gun tug-a-war. Luke had his finger on the trigger and just as Lenn ran around the backside of the house, Luke pulled the trigger.

The bullet whistled by the house, seconds before Lenn appeared around the corner. Angry at Luke's reckless behavior, I yelled, "You could have shot Lenn!"

I jerked the gun toward me, just as Luke released the weapon, satisfied that the bullet was dislodged from the gun.

In a panic, Mom whispered loudly, "Betty, we need to get out of here. Lenn and I are going to stay with relatives in Greeley. You need to get out of here too."

"I will, Mom. I'll go to Nick's parent's house. I'll be okay. I'll run and get the jeans and T-shirt that I wore today."

Mom waited outside while I ran in the house. I grabbed my shoes and clothes and threw them in the car. Mom and Lenn followed me to Nick's house and then continued on to Greeley. Nick's Mom and Dad opened their home and their arms, welcoming me to stay with them as if I was a blood relative. They harbored me in their house for weeks until things calmed down.

CHAPTER FOURTEEN

▼

FAMILY

Luke's condition was worsening and I was old enough to move out and live on my own. Carol and Larry refurbished a mobile home and sold it to me for a bargain price. I parked it next to my girlfriend Barb's mobile home in a park in north Boulder. Lenn moved in with me to keep me company for a short while.

As Jan's marriage dissolved, Jan and her husband split their assets. Within a few weeks, Jan found an apartment and called me, "Betty, how is Mom doing? Oh, by the way, would you mind taking care of my Siamese cat, Cocoa?"

"Sure, I'll take care of Cocoa. Mom's not doing very well, I'm afraid. Luke doesn't want her to work and he drinks all the time. He's so controlling!"

"Betty, I don't know what to do. I offered to buy Mom a small place to live so she would not have to put up with Luke anymore. But she said that she did not want to be a burden. Mom said she would be fine. You can't help someone who doesn't what help. The whole thing frustrates me." Jan paused, "Anyway, my new apartment will not accept animals. Eventually I will move somewhere where I can keep Cocoa, but not now. You sure you don't mind?"

"Not at all! I would love to have a little company."

Within a couple of weeks, Cocoa arrived in an airline animal carrier. Cocoa was a good houseguest. Jan would call weekly to get behavior reports.

"Jan, you know I'm not used to caring for indoor animals. Guess what happened yesterday?"

"I don't know, Betty. What happened?"

"Well, I put Cocoa's used litter waste in a paper bag and I set the bag on the front deck to keep it from stinking up the whole house. As luck would have it, it rained that night. The next day, I was in a huge hurry when Mom arrived with some groceries for Lenn and I. I carried the groceries from the car to the porch and set the bags on the porch. Lenn carried the bags to Mom who was in the kitchen putting everything away. Over zealous, Lenn picked up a soggy bag of used cat litter. It barely made into the front room when the bag split and stinky cat litter was spilled all over the carpet. I wish you could have the look on Lenn's face, Jan! It was priceless!"

"I'm sorry I missed it. What a mess! Jan paused, "Well, I have some good news, Betty."

"I'm always ready for good news, Jan. What is it?"

"I think I'm going to move back to Colorado. I would like to live in Boulder. I love the Flatirons."

"You're kidding! That's great! You need to call Mom and tell her. She will be real happy to hear that you are coming home."

As I hung up the telephone I felt relieved that Jan chose to live near us again. It would be fun to have my sister close enough that we could visit on a daily basis. I looked forward to building our relationship.

PART III

▼

YOUNG ADULT YEARS

CHAPTER FIFTEEN

▼

GINGERBREAD HOUSE

By 1979, Nick and I were married four years and living in a mountain chalet called the Gingerbread House. Nestled in an Aspen grove, the majestic home enchanted most of our family with its three private decks and loft. Secluded by miles of mountain roads, Nick and I shared intimate winter evenings alone.

But the harsh winter created havoc in our lives and the Gingerbread House's sewer-line and well-water piping froze. The ground was frozen and no rental company would rent Nick heavy equipment to dig into the ground to repair the pipes. With no other choice, Nick tackled the problem using primitive tools. Five months pregnant, I stood outside with my coat barely buttoned over my swelled tummy and held a flashlight in my hand as Nick warmed the ground with a fire and dug a six foot deep, two-feet wide, thirty-foot long trench with a pick and a hammer.

Our relationship entered another dimension. My respect and love for Nick grew as I helplessly watched Nick's powerful body as he worked to bring utilities back into our home. By the time that Nick completed the project, we were convinced that we needed to move before the baby was born.

We rarely had company, so we were glad when Jan stopped by. Jan and I sat at the table in our small dining area while Nick grilled the meat for supper. I was rambling on about my pregnancy, "Jan, I remember when Nick and I were seventeen. It was so strange for me to see a guy as comfortable as he was holding a newborn. You know, I figured I should have a natural motherly instinct that would make me that comfortable holding a baby, but I'm always afraid the baby is going to break or something."

Jan's hands were fidgeting with a piece of paper, "Oh, I've seen you hold babies before. You're not *that* bad."

"Nick is clearly more comfortable holding a newborn than I am. I realized that he would be a good father ten years ago. I watched him as he held his niece as naturally as if she were a football. I watched his eyes sparkle and dance with all the joy of a proud papa. His love for babies radiated across the room."

I sensed that Jan was uncomfortable but I didn't understand why. She seemed distant but was very cordial, "I'm sure Nick will be a wonderful father, Betty."

"Nick always said that he wanted a whole football team. I told him early in our relationship that he was the one that would be giving birth to eleven babies, not me. Can you imagine? Eleven babies!"

Jan grinned at the thought, "He'd have the first one by natural childbirth and backtrack real fast. Holding a baby and giving birth to a baby is a whole different story!"

"You should see him. Nick wraps his big hand around my stomach and holds on to my stomach while he's talking to my belly button. There are times when I just have to say, "Hey Nick, I'm up here. Talk to me.""

"I wish he could experience the feeling of the baby flutter in the womb. There's nothing really like it, nothing compares."

Jan tilted her head down and I noticed her eyes saddened as she sank deeper in her thoughts. I realized that I shouldn't have talked about the baby so much. I felt like a total idiot. I wondered what she was thinking. I wondered if she could hear her biological clock ticking away.

"I pray to God that someday, I too, will have a baby. You know, I was supposed to have a baby before you. I'm the big sister you know. You're five years younger than me and you're the one having the baby."

I looked sadly at Jan. I was sorry if my pregnancy caused her pain. I suppose Jan was wondering if she would ever have children. Not knowing what else to say I said softly, "You'll have a baby someday, Jan, and you'll be a good Mommy."

Nick barged into the room. "Ready to eat? We're having elk tenderloin steaks!" I could see that Nick felt a tremendous sense of accomplishment from using his newly acquired primitive hunting skills. The great hunter has come home with the kill.

Jan stared down at the steak on her plate as if the entire carcass lay before her dressed in mushrooms and garnish. I took one bite of my steak and noticed it was extraordinarily gamey tasting, "Can I get you something else, Jan? The baby is telling me to send down an egg sandwich instead of this meat. Sometimes I'd rather get my protein by eating eggs."

"No Betty, really, this is fine. It's just been a long time since I had wild game."

Nick asked, "Jan, now that you've sold your California property and bought a nice new car, what are you planning to do?"

"I'm going to look for a place in Boulder and settle down here in Colorado."

I blurted, "Have you found a home?"

Jan nodded her head. "In fact, I bought a small mobile home in Boulder.

"Great Jan, I can't wait to see it. I go to Boulder all the time to visit my doctor. In fact, Nick and I are selling this house so our baby can be closer to the hospital, schools, and sporting events."

"Good, maybe we will see each other more. This place is enchanting but it is too far from the rest of the world." She quickly glanced at her watch, "Which is why I should probably head home."

"I'm really glad that you came for supper Jan. Next time we'll have beef steaks instead of elk steaks, okay?"

"It doesn't matter, Betty. Well, thank you for having me over. Let me know if there is anything you need."

With a tinge of regret, I walked Jan to her car and watched as she drove down the curvy dirt road. We had a brief, awkward moment. Our family was never comfortable with good-byes.

CHAPTER SIXTEEN

▼

LIFE IN TOWN

We sold our home and the closing was set one week before my due date. My doctor appointment was near Boulder Community Hospital so I stopped by Jan's new home afterwards and knocked on the door.

"Hey, come on in Betty. I heard you sold your house and they want to move in already. What are you going to do? That baby is due any day now?"

"I can't believe the timing. We were anxious to get closer to town so we didn't negotiate an extension for the closing. I guess we'll look for an apartment until we can find someplace to live."

"I wish you would consider staying in my home until you have your baby, Betty." The hospital is just down the road from here. You could be there in less than 10 minutes. In the meantime you can look for a place to live. I really don't mind!"

"I don't know, Jan. Your offer is tempting."

Jan sipped her ice tea as she stared out the window at the summer flowers, bright and vivid and full of life. "Boulder is truly God's country. Betty, I am so happy to be here in Colorado, California seems so plastic in comparison.

Now that I've received the money from my property in California, I can help Mom out a little. I've asked Mom to let me buy her a little mobile home so that she can get away from Luke. His alcoholism seems to be getting worse. I want Mom to move away and start all over, she should never have married that man! Mom doesn't want to be in anyone's way. I manage to slip her a little money now and then though, just to help her out."

"Jan, you are so much like Mom. You have a servant's heart. You'd give away your last dollar if someone needed it more than you."

I thought about staying with Jan for a while, just until the baby comes so Nick and I could find a place to live. I realized that with the baby coming any day, I had few choices. "Oh Jan, I don't know, Nick and I don't want to be in your way. We sure didn't expect our house to sell one week before the baby was due! We do need a place though and your home is awfully close to the hospital. Well, maybe for a couple of weeks. Let me ask Nick and see what he thinks, okay?"

Jan smiled and walked me to the door, "Good, I'm gone all day at work anyway and we'll just be together in the house in the evenings." It's really not a big deal, besides I want to be by that baby…after all, I'm the baby's aunt.

Well, Jan I have to go now. Let me call you with the answer. I think Nick will like being close to the hospital.

Within a week, Nick and I sold our home in Coal Creek Canyon and placed our furniture in storage. Although Nick and I didn't want to inconvenience Jan, we accepted her offer and moved in with a suitcase full of clothes.

On August 2, 1979, we walked to the clubhouse and noticed four seven-year-old boys swimming in the pool. I looked at one of them and whispered to Nick, "That little boy looks just like you, he has the same beauty mark on his face as you. That's what I think the baby is going to look like. He sure is a handsome boy."

Nick looked at the boy with new interest, then smiled with satisfaction.

A little butterfly flutter tickled my stomach, "Nick, I feel a little strange. Let's go home, okay?"

"Oh boy! This might be the night, Betty!"

"Well, I don't know about that, I can't explain the feeling. I just feel strange." Then I smiled at him with my eyebrows raised. "Maybe you're right! It just might be the night!"

Nick walked slowly as I waddled next to him, when we arrived at home we both changed into dry clothes. I called my Mom on the telephone, just as she answered the telephone my water broke. I was scared and for a moment I didn't know what to do. I felt dirty. I had a peculiar substance on my legs and feet. I had to take a shower.

Nick was pacing back and forth by the bathroom door, "Betty, I don't think you are supposed to take a shower when your water breaks, we better go to the hospital. How are you feeling anyway? Are you having contractions?"

"Yes, I'm having contractions and I'm getting out of the shower. I just couldn't stand that stuff on my legs."

Pacing back and forth on the other side of the door, Nick reported, "I called the doctor and he said that we should come in to the hospital when your contractions are ten minutes apart. The doctor isn't too worried about the baby coming too soon, first babies often take their time."

Nick carried my hospital bag to the car. I had just settled on the couch when Nick came back into the living room. "How are you feeling, Betty? When was your last contraction?"

"I'm having one right now."

Nick placed his hand on my stomach and looked at his watch. "Okay, let me know when you have another one."

"Okay."

A half an hour past before another contraction came. Nick still had his hand on my stomach as I said, "Here comes another one."

"I can feel your stomach tighten, Betty! It won't be long and we're going to see that baby!" Nick said with anxious anticipation.

We timed the contractions for two hours and finally it was time to go to the hospital. We arrived at the hospital at 9:00. Nicholas Shawn didn't decide to meet his parents until 3:10 a.m. Six hours of pain forgotten at one glance of our beautiful baby boy.

Nick lifted Nicholas Shawn's arm and proudly said, "Look at these biceps! He's a perfect boy. Isn't he beautiful?"

I admired Nicholas Shawn for an all too brief moment before the hospital staff whisked Nicholas Shawn away to poke and prod him. I felt an empty feeling that I never knew before as I watched Nicholas Shawn leave my sight.

Nick stroked my hair with his hand and said, "You should try to get some sleep, Betty. I'm going to go with Nicholas Shawn and we will both be back in an hour or so.

A few hours later, the nurse wheeled Nicholas Shawn's crib in my room. Nick and I counted his fingers and his toes and stared lovingly at his face. We promised to protect him and love him the rest of his life and promised to do everything in our power to keep him from harm, physically, mentally, and spiritually. We vowed that we would give Nicholas Shawn the best possible life that we could.

The next day, Nick sat at the edge of my hospital bed. "I have something for you, Betty." He handed me a cute yellow short set. "You can wear this home from the hospital.

Nick knew that I was looking forward to getting my slim figure back and seeing my toes once again. I was tired of looking like I swallowed a basketball. I tried the short set and walked over to the full-length mirror. Immediately my mood changed. The 5'10" reflection had a big belly and skinny legs! I whined as I looked in the hospital mirror. "Oh Nick, I looked like Big Bird."

Nick frowned at me, "No you don't."

"I know now that I can't wear yellow or gray. If I wear gray, everyone will mistake me for the Goodyear Blimp!"

"I don't like when you talk bad about yourself, Betty. You look nice."

I *was* fishing for a compliment. I needed a little ego boost from my husband, I wanted Nick to think that I was sexy again. I bent over and kissed Nick on the cheek, "Thank you for the outfit, I am just disappointed that my stomach isn't flat yet." In the back on my mind I wondered if Nick was telling me the truth. I wondered if he still found me attractive.

There was a light knock on the door. Jan walked in the room carrying a baby present. I was happy to see her but I looked at her 5'3" 100 pound body. She looked so petite and feminine. I began to feel even bigger and frumpier.

She smiled at me and said, "Where's that baby?"

"The nurses are performing some required tests on him, you can probably see him from the nursery window."

The doctor knocked on the door. "There's nothing to worry about but you're son has yellow jaundice. He should be okay in a few days, he just needs to stay under some special lights until the symptoms go away." He turned and looked at me, "But I understand that you can go home, Betty."

"Without the baby? I can't leave the baby." It seemed unreasonable to make a mother go home without her baby.

The doctor said reassuringly, "Your baby will be able to come home in a few days, there's no sense in you being here."

Nick and I were disappointed and afraid to leave our baby. I slowly packed my clothes and Nick and I walked down to the nursery. Nick and I just vowed to take care of our baby and now we were leaving him alone in the hospital. We put gowns on over our street clothes and walked up to the glass crib. Nicholas Shawn had a blindfold over his eyes and his ear was folded under the blindfold. I asked the nurse to fix his ear so he would be more comfortable. Nick and I touched Nicholas Shawn's little hand and promised him that we would be back first thing in the morning.

Nick and I decided we needed to do what we could to show our baby that we there for him. We visited Nicholas Shawn every day, and I decided to do something special for Nicholas Shawn's week old birthday. On the night of August 10 we set the alarm clock for 2:30 a.m. and drove to the hospital with a cupcake and candle. At 3:10 in the morning we were standing by the lighted plexi-glass crib holding Nicholas Shawn's tiny hand. Nick lit the candle and the nursery staff joined us as we sang, "*Happy Birthday to You, Happy Birthday to You, Happy Birthday dear Nicholas Shawn, Happy Birthday to Youuuuuuu!*" Nick and I felt good about doing something special for our little baby.

The doctor released Nicholas Shawn to go home a few days later. "Give the baby a little sun every day and if you see that his skin is turning a little yellow make sure that you call me."

On the way home, I started singing in a voice that resembled a frog singing alto off-key to the tune of what later became Barney's theme song, "*Nicholas Shawn, Nicholas Shawn, Nicholas, Nicholas, Nicholas Shawn, I love you, you love me, and we're as happy as we can be!*" Nick smiled at the baby and I with apparent approval as we pulled in Jan's driveway.

Jan opened the door to greet the new arrival. She peeked through the receiving blanket and softly said to the baby, "It's so good to have my sweet little baby Nicholas Shawn home. You gave us a little scare at the hospital though." Jan grabbed my hospital bag and said, "Make yourselves comfortable. Meanwhile, I want to hold my little boy."

Nick handed Nicholas Shawn to Jan. I watched Jan as I put all the baby paraphernalia away. Jan looked so cute holding Nicholas Shawn. She acted like she was weighing the baby, "Wow! What a chunk! He's going to be a big boy. That reminds me, I bought Nicholas Shawn a few things. I guess I got a little carried away. Judging by his size, you better put him in some of those clothes before he out grows them."

I shook my head in disbelief, "Jan, I think you've already done enough. You are quite the aunt! By the way, Jan, we've found a condominium in Arvada and are scheduled to move there in about four weeks. The condo is real close to the property that we bought. We'll start building our house in a few months."

Jan smiled at me, "I'm just happy I could help you out."

"Jan, I'm worried about Mom, have you been able to convince mom to move here yet?"

Jan looked out the window and watched as a car passed by, "Well, I am still trying to talk Mom into moving in but I guess Mom told Luke where this place is located."

"Oh no, you're kidding me. It wouldn't be safe for Mom to move here now, not if Luke knows where it is."

Jan shook her head, "I guess I'll just sell the mobile home and maybe buy something later."

CHAPTER SEVENTEEN

▼

RELIGIOUS BOND

Jan and I frequently discussed the Bible. Our topics ranged from speaking in tongues to a wife's subservient duty to her husband. Jan and I agreed to disagree on the subject of tongues, but agreed that the Bible instructed wives to be subservient to their husbands.

I watched Jan's life gravitate toward becoming a full-time subservient wife while my life was divided between being a subservient wife and women's fight for equality. While I was subservient to the male species in my home, I worked in a male dominated career, analyzing welds and supervising both men and women. I told men what to do during the day and during the night my husband told *me* what to do.

Some of my independent female friends couldn't understand why I would take such a giant step backward for equality for woman. They associated a subservient wife with weak-mindedness. I briefly explained that in theory, the relationship resulted in mutual respect and a lot less stress for the wife. But, I knew when I was speaking to my friends that they chose another life, and that was okay. I had no interest in tackling the woman's liberation movement.

Jan arrived at the condominium ready for our Bible study just in time to see baby Nicholas Shawn before he fell asleep. Nicholas Shawn was a large baby and when Jan held him, Nicholas Shawn seemed even larger.

"The pediatrician commented that Nicholas Shawn was in the 90 percentile in weight and off the chart in height." Nick said proudly, as if having a large baby boy was a major accomplishment that was directly connected with Nick's virility.

We settled down in the living room and studied the Book of John in the Bible. Nick read John 3:16 from the Bible. We summarized the verse by rephrasing the words in a simpler format. The Bible says here that all you have to do is believe that Christ died for our sins so we may be saved. There's no mystery to this verse; it means exactly what is written.

Jan said, "You know, Nick and Betty, you do not have to be baptized, but you get baptized to show the Lord and witnesses that you have accepted Christ as your Savior and that you love the Lord."

Nick responded, "Well, I was raised a Catholic and I already have been baptized. My Mom and Dad would not recognize another baptism, especially in another church. But you know, all this does make sense to me and I want to be baptized again to show the Lord that, as an adult, I have chosen to accept Him as my Savior."

I added, "I think we should talk to our pastor and see when he can baptize us, Nick. I've never been baptized but I accepted Christ as my savior in Sunday school when I was a little girl."

Jan smiled and looked up from her Bible, "Good! I think it would be wonderful if the two of you both got baptized on the same day!"

"But what about Nicholas Shawn?" I asked Nick, "Should we have him baptized?"

"I think we should let Nicholas Shawn decide when he grows up. He can make his own decision on what denomination he wants to follow," Nick commented.

Satisfied with our decision, Nick and I planned a date and time to get baptized.

"Don't be surprised if Satan tries to change your plans, Betty. Satan likes to keep you from seeking the Lord. Just be aware of Satan's evil plotting."

Sure enough, the day came for Nick and I to go to church to be baptized and Nicholas Shawn was very ill. I remembered Jan's warning and Nick and I decided that since the baptism would only take a couple of hours, Nick and I could follow through with our commitment while Aunt Jan watched Nicholas Shawn.

After our baptism, Nick, Jan, and I celebrated with a quick lunch and then hurried home so that Nicholas Shawn could get some rest. I felt good about publicly accepting Christ as my Savior.

I bent down and kissed Nicholas Shawn on the forehead and wondered if we should have baptized him as I made the sign of the cross over Nicholas Shawn and prayed out loud, "God please bless this boy."

CHAPTER EIGHTEEN

▼

THE ART OF DYING

In March 1980, Nick and I drove to Carol and Jack's house to help butcher two hogs. At a time when living off Mother Earth was cult-like, Carol and Jack loved to grow their own vegetables, can food in the fall, and raise small farm animals. Eating homegrown food was the recipe for a long, healthy life. Nick and I admired their lifestyle, I dreamed of growing vegetables and canning during harvest and Nick was interested in learning how to butcher a hog.

We really didn't need an excuse to visit Carol and Jack. They were our favorite couple to chum around with and we couldn't help admiring how they raised their four lovely children and their adopted handicapped child and still had room in their house and hearts for foster children. I watched them care for babies who were unwanted and after getting attached to them, Carol and Jack let them go with only a prayer and a hug, and a few clothes in a bag.

When we arrived, Nick took Nicholas Shawn out back and showed him the farm animals while Carol showed me her latest craft project. We barely started when Mom and Luke drove in the driveway.

"Oh good! Here's Mom and Luke, let's go see if they need any help bringing anything in." Carol said as she turned to walk out the front door.

We met Mom as she was climbing out of the cab of the truck. "Hi Mom, I'll be back in the house in a few minutes, I'm going to go get baby Nicholas Shawn from Nick."

Mom was rubbing her side as she walked up to Carol, "We brought Luke's 22.caliber rifle. Luke doesn't have a gun rack in his pickup so he laid the gun across the seat. That stupid gun kept sliding across the seat and hitting me in the side. Each time I moved the gun it would slide over and hit me again. I'm so glad to be here."

"We're glad you're here too!" Carol motioned to follow her, "Come on in and visit while I peel the potatoes."

Mom followed Carol into the house as Luke and I walked back to the barn.

"Nick, I'll be in the house with Nicholas Shawn and we'll call you guys when it's time to eat."

Nick handed me Nicholas Shawn and I walked back to help Mom and Carol fix supper while everyone else stayed in the barn to watch the slaughter. A few hours passed and dinner was ready. Carol yelled out the back door, "Come in and eat. The food is going to get cold. Everyone, come in...*now!*"

The butcher gang filed in to the house. But Luke and Nick remained out in the barn. I thought Nick and Luke were civilized to each other but I started to worry if everything was all right. I panicked. I started to go to the barn to see what was wrong. I walked out the backdoor just in time to see Nick at the doorstep.

Nick said, "Luke wanted to kill the pig himself. I was pretty nervous about Luke having a gun in his hand so I insisted on shooting the pig myself. You should have seen Luke's eyes, Betty, it seemed like he was in a trance as he watched the blood dripping on the ground. That's what Luke's doing right now, just staring at the pig, mesmerized. With each drop of blood that fell on the plastic below, Luke seemed to go deeper and deeper into the spellbound fascination of death. It scared me so much that I was afraid to walk away from him. I was afraid that Luke would shoot me. I remember Luke's and my confrontation all too well."

I was horrified, "Oh my gosh, Nick! Luke is *still* watching the pig die?"

"I guess so. When I was standing by Luke I thought to myself…Oh my God, Luke has lost it. He has really lost his mind. How can I turn my back on him now?" Nick looked afraid as he continued, "There wasn't anyone else around. I couldn't stay with a mad man and a dying hog, so I decided to take my chances and walk as fast as I could without looking obvious. I swayed my steps so that I would be a moving target and harder for him to hit. I even threw my arms up occasionally to increase my odds, for crying-out-loud!"

Nick took Mom to the side and whispered "Mom you need to stay away from Luke, something just isn't right with that man."

Mom looked in horror at what he had to say. "He's not been right in the head for some time now, I know that I need to get away from him."

Luke stayed with the pig until the blood stopped dripping. When the motion of death was over there was no more to see. Luke walked to the house. There was something about the look in his eyes, something that I had never seen before…

I warned Mom again not to go home with Luke…but she did.

▼

CHAPTER NINETEEN

DEATH CHILLS

A week later, Mom called me in a panic, "Don't call me over at Luke's because I'm leaving, I'll be at Aunt Pearl's house. Luke got drunk…again. Shoot Betty, Luke's not even trying to get well. I'm so sick of it all. I'm going to let Luke dry out a while before I go back. Don't worry about me."

"Will you be at Aunt Pearl's house the whole time?"

I'm either going to Aunt Pearl's house or maybe Jan's house, I might even go over to Aunt Barbara's or your Aunt Betty's house in Greeley. I don't want to stay in one place too long or he'll find me. Just don't worry about me. I have enough clothes to get me by for a while…everything's okay."

Mom was obviously upset. I was reflecting on all the pain that she had been through since we moved to Boulder. Mom should have left Luke a long time ago. She knew how I felt so I simply said, "Okay Mom, be real careful okay? Let me know what's going on with you…love you."

Mom had planned her escape months before and her bags were packed and waiting in the car. She hung up the telephone and walked into the living room to tell Luke that she was leaving him. She told him that she hoped that he would try to stop drinking and get control of his life. Angry, Luke disappeared into the back room as Mom quickly ran out the door. Once she was safely in the car, Mom looked back at the house and saw Luke through the living room window. He was jumping in an uncontrollable rage, shaking his fists and shouting a silent but potent message.

Afraid, Mom quickly backed out of the driveway and drove away vowing not to look back.

The next day Mom continued her normal routine. Mom loved her job and took pride in the fact that she was in charge of filling international greeting card orders. But as she drove to work from Aunt Pearl's house she felt strange. The feeling intensified as she drove past a fatal automobile accident involving a preacher. Disturbed by the recent events, Mom decided to stay overnight in Boulder at Jan's house.

The next morning, Jan's new husband warned Mom that he had a premonition that something terrible was going to happen to Mom. Mom spent the morning trying to forget the warning.

A few days passed and Luke's truck hadn't moved. There was no movement around the house. Luke's mom, Grace, lived next door and noticed that something was wrong. She called a neighbor to check on Luke. The next thing Grace saw was the neighbor running from the house, crying uncontrollably and screaming in a frantic rage the bad news.

Grace volunteered to try to find Mom, and called around to all Moms' relatives that she knew. Finally Grace found Mom at Jan's house. She gently said, "Sweetie, you need to come home, they found Luke. He's dead."

When Mom arrived at the house she found the police waiting for her. The police took Mom to the side started their routine questioning. There were a few odd things about Luke's death that didn't add up. Luke was found lying on the bed, covered with an electric blanket. The controls to the electric blanket were turned to high.

The electric blanket heated Luke's body and accelerated the decomposition of the body. Mom recounted the night she left Luke and told the police what time she left the house and where she went. But the rapid decay of Luke's body made it look like Luke died before Mom left.

The police continued to interrogate Mom. They wanted to know how Luke could receive a gunshot blast to the head and before Luke's body grew limp, he could fold his hands across his chest while the 22-caliber rifle fell to his side. "Normally, people who kill themselves do not place their hands on top of each other," the policeman said as he waited for Mom's reaction.

Mom was noticeably distraught and explained to the police that she was nervous about Luke's obsession with guns. Mom told them that she gathered all of the guns she could find and wrapped belts and rope around them so Luke couldn't get to a gun very fast.

After hearing Mom's story the police determined that Mom didn't have anything to do with her husband's death and discontinued the interrogation.

Mom drove back to Jan's house. Still overcome with grief, Mom called me to tell me that Luke committed suicide. "Betty, Luke shot himself. He's dead.

"Oh no! He did?" Tears swelled in my eyes.

Mom said gravely, "Yes, I'm over Jan's house now. I just got back from Luke's place. The police interrogated me. I wonder if it was possible that the police saw my fingerprints on the butt of the gun from pushing it aside the week before? Or maybe they suspected me because I wrapped the guns with belts and ropes."

"Mom, it's a good thing you wrapped those guns. Who knows what would have happened if you didn't. The police have to do routine questioning to make sure that there isn't any foul play. It's over, try not to think about it. You need to finally let go of this terrible episode in your life."

"The funeral will be in a couple of days, Betty. I think you should meet Luke's girls, Jan and I at the mortuary so we can plan the arrangements."

"Okay Mom. I will be there for you."

▼

CHAPTER TWENTY

HEAVY AIR

Under the circumstances, it was necessary to have a closed casket funeral. Nick and I sat among friends of the family in the large room facing the casket. I was emotionally detached as I stared at the coffin, my imagination drifted out of reality. I leaned over and whispered to Nick, "How do we know Luke's really dead? I've never been to a closed casket funeral before. Maybe he staged his death and is fishing in some secluded Colorado mountain-lake."

Nick gave me a disbelieving look. "That's crazy, Betty. Besides, there was a body."

"Yeah, I guess so." I shuddered as I realized Nick was right. I wondered why my mind wandered. I'm not crazy, I reasoned, insensitive, and maybe creative, but not crazy.

Mom moved back into the house a week after the funeral. Jan offered to help Mom find a place to stay and give her money to help with the rent payments. I offered to have Mom move in with Nick and I, but Mom refused. She insisted that she would be all right living in the house and said that she had a lot of business that she needed to finalize.

It took me a couple of months to gain the nerve to walk into the house after Luke's death. As soon as I walked in to the porch and opened the kitchen door I knew what it was like to sense death. The air in the house was heavy, and although the house did not have a strong odor, I acknowledged a distinct smell. "Mom, you can't live here anymore."

Mom stood in front of me with a curious look on her face, "Betty, I'm not afraid. There's nothing here that will hurt me. Don't worry so much."

"No Mom, it's wrong. You can't live here. I can't explain it, but you can feel that someone died here." I walked to the bathroom next to the room where Luke killed himself and glanced at the mirror on the door, through the reflection was the bed without a mattress. My imagination went crazy and I imagined Luke lying on the bed, the color red all around him. I decided that I didn't need to go to the bathroom anyway and came out to the kitchen. "Mom, you have to get out of here. It stinks in here. You can feel death in the air. You don't need to be in this environment, anymore. I want you *out* of here!"

"I guess you're right, I need to move. You know, I'm going to make sure that Luke's girls get their share of this place. It's the right thing, besides. I don't want anyone's money."

"I know, you're always looking out for someone else. Do whatever you think is right and I know that the Lord will bless you, Mom. Just move away from here, okay? You are done living this Hell. I don't want you here another night."

"I'll move, but I don't want to burden anyone. I'll find an apartment in Boulder."

After a few weeks of searching for a place to stay, Mom moved out of the house and into an apartment in Boulder. She spent her spare time visiting relatives, keeping her promise not to "burden" anyone. She was determined to be a wanted guest, one who helped out around the house so everywhere she went, Mom cooked and performed light housework. It was Mom's way of helping out, and also giving love. When her hosts had nothing else for her to do, she moved on to the next friend or relative.

CHAPTER TWENTY-ONE

▼

TWO SISTERS, TWO BABIES

On August 1, 1982, I looked like I swallowed a basketball and was about to have my second baby at anytime. I walked in Jan's hospital room. Jan was sitting up in bed holding her tiny baby girl. The look in Jan's eyes said it all. She looked as if she was determined to protect and love her new baby girl for the rest of their life. Jan would see that nothing in the world would ever harm her baby.

I walked over to peek through all the blankets, "Oh Jan, she is beautiful! I've never seen anyone so small and so perfect. She has your breathtaking blue eyes. What a little charmer! Here, I had so much fun buying this little dress. It's the smallest one I could find."

Jan looked at me with determination, "Betty, you took the name that I wanted for my baby. I hope you don't mind, actually it doesn't matter if you mind or not, we've decided to name our baby girl Nicolette LeVee, we'll call her Nicky. We are naming her after her daddy's Uncle Nick and his wife LeVee."

I responded, "Jan, I don't care, I love the name Nick. You can never have too many Nick's in your life! You just had to beat me though, didn't you? Little Nicky came out before my little bundle of joy."

"You beat me." Jan smiled, "Nicholas is going to be three years old in two days."

"Yep, the big boy is going to have a birthday party pretty soon. It doesn't look like you're going to be there. Nicholas will miss his Aunt Mommy, but I can't think of a better reason to miss a birthday party. In fact, I better go and pick up the party favors. Call me when you get home, Jan. You have a beautiful baby girl!"

Exactly two weeks later, nine pounds, thirteen ounce, Kristopher Lenn was born. Jan and I wanted Nicky and Kristopher to have a close relationship so that they could feel the love that a brother has for a sister and a sister has for a brother. Jan and I made a promise to make sure that Nicky and Kristopher shared plenty of time together.

CHAPTER TWENTY-TWO

▼

SEXY FEET

Not long after the birth of her daughter, Jan found herself as a single parent. But Jan was strong and determined to make Nicky's life happy and complete as she could in a broken home. Bills were piling up so Jan was forced to return to work. Jan made a respectable salary working for an insurance office but struggled to make ends meet. Money and relationships were not important to Jan. She placed her entire focus on Nicky. By the time Nicky was two years old, Jan was working as an administrative assistant for a company not far from the Crossroads Mall in Boulder.

I was working the night shift when Jan called, "Betty, do you want to meet me for lunch at Jose Muldoons Mexican Restaurant?"

"Sure, I'll see you at 11:30!"

When I arrived at the restaurant, Jan said, "I have a friend that I want you to meet. This is John, Betty...John works in the office, he's a real computer whiz."

I looked across the table at a distinctive-looking man a few years older than Jan. "Nice to meet you, John."

John acknowledged my greeting with a nod. I studied John as we talked. John injected a laugh in almost every sentence. Such a jovial man, he seemed very intelligent, I thought. Finally, Jan met a good man.

We got back to the office and Jan whispered to me with a giggle, "My boss is at lunch right now but you just have to meet him. He's got a foot-fetish."

I crinkled my nose, "A what?"

"You know Betty, he like's feet. People say that he takes his secretaries shopping and buys them shoes. You should see the pictures on his wall, Betty, the pictures on his wall are pictures of feet!"

Smiling at the thought I said, "No, you've got to be kidding me. I've never heard of such a thing!"

"Really! It's true! It's the funniest thing!"

"Well, I'm wearing sandals, I think I'll pass on meeting your boss," I said laughing. "I'll see you later, Jan."

CHAPTER TWENTY-THREE

▼

SECULAR HOLIDAYS

After a few months, Jan and John had a private wedding ceremony in a friend's house in east Boulder. They both stood in front of the copper fireplace and recited their wedding vows as John's children and my family looked on. The reception immediately followed the wedding and took place in the dining room. Perhaps a faux pas, but Nick and I gave John and Jan a wedding card with a $50.00 bill tucked inside.

Jan tried to slip the money back to me, "We really don't need the money, Betty, keep it."

I scolded, "Jeez Jan, you don't give wedding presents back."

Jan whispered in my ear, "Betty, John has money. He kept it a secret while I was dating him. Who would have thought? After all, John was working with me, I didn't know he didn't have to work."

"Jan, I wanted to give you something. Keep the money. I know it's not much."

"Well, thank you Betty. It's a very nice gift."

Shortly after the wedding, Jan and John purchased a beautiful home in prestigious Pinebrook Hills in Boulder, Colorado.

I was happy for Jan. She was very much in love and had a wonderful husband. It was obvious to me that John loved Nicky as if she were his own child. The three of them began a fairy-tale life.

That following September, Jan and I were planning what costumes to make the children for Halloween. Jan and I sat on the couch in the living room of her Pinebrook Hills home, thumbing through pattern books and commenting how funny our children would look in various costumes. Like most parents, Jan and I wanted our children to experience the same joys we did as a child. We were cautious, the world had changed dramatically since the late 1950's. We did what we could to minimize our children's exposure to evil and corruption.

Like other children their age, Nicholas Shawn, Nicky, and Kristopher liked to dress up for Halloween. They never expressed an interest in masquerading as anything evil which was good because Jan and I would only make costumes of animals and other non-frightening characters.

One of Nicholas Shawn's favorite movie characters was ET the extraterrestrial. When Jan and I came across an ET costume in the catalogue, I wanted to make it for him. "Jan, Nicholas Shawn loves ET. My gosh! Look at the number of pieces…and then there's the padding! Um, not this year! This pattern is way too complicated. The face alone is more complicated than an entire suit! There's no way!"

Jan paused for a moment and after calculating her schedule said, "Oh, let me make the costume for my Nicholas Shawn. I can do it."

"You're kidding, Jan. That's a big job! It'll take you a long time. Are you sure you have the time for such a complicated pattern?"

"I want to do it for my Nicholas. Just pick out the material and I'll get started."

Jan spent weeks sewing costumes in an effort to get both Nicholas Shawn's ET costume and Nicky's bunny costume done in time for Halloween. Meanwhile, after work and on weekends, I was busy sewing two-year old Kristopher a kitty costume. When the costumes were done and Halloween came, we enjoyed the fruits of our labor. Jan called me on the telephone, "Betty, I just finished Nicholas Shawn's ET costume. Why don't you and the boys come over for supper so Nicholas can try on his costume."

"Nicholas Shawn will be so excited when I tell him you have a surprise for him. I really appreciate your hard work, there's no way that I could have finished that pattern. Thanks, Jan."

"I'm happy to make Nicholas Shawn his costume. I don't do very much for him now that Nicky and Kristopher spend so much time together. I really don't know what a child his age likes to do."

"Nicholas Shawn likes to do anything. He's not particular. I'm excited to see the completed costume. By the way, I finished Kristopher's costume. He looks real cute in it."

"Betty, ever since you made Nicky that first stuffed bunny named "Hoppy," she can't sleep without it. Now, she's going to be "Hoppy" for Halloween."

"That'll be cute. I can't wait to see her in her little costume. I better get going, talk to you later Jan, and thanks again."

"Okay, I'll see you about six o'clock then. You owe me," Jan laughed as she hung up the telephone.

We arrived at Jan's house fifteen minutes late. Jan made a special ethnic meal with exotic spices. She was always experimenting with cooking. She had a knack for making even the simplest dishes special and fancy meals elegant. It was obvious that Jan enjoyed being creative in the kitchen.

"Oh, Betty, I can't wait. I want to see Nicholas Shawn in his costume before supper." Jan walked to the edge of the room and called out, ""Nicholas Shawn, I have your costume done. Come see it."

Nicholas ran over to his Aunt Mommy bubbling with energy, anxious to see his new costume. Jan handed Nicholas Shawn the costume. "Do you mind trying it on for me? It's an ET costume."

His large brown eyes sparkled as he grinned from ear to ear. "Oh wow! This is so cool! Look at this Kris, look at my ET costume! Wow!"

He ran in the bedroom to try on the costume and before we knew it a brown alien with a large fluorescent red heart was standing in front of us, his smiles hidden behind the padded round face of ET. We knew that Nicholas Shawn was experiencing one of the highlights of his young life. "Oh thank you Aunt Janet," he said as he put his short arms and long ET fingers around his Aunt Jan. "I love you."

Meanwhile, I was having fun taking pictures and watching them parade around the house in their costumes. I thought to myself, this is what it's all about, kids laughing and having good clean fun. Memories are made of happy times like this. Jan always treated my children as if they were her own offspring and I knew that I could never repay Jan for her generosity. I was just thankful that I had Jan in my life. Jan unselfishly demonstrated her love once again.

CHAPTER TWENTY-FOUR

▼

BEGINNING TO DE-PROGRAM (1986)

Halloween, 1986 was very different from the past. There were no jack-o-lanterns or any other customary symbols associated with the holiday. Jan and I changed our traditional Halloween celebration and both opposed society's promotion of secular holidays.

Jan was becoming very active in her church. She spent countless hours typing the ministry's newsletter and mailing out audiotapes. Jan was a humble and obedient servant and never complained or boasted about her contribution to the ministry. Every time I called her on the telephone, she was busy working on something for the church. She was busier than most paid employees that I knew.

Focused on living to please the Lord, Jan was at peace with her walk with Jesus. Jan's stubborn nature was one of the ministries greatest assets. She was determined to work through a project until the end. Her way of glorifying the Lord was to serve the church. As Jan and I continued to share our views about the Bible my own walk with the Lord was strengthened. Jan and I occasionally had opposing theologies. We considered our differences a process of growing in Christ. Jan made sure to include me on the mailing list to receive newsletters and audiotapes. I intended to study them all, but I had never taken the time.

Jan and I talked to each other nearly every day. We discussed the problems with bringing children up in a crazy world filled with violence. Jan sent me newsletter explaining why we shouldn't celebrate secular holidays. I was already concerned about Halloween so I read the article. The message warned that Christmas trees, wreaths, and of course, Santa Claus did not belong in our Christian life. Halloween seemed evil to me anyway, but after reading the article, I felt that I had to decide whether to allow my children the same childhood experiences I had, or never permit my sons to celebrate any holidays. I hated for Nicholas Shawn and Kristopher to miss out on the benefits of playing make believe and to exercise their creative minds.

Since the drug years of the 1960's, Halloween was increasingly violent and horrible things happened to children every year. I dreaded reading the paper every November 1st fearing that something terrible had happened to an innocent child the night before…and it usually did…somewhere. My heart would break each time that I read that a child was poisoned, ate an apple with a razor blade in it, or was shot while enjoying the holiday. I noticed that other parents started throwing Halloween parties as a safe alternative to traditional *trick or treating*.

Kim Miller, of the Concerned Christian ministry, warned that Halloween was evil. The ministry attempted to educate people about the history of Halloween and how it was a celebration rooted in entertaining spirits of the dead that inhabited bodies of animals. If the spirits did not feel entertained, the spirits placed spells on the hosts of their bodies, a *trick*, and if the spirits were pleased, they *treated* their hosts well…the original *trick or treat*.

Nick and I read through the description about Halloween's twisted origin and decided that Halloween didn't glorify the Lord and that evil characters really didn't have any place in our own little family's tradition. Witches represented Satan worshippers and black cats housed the spirits of witches, ghosts were the spirits of the dead and jack-o-lanterns reportedly originated from the actual practice of filling a human skull with human fat to watch it burn during Satan worship. The holiday began to frighten me even more than before. I was afraid of the real Satan worshippers in the world.

Nick and I decided to modify the Halloween to suit our beliefs. We enjoyed watching Nicholas Shawn and Kristopher dress up in their favorite fantasy costume. We limited their costume selection to non-threatening characters. And although many people will say that Halloween's all in fun, we had other more positive ways to have our fun. Nick and I felt at peace with our decision to eliminate the unnecessary evil from our innocent children's lives.

Jan needed a clear-cut division between celebrating Halloween and not celebrating Halloween. Jan decided to eliminate the celebration of Halloween all together.

Jan was fortunate that she had the luxury to devote every hour of the day to Nicky. Jan's life was caring and nurturing Nicky. I knew that she understood the importance of letting Nicky express her creative talents and let her act out healthy make believe. Although the traditional pagan way of expressing creativity during Halloween was out of the question, Jan started a new wholesome activity for Nicky and other children. Kristopher attended one such occasion in a month other than October.

Jan said, "Any month but October, I don't want this to turn out to be another form of Halloween. You know, Betty, we've been studying in Bible Study about how Satan is subtly entering into our children's lives through cartoon characters and even seemingly non-threatening cartoons. You know those "transformers" that are so popular? Well, it's part of a master plan to get children comfortable with aliens and demonic creatures and to take the children's focus off the Lord. After a while, when demons come to Earth, society will accept them and allow them into their hearts and mind. It's a scary thing. But that's why a person cannot fight the devil. Satan is involved in everything."

"Gee Jan, I'm sure I will look at all the characters that Nicholas and Kristopher are exposed to differently now."

Jan explained to me that holidays that were meant to glorify God, were never on the right historical date and the holidays always had a secular celebration as an alternative. For example, Christmas is often spelled Xmas and is celebrated on December 25th, but Jesus Christ was not really borne on the 25th of December. The alternative secular celebration is with Santa Claus, the Christmas tree, wreaths, and commercial gift giving. The date that Good Friday and Easter are celebrated is not historically correct either. These Christian holidays are celebrated with a secular Easter bunny and hunting for Easter eggs with the kids and result in de-emphasizing His gift of dying on the cross for our sins and rising from the dead.

"That's interesting, Jan. So what do you have going on?"

"Well, I'm just calling to invite Kristopher and Nicholas to a masquerade birthday party for a large bright red dog featured in children's books. Nicky's is inviting other children too."

"I'm sure Kristopher would love to come, but Nicholas has something else planned."

After a month, the day came for the party. The children played party games and dressed up in their favorite, but not scary, costumes. Toward the end of the party the children shared birthday cake and ice cream in honor of a big red dog named Clifford.

CHAPTER TWENTY-FIVE

▼

TELEVISION AND EVIL CHARACTERS

Once Jan's ministry re-programmed Jan's and my traditional holiday celebrations, the church moved on to direct other aspects of our lives. Jan and I spent countless hours planning how we could raise our children in a complex world full of mean people. It was soon evident that television was the gateway to innocent minds. Jan and I planned our defense strategy against the evils of modern day media and although Jan recognized that there were some good programs on television, there were far more secular shows. To adjust to the identified problem of secular television shows, Jan would only allow educational channels and pre-approved programs to air from her television. I chose to be less conservative and unsuccessfully attempted to limit Nicholas and Kristopher to a few pre-approved programs.

As a public service, the Concerned Christians attempted to educate parents about the danger of children watching cartoons. Cute little animated cartoons that parents grew to love while growing up were replaced by terrifying animated monsters that transformed from one identity to another. Even the most famous cartoon characters were under the suspicion of having a darker side. The ministry's newsletter encouraged parents to guard the entrance of their children's minds and warned that evil forces were covertly altering our children's mind. The ministry reported that television producers had evil motives for changing cartoons characters and ultimately the evil television producers would control younger children and make them think and do what a satanic group wanted them to do. Cute innocuous cartoon characters and toys that transformed from action heroes to monsters provided an avenue to infiltrate the minds of thousands of children at one time. Parents were warned that the purpose of these toys and cartoons was to get children comfortable with strange and evil looking characters so that they will accept the anti-Christ and demonic aliens when they are introduced in the future.

The Concerned Christians stressed that Satan uses a variety of subtle tricks to enter a person's life. As the world accepts an increasing number of secular programs, and Satan removes everyone's focus from the Lord, Satan would slowly invade the minds and souls of the world.

The ministry attacked every group known to man. Holistic health was a product of Satan. Meditation practices such as yoga and all forms of martial arts were criticized as being a form of worshipping the devil. Public schools cultivated and promoted Satan worshipping by not allowing prayer in school, while allowing the introduction of Buddhism and other religions and barring Christianity from the schools. The deprogramming continued with the core message warning that everything needed to be examined for elements of satanic influence. People in the world were in danger of losing their ability to discern good from evil. The Concerned Christians feared that people would eventually accept any and everything and that the Gospel would mean nothing.

Jan and I continued to analyze other aspects of our life and other programs on television. We analyzed popular sitcoms and noticed how the sitcoms were often based on a story that glamorized children rebelling against their parents. More often than not, the script demoralized the respected relationship between parent and child.

Jan and I independently decided that we could not be defeated in our battle to instill Christian morals and common respect for elders in our children. I continued to closely scrutinize the television shows Kristopher and Nicholas watched. As the boys and I watched the television shows, I critiqued the message to point out the good and illustrate how some of the stories undermined parents and authority. I explained to Nicholas Shawn and Kristopher that there would always be consequences to the choices they make. I asked them both to base their decisions on the golden rule.

Nick and I placed less emphasis on television and more emphasis on sports. Nicholas Shawn had a strong desire to learn karate. After an extensive search in the surrounding area, we identified an instructor who did not make the children bow to the east and worship a foreign god, we allowed both of our sons to take karate lessons. In order to maintain a close watch over our children's spiritual education, Nick and I enrolled in the classes. We monitored the Karate classes for repetitive mindless chanting and practices that would cause Nicholas Shawn and Kristopher to digress from their Christian education. In addition, both our sons were interested in acting so we enrolled them in acting classes. Meanwhile, Jan limited the television stations that Nicky could watch and involved Nicky in music, voice lessons, and a variety of sports activities. We all did our best, under the circumstances, to reduce the number of hours our children were exposed to negative influences.

The Concerned Christian's warned about the danger in listening to music, evil music. "You have to be careful what you listen to Betty, some songs have subliminal demonic messages. You don't want your innocent children to be subject to some demented person's scheme to destroy them."

Jan gave me a few examples of what she was talking about. My awareness heightened, I monitored the radio and found they played blatant satanic messages in songs that glorified murders and deviant sexual practices. Satan's subtle presence surprised me. I used to read horoscopes but I stopped because horoscopes were not of the Lord. I asked myself why I had to go to a newspaper to find out what some mere mortal is predicting in my life and take away my focus on Godly living. Besides, horoscopes were so generic that they could apply to anybody any day. Other examples of seemingly harmless or fascinating draws away from the Lord, were things like palm-readers, channelers, and people who worship Mother Earth. There were endless, seemingly harmless avenues for Satan to control a person's life and take the person's focus off the Lord.

I agreed with Jan that we needed to protect our children. I chose to send my children to private Christian schools. She chose to home school Nicky. Of course, Nick and I were interested in protecting Nicholas Shawn and Kristopher from the evils of the world but we also wanted them to enjoy being children. Jan could afford to make sure Nicky had all these things in a non-conventional way, because she didn't have to work.

▼

CHAPTER TWENTY-SIX

GROWTH ACTIVITIES (1985-1995)

I arrived at Jan's Pinebrook Hills home on an early Sunday afternoon in July 1988. As soon as I stepped out of the car I heard, "Come see the parade of lizard houses and condominiums! Each home is built to please even the most finicky lizard," Nicky and Kristopher said in unison.

"You two are something else, give me the VIP tour," I exclaimed. "Then Kris, you need to go get your clothes so we can head for home."

With smiles on their faces, Kris and Nicky explained the features of the pile of flat sandstone rocks called "lizard houses." Their eyes interpreted my facial expression as I examined their architectural talents.

I bent down to look inside one of the lizard condominiums, "Those are some lucky lizards if you ask me! I turned my head and looked up at both Nicky and Kristopher, standing with their little hands on their hips pleased with their creative housing project. "Well," I sighed and stood up and dusted the dirt off my knees, "I have to talk to Aunt Jan. Kris, go inside and get your clothes ready."

I walked up the driveway and met Jan at the front door. "Hi Jan, how were the kids? Nicky and Kristopher never fight, so I'm guessing they both enjoyed each other's company. I just toured the latest lizard houses. Those two certainly do not lack imagination."

"They both had a good time. Oh, Betty, they're not done. Nicky and Kristopher have a play they want you to see before you leave. It's hilarious!" Jan always beamed when she talked about Nicky and Kristopher. I could tell that they were a true source of joy for her. "Sit down on the couch, Betty, they worked on this play all weekend. They made their costumes and everything. You'll laugh, just wait and see."

Jan and I sat down on the couch smiling in anticipation of some silly production filled with wiggles and giggles. Soon the first star ran out and stopped with a bounce directly in front of our seats. "Ladies and Germs!" snorting with laughter between words, "I now present to you Tweezzers!"

Tweezzers came out in a flamboyant feathery number, laughing and swaying back and forth with her hands over her mouth and trying to stop smiling as she recited her lines. The play ended with the two of them trying to sing a song in tune, a perfect finale.

Jan and I clapped our hands and shouted, "Encore, encore!"

Both of the children ran into the bedroom pleased that they presented another grand performance. A person couldn't pay to have as much fun as Kristopher and Nicky had together naturally. Cousins or brother and sisters, the relationship and the memories were priceless.

Jan creatively sought ways to enrich Nicky's life. I was thankful that she included Nicholas Shawn and Kristopher whenever possible. "Before you go Betty, the University of Colorado has a summer program for children. They have astronomy, biology, oceanography, and several more programs. Do you want to send Nicholas Shawn and Kristopher? I'll pick them up every day and take them to lunch either before or after class."

"I can't believe it! Our kids will be going to a university?" I laughed, "I knew those days would come quick enough, but I didn't think it was going to be this fast. Why don't you send me the information for Nick's and my review."

"I'll give you a copy of the flyer, but you have to sign up soon because I think it's a very popular program."

Jan and I discussed the classes that were available and which one's Nicky wanted to attend. The courses were expensive but as long as we could afford to have our children participate in wholesome activities that enhanced their learning experience, we made it happen. When Jan and I told them what we had in store for them that summer and they screamed in delight. It was going to be fun for them to go to college to learn advanced studies, designed for inquisitive six to twelve-year-olds.

As time went on, all three children enjoyed the classes and looked forward to the next one. Nicky wanted to pursue a career in Oceanography. Jan encouraged her to learn more about the ocean. In addition to getting Nicky books from the library and bookstore about oceanography, Jan set up a field trip to see the ocean. Her field trips were so well planned out that Nicky had an itinerary, a workbook, a journal, and could take pictures of what they saw and learned.

Kristopher and Nicholas Shawn enjoyed visiting Aunt Jan's house. Most of the time Nicholas Shawn would play on one of Uncle John's many computers while the two younger ones played together in another room. Uncle John painstakingly showed Nicholas Shawn how to find information on the bulletin boards, the precursor to email. Whenever Nicholas Shawn had any questions, he called his Uncle John and asked him for help.

Jan usually had a ton of fun things planned for the children. She would either take them to the park, the zoo, museum or swimming to keep their minds clear from satanic influences. One thing for sure, the children were going to have a good time. She was a master at coordinating child activities and planned all extracurricular activities as if it were a class.

I always thought I should be more like her. I remember whenever we went anywhere together, Jan was prepared with all the right paraphernalia.

Whether it was a raincoat, a blanket for the park, or just sunglasses and sunscreen, Jan had it in the bag. She was famous for her emergency stash of nutritious snacks in case one of the children became cranky or hungry. When Jan pulled out her bag, I hid mine out of embarrassment. I used the excuse that my schedule was too hectic, but I learned from her good example and came better prepared on future outings.

CHAPTER TWENTY-SEVEN

▼

JOBS FOR THE RICH

Jan and John had a very unique lifestyle. Neither one of them worked a "regular" job but yet they were busy all the time. Jan immersed herself in volunteer work and John spent hours on the computer. It was hard for me to imagine what they did all day, their lives were so foreign to mine.

Early one October morning after dropping my children off at their private Christian school, I gave Jan a phone call.

"Jan, I hope I didn't wake you."

"Are you kidding me? I've been up since before daybreak. I always get up and study the Bible for a couple of hours before I get Nicky up for school. It's good to have some quiet time."

"I know you are busy home schooling Nicky during the day, but I thought I'd stop by and see you real quick while I was in Boulder. I know you said that you didn't want to be interrupted during school hours, but to tell you the truth…I don't know when your school hours are and I didn't want to disturb your lesson plan for the day."

"Oh I'm sure Nicky wouldn't mind the interruption. That's the nice thing about home schooling Betty. We turn everything into a lesson plan. You know, there's a lot to learn about life. Sometimes the things that seem so simple to you because you do them everyday, are a tremendous lesson for your son or daughter. Nicky studies History, English, Math, Spanish, but she also gets lessons in typing, cooking, sewing. There are endless opportunities to teach, and at our children's age, they are so hungry to learn."

"Jan, how in the world do you teach Spanish? You don't even know Spanish."

"Tapes, books, field trips…whatever it takes Betty."

"You have quite the life Jan. While the rest of the world works making someone else rich, you are enjoying every aspect of your child's life and still finding time to do things for your self and your family. But you know what Jan? You work harder in your volunteer job for the church than any working person I know."

"Well, as Christians we are to place the Lord before everything else in our lives. I will do what I can to raise Nicky in a good Christian environment. The way I see it, home schooling is the only way that I can teach Nicky how the Lord made everything possible. It seems to me that public schools can talk about any religion but not Christianity. I want Nicky to appreciate how the Lord created Heaven and Earth and spare her from Darwin and his band of idiots. By the way, you've been getting the tapes that I've been sending you, right? Well, Are you listening to them?"

"Yes, I've been getting the tapes, but I've been real busy. I don't have a lot of time to listen to tapes. I've been studying for my job. I think you're right about school though, kids now a-days don't know what to believe. They go to church to hear one thing, and then the children go to school and hear conflicting stories. Although I agree with you, I really can't stay at home. We need my income. We do the best we can, we send Nicholas Shawn and Kristopher to Christian schools to be focused on the Lord at school and we try to live a Christian life at home."

"I send tapes to Carol, too. At least Carol listens to them!" Jan scolded.

"I know, Carol mentioned Kim a couple of times. Nick and I are going to visit Carol and Jack this weekend."

"I don't get to see Carol much. I talk to her on the telephone and send her tapes, but I don't see her very often," Jan said and quickly changed the subject. "I was in the doctor's office the other day Betty and I was so mad. The doctor was questioning Nicky like I was abusing her. He interrogated Nicky! I just sat back and listen to the doctor's questions and Nicky's answers. The doctor wanted to know how many hours a day she studied, if she ever saw any other children, and if she got any exercise. He asked her to name all the subjects she was studying."

"Jan, I kind of get the same thing with the private school. The general population thinks that we are sheltering our children too much. So, what was Nicky's response?"

Well, she told him how many hours she studied and what specific classes she is taking. I really enjoyed watching the doctor's expression when she told him that she was taking piano lessons, voice lessons, swimming and gymnastics with other children. Betty, you know that Nicky is a very busy little girl."

"Yeah, I know. And she is involved with more people than the average public school child. Shoot, she can communicate with adults as if she were a four foot tall grown up."

"Anyway, I just get tired of all the accusations, let Nicky's test scores and talents speak for themselves. You know, she is past the traditional public school grade for her age and at the top of her class…that's why I have to keep such good records. If I didn't the government could take Nicky away from me for not sending her to school. I would document her progress anyway, but I hate the threat hanging over my head all the time."

"Jan, Nicky is the most privileged little girl I know. It irritates me to hear that people are cross-examining you and her like that."

"I'm glad you're coming over today Betty. John, Nicky, and I are going to our Ouray home for a few weeks and we will not be around. It's one of the benefits of home schooling, we can travel and still not interrupt

Nicky's school. Nicky kind of enjoys the change in scenery anyway and she gets to visit her little girlfriends in Ouray."

"Well I'm glad I caught you before you left. You've been traveling a lot this year. Connecticut, Florida, Ouray, Boulder, and where ever else…you have quite the life."

"Betty, you should really consider home schooling Nicholas Shawn and Kristopher…really."

"Jan, I don't have your lifestyle…remember? I have to work."

"You only have to work because you want to. Anyway, I guess I better wake up Nicky and I'll see you when you get here."

"Okay Jan." I hung up the phone and gathered the chocolate chip cookies I baked and placed them in a plastic container to take to Jan. I placed them safely in the back seat of my Audi.

I enjoyed driving into Pinebrook Hills, the big expensive homes intrigued my curiosity. I wondered, as I pulled into Jan's driveway, what do these people do for a living to live in such luxury? I walked up to the door and knocked. Jan came to the door and let me inside. "Hi Jan, here are some cookies, am I here at a bad time?"

"Oh Betty, now I'll have to fight these off! And no, it isn't a bad time. Nicky's downstairs finishing an assignment and will be finished soon. I was working on something for the church until it was time for Nicky's next class. You would be surprised how much you can get done when you home school your child. While the child is finishing a lesson plan, you can be working on something too. Don't get me wrong, it's hard work, but there is a tremendous payoff."

I shook my head no, "I would be fighting with Nicholas Shawn all day if I home schooled him. He is such a gregarious socialite. There is no way he would put up with me twenty-four hours a day. I don't think Kristopher would appreciate it either."

"Well, Nicky doesn't have to put up with me the whole time, John takes over when the subject is more his expertise rather than mine. And then of course she has classes outside the home."

I walked over and sat on the couch, "Nicky loves John so much, I'm sure it's a treat to have his participation. But as far as Nick and I doing the same thing Jan, forget it. It just wouldn't work for us."

Jan followed me and sat on the chair next to John. John was concentrating on his laptop computer, he was always working on his computers. I guessed that he was checking the stock market. "John, Nicholas Shawn really appreciated you letting him use one of your computers the other day, Nicholas Shawn said that you taught him a lot. Thank you for doing that with him."

"It was no problem, I was glad to show him a few things."

"Nicholas Shawn asked me if you would mind if he called you when he gets stuck on our computer. Nick and I wouldn't be much help to him and he admires you a lot."

John smiled, "I don't mind at all."

"Thanks John, Nicholas Shawn has really taken an interest in our computer. He set it up in his room and now Nick and I are lucky if we get to use it for our advanced studies at college."

Jan shook her head. "You know Betty, I don't know why you are wasting your time going to college. The world is going to end soon anyway."

Confused, I said, "Jan, I don't understand you. You do a lot of advanced classes for Nicky and then you say that the world is going to end anyway. It seems like you're living a contradiction."

Jan looked at me in disgust. I felt uncomfortable and said, "Well, I better get going, I'll give you a call later. Thank you for visiting with me, Jan and John. It's always good to see you."

CHAPTER TWENTY-EIGHT

▼

THE MEETING

Jan didn't seem to mind when I dropped by to visit unannounced. One particular day, in the late 80's, I came to Boulder to shop at the Pearl Street Mall. After shopping, I decided that it would be fun to see Jan for a while. I took a short detour down Broadway and up to Pinebrook Hills. I knocked on the door. Jan came quietly to the door and she whispered, "We're having a Bible study in the front room. I can't visit right now. Oh follow me, I have something I want to give you."

Jan always had something for me. Sometimes it was an article from a newspaper, an audiotape of a story by Nicky, clothes that she no longer wanted, or maybe a piano concert audiotape by performing artist, Nicky.

I followed Jan past the living room and into the kitchen, there were several people surrounding a guy that was a sitting a little higher than the rest. It reminded me of a time when a friend told me that if I wanted to have the psychological advantage over my employees, that I should elevate my office chair higher than theirs. My friend told me to always face toward the door so that I have the advantage of controlling distractions.

Although I never felt the need to take his advice, I could recognize a player.

As I walked by the group in the living room, I thought to myself, this player's no dummy, he knows how the game works. The player slowly turned his head and gazed my way, looking at me as if I were invisible and continued talking to the group. I had a strong premonition. I couldn't have felt more uncomfortable about the player if he were to slither over my shoes. Strange…I thought, I felt this way only one other time, and Jan introduced me to that man too.

"Did you want to stay for Bible study? I'll get you a beverage and you can come and sit in the front room with us."

"Oh no, I just bought some clothes at the mall and I thought I would stop by to see you a minute. I'll just go home and check in with you another time."

"Well here, take these cookies. I want them out of my sight, they're too tempting. Nicky and I made them last night."

"Thanks Jan, make me fat instead. You know I hear food screaming at me from the other room. I'm the one that will end up eating these cookies, no one else."

"Better you than me!"

I started walking to the door. Jan insisted that she introduce the members of her Bible Study group. She introduced the group leader last, "Betty, this is Kim Miller."

Kim looked down at me and said rather snobbishly, "Huh, it's nice to meet you."

"I've heard a lot about you Kim, please excuse me, I was just leaving. I'm sorry to interrupt." I walked away thinking…um, so this is the guy.

Kim turned his attention back to the members of the Bible Study as Jan walked me to the door, "Sorry Jan, I didn't mean to interrupt your Bible Study."

"That's okay, I'll give you a call later."

"Okay, bye."

As I drove home I couldn't get over the feeling that I had in the pit of my stomach when I met Kim. It's strange that I should feel so repulsed about someone I had just met. I thought, Jan likes him, he hasn't committed a crime, so I asked myself, what's my problem? I needed to give Kim the benefit of the doubt.

No, there's something real about how I feel, I will just have to pray about it.

CHAPTER TWENTY-NINE

▼

BLIND LOYALTY

Later in the evening, I couldn't get Jan out of my mind. I thought, Jan doesn't have to work outside the home. She has the opportunity to do anything she wants to do all day. Yet she chooses to work harder than most any body I know. She types newsletters and donates money and time to improve Kim's quality of life. She seems to enjoy her volunteer work but she never gets a break. Between home schooling Nicky, and her volunteer work, Jan has no time for anything else.

So, this is the guy that Jan said didn't have a car, didn't own anything, and lived very frugally. Jan said that Kim was just simply devoting his life to the work of the Lord. She said that Kim went through some transformation after fasting and depriving himself of life's necessities. She seemed convinced that Kim was a man of God. But I couldn't get over the gut feeling that I had when I first met Kim, the hair on my neck stood on end.

Anyone who really knew Jan could see that she was a devoted Christian, wife, and mother. I couldn't criticize Jan for what she was doing and I would normally stay out of her business, but my soul was disturbed.

I could not understand Jan's loyalty to Kim. Jan and I had blood relatives who were very ill and could use her help, not charity, but a kind sisterly gesture now and then. I understood Jan's loyalty to God. Jan did not have a brick and mortar church so Kim essentially became the "church." It appeared to me, that Kim and his wife, Marsha were taking advantage of Jan's kind heart. They received money, furniture, and God knows what else they could squeeze from the good hearts of Jan and John. In turn, Kim taught his version of the gospel.

I knew that a "Marsha" was Jan's hairdresser, but I didn't realize it until later that the Marsha that cut Jan's hair was probably Kim's wife. Jan said that Kim and Marsha live so frugally and didn't own a car, so as a service to the church, Jan would taxi Marsha to the store or wherever she needed to go. In turn, Jan felt good about herself and her ability to make a difference in their lives and for the betterment of the church.

As time went on, I noticed that Jan began to have an increased sense of purpose and felt that her work with the church was tantamount to saving the world. With the dedication of the most loyal employee, Jan worked night and day to type and assemble Kim's message in the form of a newsletter that would, in her mind, save souls. Her tireless service included mailing audiotapes to potential members. Sometimes she served Kim by helping free up his time by running errands so the voice of the church could dedicate more time saving souls and from my observation, solicit more money.

Part of me was happy that Jan found something that she could be so passionate about. I couldn't relate because much of my identity came from my children, my husband, and my career. I could understand that Jan's identity was directly related to her child, husband and her volunteer work for the church. But I noticed a strong contrast between how much she was doing and giving of herself to her church, and her compassion for her mother, sisters, brothers and eventually her daughter. I surmised that the love and attention that she gave to her immediate family was inversely proportional to the amount of advice she was getting from Kim.

As time went on, I couldn't help but think that if my relatives were wealthy, Kim would have manipulated Jan to recruit her family members so that he could snatch them out of their comfortable lives too. But, my family was riddled with health problems in the form of heart disease and cancer. The high cost of medical care depleted my relative's assets and made them unlikely candidates for Kim's ministry.

I often envisioned Kim, as a huge parasite attached to Jan and John, leaching anything that he could get from them. The more aware I became of his sticky tactics, the more I would try to tell Jan that there was something about Kim that didn't seem right to me. Jan and I often fought about her strong allegiance to Kim. Jan adamantly defended Kim each time I tried to get her to look objectively at what he was doing. In order to keep peace between Jan and I, we usually ended the conversation by agreeing to disagree.

CHAPTER THIRTY

▼

CELEBRATING SELF

It was an unusually hot day in July. Jan asked if Nicholas Shawn and Kristopher wanted to join Nicky for an afternoon at the swimming pool. When I arrived at Jan's house, I knocked on the door. I could hear Jan shout from the other side of the house, "Come on in, Betty…Nicky's downstairs."

I don't remember Jan and John ever locking their door, on the other hand, some people would consider me neurotic about making sure doors were locked. I walked inside Jan's house and up the stairs, while the boys ran down the stairs to find Nicky.

John peeked over the rail of the loft and waved.

"Hi John, where's Jan?"

"She's up here with me. Come on up."

I climbed the winding stairs, "There you are, Jan! What are you doing?"

"Oh, I'm just planning Nicky's birthday party. I thought I'd have it in the red caboose, you know, the one by Crossroads Mall?"

"I always wanted to see inside that caboose."

"The restaurant has a birthday special. There are a couple of plans to choose from. I'm going to buy the one where the children can have lunch, cake and ice cream, and maybe have a clown to help out with activities like face painting."

"That sounds like fun. I have to plan something for Nicholas Shawn and Kristopher too. It's not easy when all three of their birthdays fall within a two week timeframe!"

"Betty, why don't you just combine both the boy's birthday party with Nicky's. I have a flyer here that you can send out to a few of their friends."

"Wow, I'm impressed, this looks really nice! Did you do this with your computer? Look all the different fonts and colors! It must be nice to have everything you want, Jan." I smiled as I made a snarling face at her to let her know that I was envious, but loved her anyway. "Let's call the kids upstairs and see if they want to share their birthdays. We'll tell Nicholas Shawn and Kristopher that they can invite a couple of their friends."

We called the children up and showed them the flyer. They all smiled and nodded their heads as they fidgeted, anxious to get to the swimming pool.

"I guess you guys are ready to go swimming!" Your Aunt Jan and I will be ready in a few minutes. Go get your towels and we'll be downstairs by the time you're ready."

The children ran downstairs and waited impatiently while Jan finalized her project. "Betty, did you want to go in my car?"

"No, we'll have to go home when the boys are done swimming. I'll just follow you to the pool."

We arrived at the pool and Jan and I stood in the shallow end of the pool as we watched our three children face-float back and forth across the pool. Their laughter and giggles reminded me of my younger days. Jan and I couldn't help smiling with our young ones, but occasionally frowned when one of the children splashed too vigorously. Four hours and five sunburns later, we packed up the car and promised that we would do it again after we recovered from sunstroke.

A week later I called Jan to warn her, "Jan, you won't believe this but I gave Nicholas Shawn the flyer you made…well guess what he did with it? He gave it to his teacher in daycare, and she posted it for all the kids to see. I can't tell you how many people will be at the party!"

I heard a nervous laugh on the other end of the telephone, "Oh you're kidding me! Well, this could be interesting."

The day of the party came and fortunately we had a small number of guests at the party. Nick, Jan, and I kept busy making sure that the children had all the hamburgers, cake, and ice cream that they wanted. Nick appointed himself as the official sticker applicator and photographer. The grown-ups were enjoying the party as much as the children.

CHAPTER THIRTY-ONE

▼

VACATION HOMES

Ouray, Colorado, a picturesque mountain community nestled in a valley of tall snow capped mountains with an occasional waterfall streaming down the mountainside was one of Jan and John's favorite get-a-ways. Since the late 1980's, Jan and John owned their own piece of paradise close to the Ouray's natural hot springs. The quaint European town offered a rich mining history, quaint shops, and gourmet restaurants.

It was almost Easter 1989 and Jan called me on the telephone. "Betty, I was wondering if you, Nick, and the boys want come up to Ouray during your long Easter weekend?"

"That would be fun. I'll ask Nick to see if he has anything planned with his family. How long does it take to get to Ouray from here?"

"Oh, it takes about five hours, something like that. Anyway, you'll be staying a couple of days, you'll have time to rest before you have to drive back home. I want you to see our little vacation home. It's real cute. I wouldn't mind moving to Ouray for good, and who knows? Maybe we will move there someday."

"How does Nicky like it in Ouray?"

"Nicky really likes it. She has little friends in Ouray that she enjoys playing with and I think she likes being in Ouray better than Boulder."

"Hey, hold on a minute, Jan. Nick just pulled in the driveway. Let me ask Nick if he wants to go to Ouray this Easter."

I set down the telephone and asked Nick if he wanted to go to Ouray for Easter. He nodded his head yes, so I ran into the house to tell Jan.

"We're good to go, Jan! I would love to see your new home. Thanks for asking us."

Good Friday was here before we knew it. Nick, Nicholas Shawn, Kristopher, and I loaded our GMC Jimmy with clothes for the weekend and drove to Ouray. When we arrived in Jan's driveway we saw a small home that sat on the edge of a cliff overlooking the Rocky Mountains village, commonly called "Little Switzerland." I was impressed as I entered the sliding glass door off the deck of the living room. "Jan, you sure must have enjoyed decorating this home."

Come with me and I'll show you the rest of the home. Jan guided me throughout the house. Every room had a blue and white color scheme that was not only in harmony with the adjoining room but also the blue sky and purple mountains visible through the sliding glass doors. "This place looks like it should be featured in the next Colorado Home magazine, you really did a good job decorating this place, Jan."

"Well, I'm glad it's over. There's no place to buy home furnishings in Ouray so the closest town that I could buy anything was in Montrose. I couldn't tell you how many trips I took driving back and forth to Montrose."

"It was worth it, Jan. Now you're done and all you have to do is enjoy it."

"Hey Betty, do you want to take the kids swimming at the Hot Springs later?"

"We brought our swimming suits, Jan. We're ready when you are!"

"Well then, let's go!"

We drove down the mountain and were in the pool in less than ten minutes. It was a sunny but cool day in April and the temperature of the water was just right. The steam hovered over the water and filtered the facial features of the hot springs bathers. Strands of my long blonde hair curled loosely on the nap of my neck. I looked at Jan. She was obviously enjoying the pool and the companionship of her family. Her soft smile seemed peaceful and content. Jan was careful not to get her head wet and it reminded me of the days of swimming in the cow trough. I was happy that Jan had learned over the years to relax and enjoy life.

The next day we drove the children to an Easter egg hunt in a small town outside Ouray. Jan, Nick, and I watched the festivities. The children stood in line at the edge of the park each with a basket in their hand. All three children were tall for their age. Nicholas Shawn was in the oldest age bracket allowed to participate in the Easter egg hunt. Towering over many of the parents, Nicholas Shawn stood holding his basket innocently waiting for the race to begin. Nick had a sad look on his face as he looked at his son and said, "Nicholas Shawn doesn't realize that he looks out of place among the shorter children his age, poor baby."

Jan shook her head and added, "Nicholas Shawn's growing too fast, isn't he? But, it's great that he doesn't let his size stop him from enjoying being a kid."

I aimed the camera toward Nicholas Shawn, "I know, big boys are often stereotyped as "bullies. This is a real contrast, today people are seeing a big kid getting ready to hunt for Easter eggs."

Nick smiled, "I'm proud of my boys. They don't realize how big they are. And I wouldn't change them for the world. There is not a lot of boys their age that kiss their dad in front of their friends."

"Nicky's happy too. Look at her and Kristopher. They enjoy doing everything together. The Lord blessed them with each other."

"Oh Betty! Jan walked over and touched my arm, "The race is starting! Look at the kids go!"

"That was funny!" Nick laughed, "That kid just stepped on a hard boiled egg and even though he smashed it, he still put it in his bag."

Jan, Nick, and I laughed as we watched all the children scamper around the grass and through the shrubs looking for eggs, especially the plastic eggs. The plastics ones had prizes inside. After a while the children started to slow down, still searching and sometimes walking over to a suspicious looking rock or dried leaf only to discover that the object was part of the landscape. When the Easter egg hunt was finished, a group of children stood in a small group and analyzed their loot. Inside Nicholas Shawn's plastic egg was a certificate for a free sundae at the local ice cream store.

"Okay, who wants to go get ice cream?" Nick said with a big smile on his face.

I do…I do…I do! The three children shrieked.

We climbed into the car and drove across the street. We walked in the ice cream store and two high school girls were standing behind the counter. I stood behind the kids as they ordered their ice cream. The conversation that I heard between one of the girls and Nicholas Shawn surprised me.

When I got in the car I asked Nick, "Did you see how that girl was flirting with Nicholas Shawn? Shoot, she must have been six years older than Nicholas."

"Yeah, I heard her ask him what he was doing later. I don't even think Nicholas Shawn knew she was hitting on him. If she only knew that he was in the Easter egg hunt just minutes before we walked in, she would realize that Nicholas Shawn is not even a teenager."

With their ice cream cones in hand, the kids all climbed into the car. As soon as the kids settled down Jan asked, "You guys want to go swimming again after we get home?"

"Yeah!" They all responded.

Nick and I drove home and stayed long enough to drop Jan off and grab our swimsuits. In just a few short minutes we arrived at the pool for a few hours of wet fun. Nick and I lounged around the hot section of the pool while the children enjoyed playing Marco Polo.

"Betty! Look on the side of the mountain! See it? Do you see the mountain goat?" Wildlife fascinated Nick. He could spot a deer, elk, or antelope from miles away.

"Wow! I've never seen a mountain goat before. Is there a herd of them? Or do mountain goats travel in herds? Anyway, I don't see any other mountain goats around, do you?"

"No, I can't see any other mountain goats. Isn't he beautiful? And the scenery all around us is majestic. This really is a pretty place Betty. You know, I think John is right. This really is premium property. I think I saw an old house downtown that you would like. You know how you like Victorian homes, Betty." Nick glanced at his waterproof watch, "We better head back home, it is almost 1:00. I think John wanted to take the kids sledding in Telluride. You want to go to Telluride with us?"

"Oh, it depends on whether Jan wants to go or not. If she doesn't want to go, I'm just going to stay and visit with her, but I wouldn't mind seeing Telluride. I've heard it's beautiful there and there are a lot of movie stars that are finding Telluride a nice alternative to Aspen."

"Now *that* would be a good place to own property, Betty. Hey, you brought the boys Easter baskets for tomorrow right?"

"Yes, I have them in the car. And just in case Jan didn't get Nicky anything, I bought a few extra things. I could make three baskets instead of two if we need to. I think that Jan bought Nicky's some stuff though. All I know is, we are planning to go to Easter Brunch in one of Ouray's historic restaurants"

While Nick coached the children out of the pool, I thought about how awkward it would be if Jan didn't have a basket ready for Nicky. I would have to talk to Jan to see what she had planned. I doubted that Jan was planning to go to one of the local churches. I felt guilty, we always celebrated Easter. If we did nothing else, we had a quiet worship time on Easter.

CHAPTER THIRTY-TWO

▼

EASTER MORNING

Early Easter morning, Nicky woke up Jan and John while Nicholas Shawn and Kristopher stood by our beds saying, "Come on! It's time to wake up and see if the Easter Bunny came!"

Satisfied that they successfully woke up the grownups, the children ran and sat on the floor in the living room, their eye panning across the room trying to find the clues to where the Easter Bunny hid their baskets. I overheard the children talking in the next room. "The Easter Bunny came last night. Look, the carrot we left the Easter Bunny is half eaten."

Meanwhile, Nick pulled on a T-shirt and his jeans as I fumbled through our luggage to find something suitable to wear. Nick grabbed the camera and came out of the bedroom shooting. The flashing of the camera renewed the children's energy and they stood up ready to dash for their hidden baskets. The house was alive with excitement and laughter. I quickly ran a comb through my hair and joined everyone in the living room.

"Wait!" Nick ordered, "Okay, you guys know the rules! If you find someone else's basket you have to just leave it where you found it and not say a thing. Everyone is to find their own basket," Nick explained. "Okay...get ready," he paused to heighten the anticipation, "Get set...." Another long pause. "Go!"

The children made a quick jumpstart and bolted toward the kitchen. The grown ups watched and the children searched. Occasionally one of us would blurt out "You're cold! You're hot! No, you're getting colder!" Finally, Nicholas Shawn and Nicky found their Easter basket but Kristopher couldn't find his. Kristopher was getting suspicious.

We often played practical jokes on each other but especially on Kristopher. During mealtime we often dished out enormous portions of food for Nicholas Shawn and the rest of the family and then dished Kristopher out teaspoon size portions of food and placed it in the middle of his plate. Kristopher reaction to our teasing was always theatrical, our kidding was always rewarded with a dramatic display of "Hey! Why me?"

This Easter, Nick, Jan, and I decided to hide a miniature basket for Kristopher and watch the expression on his face. Kristopher was in the laundry room when he found the very small basket. Kristopher spun around holding the small basket and said, "Hey..."

Nicholas Shawn and Nicky laughed at Kristopher as he continued to say, "You got to be kidding me! Mom, this is almost as bad as when you froze my spoon in my cereal bowl. Remember? It was April Fools' Day and I had cereal all over me when I lifted the spoon. Just wait, I'm going to get even with you guys."

"Gee Kristopher, don't you like your basket?" Jan asked with a smile.

Nick handed Kristopher a large basket. We knew the boys would keep score on everything that we did for each of them so Nick and I made sure their baskets were even in every way.

We watched as Nicholas Shawn, Nicky, and Kristopher rummaged through their Easter baskets with big smiles and a little chocolate on their faces.

CHAPTER THIRTY-THREE

▼

GOOD-BYE PARTIES

I peeked outside the double doors of Jan's Pinebrook Hills home to see if it was safe to talk about Nick's birthday, John and Nick were standing by the grill cooking the salmon John caught from his mother's yacht. I walked over to the kitchen counter and watched her for a moment as she prepared one of her specialties on the stove. Jan always impressed me with her culinary skills. I knew that I didn't spend enough time in the kitchen to be a good cook, but I always dreamed that when I had more time, I would master the art of cooking. Until then, I would have to stand back and hope that maybe through osmosis I could pick up a few pointers.

"Nick turns 40 this year, Jan"

"Are you going to throw him a party?"

"I am really thinking about it, Nick has never had a birthday party. His December 10th birthday is so close to Christmas that his birthday celebration was always included in the family's Christmas festivities. I'm thinking about throwing him a surprise party in September but I'm not sure where I'll do it, maybe a hotel meeting room or something."

"You're kidding! He's never had a party? If you want, you can use my house, that is, if you don't invite a bunch of kids. An adult party would be great."

"Really? Maybe I will. He'd never suspect a thing!"

Jan laughed, "Well, that certainly would be a surprise, Betty!"

"Since children would be tough to handle, I think I'll just invite people from work to this party and throw him another party on his birthday for so his nieces and nephews can come."

"I would appreciate it if you would, Betty."

Jan walked in the next room and came back with a pen and paper and sat on the couch next to me. Jan wrote down each detail of the party. "Okay Betty, the party will be here so lets limit the number of people to…say…twenty."

I watched her write down the number of people. Jan's handwriting rivaled the most talented calligrapher. "Twenty?" I tried to hide my disappointment. I hated to eliminate anyone, but I didn't want to take advantage of Jan's hospitality. "That's sounds good to me, Jan, I appreciate it. "Oh wow! I just had a great idea! I'm going to see if I can get a hold of Nick's old high school football tapes. I bet I can get them from our old school!"

"I bet Nick would really like that. Wasn't he All-American in football?"

"Yeah, Nick will be so surprised to see those tapes after twenty-three years!"

Jan smiled as she shifted in her seat, "Getting down to business, what kind of food are you going to have?"

"Since you and John introduced us to the exotic Indian delicacies, Nick has been bugging me to learn to make nan, and, oh what is it called? You know that spinach stuff…saag paneer? That's right saag paneer! Nick and I crave it at least once a month. What would you say if I had the Royal Peacock Restaurant cater the party."

"I'm sure the owner Shante would love to cater it for you. John likes Indian food too and it would be a treat for some of the guests."

For the next few weeks I tried to track down the football tapes. I called Jan to give her a progress report. "Jan, you won't believe this, I located the high school football tapes. Guess where I found them."

"If you found them at the high school you wouldn't be asking me to guess, so I give up."

"Jan, you know you're getting old when you find your high school records in the local museum! Can you believe it? Now that's old! Ha! Wait till Nick finds out, the old coot."

"That's really funny, Betty. We'll be sure to tell the old geezer. By the way, I picked up some Over the Hill gag gifts for him."

"I can't wait! I had Nicholas Shawn and Kristopher draw a picture of a turkey jumping over a hill. I'm going to take the drawing to the bakery and have them decorate the cake with the identical drawing. I searched through all Nick's elementary school pictures and found a picture of Nick smiling. It's really cute. He doesn't have his two front teeth. I thought we could put his toothless picture on the front of the invitation and the turkey drawing on the back of the invitation. What do you think?"

Jan laughed, "Nick's going to be so embarrassed, Betty."

Jan and I enjoyed planning the party for the next five weeks. She found a place that would put Nick's picture on the invitation. After work, I drove over to Jan's to finalize all the arrangements. To trick Nick, we told him that we were going to Shante's fortieth birthday party.

Finally, the day of the party, Nick and I arrived at the surprise party on time. It didn't seem unusual that none of the guests had arrived since we were to arrive early to help Jan and John decorate and prepare appetizers for the party. The door was unlocked so Nick and I walked into the house. A sign hung over the stairwell, *Happy 40th Birthday!* Nick laughed as he walked up the stairs, "Ha! Shante's forty years old! I'm going to have fun teasing him!" Nick looked at me sheepishly, "I guess I can't say much, huh? I'll be forty soon."

My toothy grin almost gave me away as I fought back the urge to laugh. "Yep, you're just a couple of old buzzards!"

As we got closer to the kitchen I slowed down and let Nick walk in to the room first. Suddenly, Nick stopped. His eyes widened and his mouth dropped as he looked at all the people that he knew from work and read the banner across the room, *Happy 40th Birthday Nick!* The room exploded with a loud HAPPY BIRTHDAY, followed by laughter. Nick buckled at the knees in shock.

After Nick regained his composure, I walked him over to the couch. "I have a surprise for you, just watch."

John placed the tape in the VCR and turned on the television. Nick's eyes were glued to the television set, anxious to see what was in store for him on the television. *Happy Birthday Nick Chavez, 33* flashed on the screen. Then a Louisville High School running back with the number *33* made one touchdown after another and kicked several field goals to the sound of rock and roll from the 70's. He was reliving a very special time in his life. His eyes were moist with joy. Nick tried to suck it all up and regain his composure but it was too late, we saw an open display of gratitude and appreciation that only comes from the heart. We touched Nick's heart by honoring him in such a special way.

CHAPTER THIRTY-FOUR

▼

NOTHING SPECIAL

Nick's party was one of the last parties that Jan and John would have at their house. They even stopped attending parties, including John's good friend's annual survivor party. Every year, John's friend commemorated that he survived a horrible plane crash by throwing a party using the severed wing of his plane as a refreshment table. John was so gregarious that it sounded unnatural for him to stop socializing.

Gradually Jan and John were abandoning their friends one by one. It was barely noticeable that the house was slowly becoming quiet. I first noticed the silence when Jan stopped meeting with some of the women that she knew. Then, couples who Jan and John knew and loved for years were no longer invited over to Jan and John's house. Finally, a childhood friend of John's and his wife were no longer part of their social circle.

I didn't understand at the time, but I noticed that the joy and laughter in the house was diminishing and the occasional smiles were becoming even more rare. I noticed that Jan still made an effort to see that Nicky had friends around her and that Nicky was able to enjoy being a child. But

Jan was very hard on herself. She was careful not to display any signs of depression, but I could see that there was something stressful in her life. Jan, a woman who had everything in the world was not happy anymore. When Jan was happy her personality was cute and giddy. Something was making Jan limit her celebration of life.

It was happening to John too, however he seemed to have more compassion than Jan did, or maybe it was because he was relatively new to the rules of Kim's game. But the jovial man that I had known for ten years was slowly transitioning into a more serious and detached person. The cheerful guy who enjoyed being around his friends, who enjoyed tinkering with electronics and computers seemed mysteriously different.

I tried to analyze the situation. It appeared to me that the reason both Jan and John's life seemed increasingly mundane, was because they fell into a rut. There were no special days in their lives to lift their spirits and their home was filled with deafening silence. The fact that holidays and birthdays were seldom celebrated and Jan and John were gradually removing themselves from their social circles surely was the root cause. It was becoming more apparent that an outside influence was responsible for their actions. It appeared that in order to please God, Jan had to eliminate anything that would make her happy, such as shopping, entertaining guests, or traveling, unless she sought permission first.

Jan vacillated between what was acceptable and what was not pleasing to the Lord. It would appear to a person who did not know the circumstances that Jan was not capable of making a decision, but in reality, she was an intelligent woman who chose to give up her own free will to please the Lord.

It seemed that her spiritual advisor was exercising his newfound power and would contradict his own orders out of experimentation, power, or possibly dementia. Regardless of the reason, Jan believed in her heart that she was serving the Almighty Lord. I couldn't' help thinking that Kim was toying with Jan's life as if she were a marionette, when he instructed Jan to go shopping at a thrift shop to purchase a religious statue. When she came home she was completely befuddled about why she would purchase such a thing. She called both Carol and I and shared her experience with us. Jan said that Kim told her that God changed his mind and that she should take the statue back to the store where she bought it. When Jan asked Kim why God would have her buy such a thing, Kim responded by telling her that God was only testing her or God simply changed his mind.

Jan seemed to think that it was funny that she had to buy a religious statue. I was troubled by the news, we were taught as children not to worship idols or statues and suddenly Jan left her basic beliefs and purchased an item that she never would have dreamed of buying under normal circumstances.

I should have realized that it was Kim that was giving Jan direction through the guise of God. Sometimes when Jan and I discussed something that needed resolution, Jan told me that she would have to talk to God about it. I naturally thought that she was talking to God like Daddy used to talk to God in the field. I never dreamed that Jan was using Kim as a mediator to talk to God. It didn't make sense that Jan would talk to God through any other person. I heard Jan on numerous occasions, criticize people who claimed to channel to God. I didn't see a lot of difference between someone claiming that God talked through him and someone channeling to talk to God.

I was troubled to know that Jan talked about Kim as though he was some kind of spiritual prophet, or God himself. It was confusing for me to listen to Jan speak about Kim, I often did not know if Jan was talking about Kim or God. Most of the time Jan would speak about Kim but disguise who she was speaking about by just saying that God directed her to do something, or she could not do something because it did not please the Lord. When Jan talked in abstract doctrine, I just listened. I had to remind myself that we live in a free country and that Jan was entitled to believe what she wanted to believe in.

Still, it bothered me…Jan's actions and beliefs were becoming increasingly foreign to me.

CHAPTER THIRTY-FIVE

▼

MORTALS AND OTHER CREATURES

By the early-1990's Jan became more and more defensive as I found that it was extremely difficult to be diplomatic about my opinion of Kim. I soon found the one sure way of creating tension between us was to criticize Kim.

One day as I sat on a rocker in my front room and gazing out at the lake, Jan and I had another conversation about Biblical doctrine. I came to the conclusion that I couldn't stand it anymore, I had finally built up the nerve to say what was on my mind. "I don't understand it, why do you do so much for this…this Kim guy? You give him furniture, money, you take his wife shopping, and cater to his every need. I don't understand it, your own brother has had a heart attack, a quadruple by-pass, and recently lost twins at birth, plus our sister Carol is sick with cancer. They both could use your help and you continue to focus on some guy who isn't even related to you. I don't understand, what's the attraction in Kim?"

Jan replied indignantly, "You don't understand. First of all, it's none of your business, and second, Kim recently suffered a great deal for the Lord. He fasted for a very long time, became weak and suffered tremendously.

Kim is not your average man, he is a godly man and has a personal relationship with the Lord. Kim literally gave up everything he had for the Lord and has been rewarded with the gift of Truth."

"Well, I guess I just don't see it Jan. All I see is someone who is taking you for granted. Don't lose focus on the fact that you have a brother and a sister with health problems and that could use your help. I know I don't do enough for them myself. The Lord blessed our family with each other and we should stay together. Your family is not some random man who walked off the street and has his hand out to you. You have Nicky, John, his children, Mom, and your brothers and sisters, we all love you. We all need your moral support, not your money, just your compassion…that's all, we are your family, not Kim."

"Betty, you really just don't understand and I think that we should just stay away from this subject," Jan slammed down the telephone. I tried to call her back and she wouldn't answer, she blocked my number from calling.

Jan didn't call me for several months and my attempts to call her were in vain. I tried to open my mind to what she was trying to tell me, but deep in the confines of my soul, I couldn't fathom Kim's elevated status, I still saw him as a phony. Maybe I was in denial, I gave Jan the benefit of the doubt and decided that Jan didn't *really* think that God actually talked through Kim. To me the idea was simply inconceivable.

It took Jan six months before she called me and asked if I wanted to go to lunch with her and Nicky. I was anxious to patch things up. Jan, Nicky, and I met at a Mexican Restaurant in Boulder. "I just think we need to forget about our differences, Betty. What do you think?"

"You're right. It's stupid to fight anyway. Life is way too short." I looked over at Nicky I realized how much I missed her. She was so cute and sweet. "Nicky, do you want to come and visit Kristopher?"

She looked at her mother for approval and turned to me and said, "Yes Aunt Betty, I would like that!"

After lunch, Jan invited me over to her house so Nicky could get some clothes to spend the night. When we arrived at her house, Jan walked over to a closet in the hall and looked at some things that she bought while we were not speaking. She reached in the closet and pulled out a four-inch tall macramé rocking horse. "Here Betty, I thought you might like this...I know how horse crazy you used to be."

My eyes held back the tears of joy and a tinge of guilt, "Oh Jan you don't have to give me anything but I appreciate your thoughtfulness." As I held the small horse, I thought that it didn't matter what the gift was, but the act of kindness was symbolic of her love and kind heart and I was thankful to have Jan and Nicky back in my life again. I felt guilty because I didn't buy them anything. I wanted to show Jan an expression of my love for her, but I thought that giving gifts was against her religion. I wanted Jan to know that I loved her too.

CHAPTER THIRTY-SIX

▼

HUSBANDS AND GOD

The next time I stopped by to see Jan, we discussed in length what a Christian wife was expected to do if her husband was not a godly man. Jan said, "A wife needs to obey her husband. The subservient wife sets an example for her husband and shows him how to live a godly life. Eventually the husband sees his wife's strength and happiness and accepts the Lord."

"But what if the husband is an atheist, Jan?"

"If the husband is holding you back from worshiping the Lord, then you may have to disobey your husband. The Lord must be above everyone and everything. I am not telling you that a wife must divorce her husband, I am saying that the wife must place the Lord above all else." Jan stood up and started to walk into the kitchen. "The other thing, Betty, the Bible says in Mark 10:21-31 that it's harder for a rich man to enter Heaven. I pray that John does not worship his money and that he and I spend eternity together in Heaven." Jan interrupted her Bible discussion, "I'm going to have some ice tea. Do you want a beverage?"

"No, that's okay, I've got to get home, Jan." I argued the meaning of the verse that Jan quoted, "But the verse in Mark is for those individuals who love their possessions more than they love Jesus. The people that should be worried are those who worship their money or covet money and the possessions of others. I don't believe that the Lord wants everybody to give up everything they own and give it to their church. To tithe is one thing, giving everything up is another. The real message is that we must love Him above all things."

"You just don't understand. I think that we need to just agree to disagree, I see a problem in the way that you choose to interpret this part of the Bible."

I could tell that our conversation was going downhill fast. I had a suspicion that Kim was trying to reach John to get his money, but I pushed the thought out of my mind and decided that it was none of my business. "Okay Jan, let's change the subject, what are you going to do later today? Do you want to go get some lunch?"

"No, I'm real busy today anyway. I have to get some stuff done for Kim."

"Okay, Well, I better get home, I'll talk to you later, Jan."

When I arrived home, I spoke to Nick about my conversation with Jan, "You know…I'm really worried about Jan."

"Why are you worried about Jan, she has everything?"

"It's not that, she's so involved with that Kim Miller guy. I don't understand the attraction. I think that he is using her to get to John's money. I met Kim once and he instantly gave me the creeps. I went to Jan's house and everyone was sitting around him, he was sitting high on a chair while his followers sat on the floor. You would think that he was Jesus Christ Himself by the way everyone was acting. They were pretty engrossed in what he was saying to them. I can't figure it out."

"I just don't want you to get wrapped up in what Jan's doing," Nick said as he shook his head. "There's something wrong there. I think your sister just needs to get a real job."

"Well, Jan's living a good honest life and she believes that she is pleasing the Lord. What could be wrong with that? She has the best intentions and who am I to tell her how to worship? After all, it is a free country."

"You're right, it's her way of serving the Lord. She's not hurting anybody. Just don't get involved in what she's doing."

"Well, I hate to see someone taking her for granted, I just don't want her scammed."

"There's nothing you can do about it, Betty. Just try to talk to her and maybe she'll understand."

CHAPTER THIRTY-SEVEN

▼

NEW PASSIONS

A few years later, Jan and John sold their adorable second home and bought a larger house with a small acreage on the outskirts of Ouray. Once again Jan was decorating her hide-away. She seemed to enjoy decorating Nicky's bedroom. I imagined that Jan and Nicky spent a great deal of quality time together visiting stores and thumbing through catalogues. Jan and Nicky decided to get away from the traditional feminine décor of ruffles and lace that was prominent in Nicky's Boulder bedroom and make the Ouray bedroom a fascinating retreat. The safari décor allowed Nicky a very exotic and fun hideaway.

It's hard to buy something for a little girl who has everything. Nicky was not a spoiled child and I never remembered Nicky asking for anything. She was always content with having people around to visit. August was approaching and of course so was our children's birthdays. I was finally beginning to understand that although Jan could not celebrate birthdays, Jan wanted me to remember Nicky with a gift on her birthday. It was as if Jan couldn't actually tell me, but it was expected. I was still confused about what to do around Christmas and other holidays. I was more than happy to give Nicky anything that was within my power to give. Jan hinted that if I wanted to get Nicky something she would enjoy, I should look for anything in an African motif.

I combed all the magazines and catalogues that I had lying around in my house. A few days later I received a catalogue in the mail that featured a room filled with leopards, tigers, and giraffes. The room in the picture had a fireplace with a couple of cute elephant figurines positioned on their bellies, one front leg and one back leg hung over the edge of the mantel. I couldn't resist them. I called and ordered a set of elephants from the catalogue and had them sent directly to Nicky's Ouray home.

As I hung up the telephone it occurred to me that Nicky definitely was developing her own tastes and opinions about things. Our little girl was growing up.

While Jan was furnishing her new Ouray home, I purchased a lovely 1898 Queen Anne Victorian home in Cripple Creek, Colorado. The original furnishings and majestic architecture beckoned to be appreciated. I petitioned the city to rezone the property from residential to commercial so that I could make the home into a Bed and Breakfast and name it The Victorian Lady of Cripple Creek. The town of Cripple Creek was beginning to allow limited stakes gambling and the city was changing dramatically. The gamblers needed a place to stay and I was going to have my "little dollhouse" and make money in the process.

John told me that he never liked Victorian décor because it was too ornate and had too many places to collect dust. But Jan never said anything negative about my Victorian and she seemed to be enjoying my Bed and Breakfast vicariously through me. Jan brought me a beautiful basket decorated with Victorian lace and flowers and a beautiful Victorian Bed & Breakfast cookbook. Inside the basket, I found my favorite book, "Sisters," and two Victorian cameo pictures that reminded me of the two angels I won in church when Jan and I were young. Jan's thoughtfulness was overwhelming. The antique china doll made in Germany that she gave me was too precious to leave in my distant Victorian so I insisted on keeping it in my curio cabinet in Arvada.

While Jan was busy with acts of kindness, Carol was making home-made quilts for everyone in the family. Their gracious giving overwhelmed me. I was too busy with my career to reciprocate. Every room in my house reminded me of my loving sisters.

I promised myself that someday, I would give them something to remember me by and to let them know how much they both meant to me.

CHAPTER THIRTY-EIGHT

▼

MANY REGRETS

In April 1995, I had two discs removed from my neck and both Mom and Jan was around to support me. Unfortunately, the doctor prescribed steroids to accelerate the healing and strengthening of my neck. The steroids altered my personality and made me mean. I not only hated everyone around me but I hated myself.

With a gift in hand, Jan came over to my house to keep me company. I didn't acknowledge Jan's effort to visit me. I couldn't think of anything but Nick. I was angry with him, I thought that he should be at home with me while I was recovering instead of working on The Victorian Lady. I was determined to drive to Cripple Creek to talk to him.

I grabbed my keys and headed for the front door. Mom and Jan blocked the door and pleaded with me not to leave. The medication that I was taking altered my judgement and my common sense. I felt like I had super powers. I insisted on leaving. To protect me from myself, Mom and Jan struggled to keep me in the house as I protested angrily. I looked out the window and saw Jan's Audi behind my large Ford dually truck. I threatened to drive my dually truck over Jan's Audi. Jan looked at me realizing that I meant what I said. Jan quickly grabbed her keys, ran out of the house, and moved her Audi.

I climbed in the truck and sped away.

Fortunately, the truck malfunctioned before I reached the tall mountain cliffs in route to Cripple Creek. While riding home in the tow truck, I praised the Lord for intervening and stopping me from potentially killing myself on the road. I realized that I treated Jan and Mom horribly. Jan and Mom were in Arvada to help me, acting out of the kindness of their hearts. I went crazy. My drug-induced personality caused my loved ones pain and anguish. I wished I could take my actions back and I kept asking myself, why I had to hurt the people who were reaching out to show me how much they loved and cared about me? It was such a stupid, senseless act. I wanted to apologize.

When I arrived home, Jan was gone and she wasn't interested in talking to me.

When Nick came home, he looked at the truck to find out why I was having trouble. There was nothing wrong with the truck. When Nick told me, I got a chill. I knew that the Lord was watching over me.

CHAPTER THIRTY-NINE

▼

THE ENIGMATIC GIFT

It was already May 1996, and Nicholas Shawn's last high school summer. Kristopher was going into ninth grade, and Nicky was moved up to the tenth grade. Jan and Nicky worked hard and the proof was in Nicky's progress. It would be hard to argue that home schooling was detrimental to children. I was convinced that Jan did a marvelous job raising her daughter. Nicky was a model child in every way and a mirror image of her mother.

The children were excited about getting a break from school. It wouldn't be long before all three of them were out of high school and into college. I felt a sense of urgency to spend more quality time with all three of the children. Time stole our children from us and in its place were wonderful young adults with ideas and dreams of their own. As a parent, I enjoyed this new period in their lives, but this was different, we were slowly letting them go.

It wasn't unusual for Jan to think well in advance for activities involving Nicky and Kristopher. Kristopher thought of her as his second mom. Jan called to discuss plans for the summer.

"You know, Betty, I would like to take Nicky and Kristopher on a road trip around Utah, Nevada, and California for a couple of weeks this summer. It will probably be the last opportunity for the two of them to go someplace like this together."

I thought it was a little odd that Jan said that this would be the last opportunity for Nicky and Kristopher to get together, it sounded a little too final to me. But, I figured that Jan didn't intend to say it that way, Jan probably meant that their lives were getting more complicated as they got older. "I think it would be a fun experience for them. Ah, to be a kid again…when do you plan to go?"

"Listen I'll put together an itinerary so you know exactly where we are every day."

"I'm not surprised, Jan, you are the most thorough person I know."

When it was time for Jan, Nicky, and Kristopher to leave, Jan had a complete itinerary telling me the exact locations, times, dates, and activities of their trip. While Kristopher was gone, he sent postcards keeping me informed about how much fun they were having.

When Jan and the children returned from their trip, Kristopher was concerned about something. "I don't know why, Mom, but Aunt Janet repeatedly mentioned that this trip would be the last one that Nicky and I would be able to spend together. And when I talked about going to college Jan told me that the Lord will be here before I get to college."

"Kristopher, I don't know why your Aunt Jan said the Lord would be here before you get to college. Jan's been telling me that sort of thing to me for years. As Christians, we know that the Lord is going to come, it's written in the Bible and there is nothing that we can do to change that. All we can do is live a life that is pleasing to the Lord and let whatever is going to happen…happen. You still plan for college. You can't just stop your life because you think you can predict when the Lord will be here. Don't worry about it, okay?"

"Okay, Mom. Nicky and I sure had a good time."

"That's good honey, you'll have to tell dad and I all about it at supper."

I often wondered why Jan talked about the end of the world yet she worked hard to be sure that Nicky had the best education possible. Nicky and Kristopher were scheduled to graduate in the year 2000, but now Nicky would graduate in 1999. As a mother, Jan devoted her time and energy to her daughter and worked hard to quench Nicky's insatiable hunger to learn. Jan aggressively continued to teach Nicky advanced courses. I felt that Jan felt conflict most of Nicky's teenage years. Jan wanted nothing but the best for Nicky, and wanted to give Nicky every opportunity to succeed in anything that Nicky wanted to do. But Jan believed that the Lord was coming soon, and Nicky would enter Heaven before she experienced her worldly dreams.

CHAPTER FORTY

DAUGHTER'S CHOICE

Only two months later, I sensed something was wrong. I couldn't really figure out exactly what it was. Jan drove into my driveway sporting her new Audi A4. I watched as Jan and Nicky got out of the car, I could feel the tension between Jan and Nicky. I thought that if Jan wanted me to know, she would tell me.

"Hi Jan and Nicky, it's rare to see you guys at my house. What a pleasant surprise!"

"Well, I'm on my way to Denver, Betty. I can't stay long."

I snipped, "I know, you never can stay very long."

Nicky was acting aloof. Jan was noticeably upset and finally whispered, "I'm having a little problem with Nicky. She may be going to a private school or moving in with her dad soon. I don't know what she's going to do. But she doesn't want to stay with me anymore."

"I'm so sorry, Jan. I hope everything works out."

"The Lord will bring her back to me. She just has to learn what is important."

I didn't understand what exactly Jan meant, and I didn't know what to say so I commented, "I guess sometimes a person just has to go through the trials."

I noticed that Nicky was a little distant to me too, but under the circumstances, I understood. Nicky probably anticipated that I would side with Jan if there was a problem involving her and her dad, or maybe Nicky thought I was angry with her. I tried to stay neutral about the whole problem, hoping that everything would work out.

Jan stood to leave. "Well, I really do have to go. I hope we can have lunch real soon, Betty."

"Let's do. Call me and let me know when you have time, Jan."

I watched Nicky and Jan drive down the road. I felt a heavy sorrow for Jan. I knew that Nicky wanting to leave was killing Jan. I prayed that the problem would have a happy ending.

Within a few days Nicky left her Boulder home to live with her dad and attended a public school in Lakewood. It didn't take Nicky long to reach the top of her class.

In May 1997, Jan's ex-husband took Jan to court to fight for custody of Nicky. Kim would not allow Jan to go to court to fight for custody of her only daughter. Kim told Jan that the court system was not where the members of Kim Miller's Concerned Christians belonged.

I talked to Jan a lot after Nicky left home. Jan was an emotional wreck and tormented about not being able to fight for her only daughter. Her main goal was to please God but she was emotionally torn trying to satisfy her natural tendencies to be a good mother to Nicky. Jan quickly became a recluse. I knew that Jan felt tremendous pain. She chose to sink deeper into the bowels of her religious group. I wanted to comfort her, to support her if she needed to talk about her loss. I knew what a good mother Jan was and I couldn't imagine the pain she must have felt when her only daughter left her.

I tried to give her emotional support and steer completely away from the subject of Nicky's departure. Once in a while I slipped. Nicky was always with Jan and she would be quick to remind me, "I'm not feeling strong enough to talk about certain subjects. I would appreciate it if we didn't discuss them, okay?"

I figured that Jan was talking about Nicky. I sympathetically replied, "Okay, Jan, whatever you want. I wish I could help you."

Jan and I talked about cooking, her Ouray home, my Bed & Breakfast or any other subjects that would not create any tension. Occasionally we would get on the subject of religion but by this time, we knew that our beliefs were drifting further apart so we would move on to the other subjects.

As if Jan didn't have enough stress in her life, Kim was getting more unwanted press and the Concerned Christians were becoming an increasing controversy. Jan asked, "Did you happen to see the News last night?"

"No. Why?"

"Oh never mind, I guess the Lord saved you from seeing it. It wasn't pleasant; there are some people around town that trying to cause Kim Miller and the Concerned Christians some problems. It is better that you stay out of it. They don't know who they're messing with!"

"Well, okay if you don't think I should know."

In December, Nicky celebrated Christmas for the first time in years. Jan called me on the telephone to tell me that she was furious with Nicky's father. "Nicky's dad bought Nicky a rifle for Christmas! He knows how I feel about weapons! I can't believe her dad bought her a gun!"

"You're kidding me. I can't believe it either. You don't buy your fourteen year old daughter a gun for Christmas!"

Jan repeated, "They both know how I feel about weapons. I'm am so angry!"

Kristopher tried to call Nicky at her Lakewood home a few times but she was too busy to talk, actually it seemed like someone was preventing her from coming to the telephone. Nicky was active in the school's ROTC program and with other school programs. I hoped that Nicky enjoyed her new public school life. School years can be a child's best memories. But there was still a distance between Nicky and myself and even Kristopher. I couldn't figure out what the problem was. I wanted Kristopher and Nicky to continue to enjoy each other's company. I felt like someone hammered a wedge between all of us. I kept asking myself what happened?

Nicky went from a household with two fully furnished bedrooms of her own to a one-room apartment. She excelled rapidly in school and ultimately made the decision to attend a military school for the remainder of her high school education. When I first heard that she was going off to military school I was angry. Nicky needed to just be a kid and I didn't understand why things had to be so different for her. I wished I could raise Nicky.

Nicky would try to talk to her Mom to tell her that she loved her. Jan consulted Kim Miller for advice on what to say to Nicky. Kim Miller would tell Jan to give Nicky an ultimatum to come back or she would lose her mother. He promised Jan that Nicky wouldn't be able to stand the treatment and come home. Jan frequently commented to me that the Lord said that Nicky was breaking down and would be coming home soon.

It was evident to me that Kim told Jan to hurt Nicky with mean words and by threatening to widen the gap between them. I watched silently, as Kim caused Nicky and Jan a tremendous amount of pain.

Nicky said that when she called her mom and she told her mom she loved her but didn't believe in Kim. Jan responded with what Kim Miller would allow her to say. Then Jan would hang up leaving Nicky in tears. Jan told me later that she had an emotional conversation with Nicky and believed that they would be together soon.

Nicky only wanted a normal relationship with her Mom. But Nicky was with her Mom through a third party, the master of spiritual blackmail. Nicky dreamed that she could have her mom back, the way her mom was before Kim Miller controlled her. Nicky was only a child and her happiness was under the manipulation of someone who didn't care if he ruined a mother-child relationship.

When Nicky was finally allowed to talk to Kristopher, Nicky sounded genuinely interested in attending a military school. I didn't understand it.

I didn't have any knowledge of what Military school was like. I thought children were sent to Military school when their parents didn't want to raise them or if their parents couldn't raise them because the child was out of control. This was not the case with Nicky. Her Mom loved her more than any earthly thing and Nicky's real father did the best he could under the circumstances. But, Nicky and her father were happy with their choice so Nicky finished her last two years of high school at a military academy.

CHAPTER FORTY-ONE

▼

IMPORTANT VISITORS

After Nicky moved from Boulder, Jan invited a couple of young girls from their church to live with her and John in their Pinebrook Hills home. Jan kept busy doing "important work for the church" and focused more on the girls that lived with her and less time on losing Nicky. My time was spent operating the Bed and Breakfast as a result. Jan and I rarely made time to see each other. I thought that Jan was harboring bad feelings about my crazy behavior while I was on medication. Jan and I were slowly drifting apart.

One day my emotions got the best of me, I was overwhelmed with emptiness from not seeing Jan so I called her on the telephone. "Jan, I haven't talked to you for a while. What have you been doing?"

"I've been so busy Betty. I've been remodeling the room above the garage in Ouray."

"Jan, I thought that was Nicky's room. Didn't you just decorate it for Nicky?"

Jan avoided the comment and as if to refuse to talk about Nicky she said, "Oh Betty, you would be surprised to know the important people who will occupy the room. I can't tell you much about it. But, you know the personalized soaps and lotions you buy for your Bed and Breakfast?"

"Yeah, the hand soaps are actually embossed with the name *The Victorian Lady of Cripple Creek.* You can order individual sizes or large economy sizes with your own logo or name. Do you want me to get you the address so that you can contact the company? I think they are out of Georgia or South Carolina. Anyway, the company will design your label at no charge."

"I wish you would give me that information, Betty. I've been really busy traveling to Montrose and Grand Junction to get what I need for the new room."

"I know Jan, you're the busiest unemployed person I know. Nick and I've been busy too. We are in Cripple Creek at least every other weekend. It takes us three hours to get there, we register our guests, and the guests leave for the evening to gamble in the casinos and the next morning Nick and I make breakfast and entertain the guests. When they leave by 11:00 in the morning, Nick and I scrambled to wash the china used at breakfast and clean the rooms. We start all over at 4:00 in the afternoon. It's a busy life but we really get a kick out of doing it. Then we drive back to Arvada to work our 40 hour a week jobs."

"When do you get to see the boys, Betty?"

"That's the problem. Dear sweet Nicholas Shawn had about 150 people over the other day for a party. Jan, you know our house is on a well and septic, the system is fifteen years old. Anyway, Nick, Kristopher, and I were at the Bed and Breakfast and Nicholas had a party. The only way I found out was because the neighbor came over to get his *For Sale by Owner* sign. I told the neighbor that we didn't have his sign. But he quickly told me, "Oh yes, the other day when you had that party…the kids thought it would be funny to put your home up for sale. So they borrowed my sign." I told him that we didn't have a party. I felt really stupid when I found out that there was a party and there were so many people that the entire block was lined with cars."

Jan laughed, "They put your house up for sale?"

"Cute huh? Anyway, I think we will probably sell the Bed and Breakfast. I thought that our innkeepers would be less maintenance and that owning the Bed and Breakfast wouldn't impact our family as much as it does. Nick and I are tired of traveling back and forth so much. Besides, I'm starting a new job soon and it looks like I'll be traveling to New York occasionally, often on the weekends to take advantage of the low airfare. I can't run the Bed and Breakfast and travel, it's just too much. Besides, I would never see the boys."

"Sounds like it's a good idea to simplify your life, Betty. Well, I have to run. I would appreciate it if you would get me the information on the personalized soaps."

"No problem Jan. I'll stick it in the mail today. I'll talk to you later."

CHAPTER FORTY-TWO

▼

THE CLUES

The clues of Jan and John's plans were masked by a lifestyle that had its own peculiarities. Extraordinary circumstance occasionally exposed hidden messages, and the Concerned Christians were getting a small amount of media attention in the first part of 1998.

I stopped to visit Jan and John. When I walked into the living room, they were noticeably upset about something, and they stood side by side looking at me. Jan asked, "Have you seen anything about Kim on television?

It was rare that I had both Jan and John's undivided attention at the same time, usually John was busy on one of his computers and tuning in and out of our conversation. But today, John was as interested as Jan in knowing if I heard anything about Kim.

"No, I haven't. Why is Kim in the news?"

"Oh never mind. I guess the Lord protected you from seeing it, Betty."

I joked to Jan and John, "Well, you're not going to drink poison Kool-Aid or anything like that are you?" Surprised, they stared uncomfortably at me for a minute and then laughed nervously. I felt Jan and John's discomfort as the room grew silent. I hated the awkward moment and didn't want either of them to be uncomfortable.

Before either Jan or John could answer I said, "Well, that's just absurd. If Kim is getting negative press, someone must have some kind of vendetta against him or something. There must be an ulterior motive."

For some reason, I assumed that someone wanted to give Jan and John grief. I felt the whole incident was associated with Nicky leaving her mom and was related to gaining more child-support, "I'm calling the news and I'm going to tell them that they should make sure their information source is legitimate before they make announcements to the world."

Jan and John appreciated my spunk. Jan said, "Well, John and I can't do anything about what the media says because it would not be pleasing to the Lord. The Lord doesn't want John or I to intervene with the media or the governmental system."

"Well, I don't have a problem calling the news. I think the media should stay out of harmless domestic disputes!"

Later, I went home and called the news. I called Jan to tell her that I left a message for the news anchor that reported the story and told him that he could very well be listening to someone who is involved in a custody battle or someone who has some other self-serving motive. I told him that he should verify the legitimacy of the accusation before literally broadcasting it to the world."

Jan said, "Good. The Lord is using you to speak for us. We simply cannot come to our own defense. Believe me Betty, you do not want to get mixed up in this. This is big. This is just huge!"

When I hung up the telephone, I was happy that I could help Jan. Jan seemed pleased with my interference but I thought her comment about the Lord was a bit of a reach. To think that the Lord used me to speak for the ministry…regardless, it felt good to come to Jan and John's defense. I would have fought any battle for them. Besides, I didn't see where the Concerned Christians were doing anything wrong or anything newsworthy for that matter. I couldn't understand why the Concerned Christians couldn't just worship the way they wanted. The last I heard, it was still a free country.

Weeks went by before Jan and I talked again. Jan was visiting her Ouray home more and more. She was keeping herself busy and trying to keep her mind off Nicky and mentioned how much she enjoyed the girls that were living with her. I couldn't fathom why Jan wanted boarders. The girls were in their late teens and early twenties. I didn't think it was healthy for Jan to use strangers to replace Nicky and to erase her only daughter from her memory. Jan reasoned that the girls were helpful and that it was nice to have someone watch their home when John and she traveled.

I needed to call Jan to see how she was doing. I had a nagging feeling of discontentment in the back of my mind. Was everything okay with Jan? I needed to give her a call.

"Hi John, is Jan home?"

"No, she cannot come to the telephone right now."

"Oh, do you know when she can talk?"

"No, I don't know. She's been pretty busy."

"Well okay, I'll call back another time."

At first I didn't think anything of it. So Jan was busy, she's always busy. I continued calling for a few weeks, determined not to give up. Something wasn't right.

Finally, I called again.

"Hello?"

"Jan! How are you doing? I've been worried about you. Are you okay?"

"I'm fine. I can't give you any of the details, but John had what you might call a "religious experience." He was tormented for several days and now he has peace with life."

I paused trying to make some sense out of her cryptic message. I asked myself what kind of religious experience? This is just too strange, I thought. "So Jan, what happened?"

"I can't really get into it, I. All I can tell you is your brother-in-law has accepted Jesus."

"I think that's wonderful, Jan. He's a good man."

"We've had some strange stuff happen around here, they were messages from the Lord. You know our dog had puppies and one of the puppies had a disability."

"You had a puppy with a disability? Oh, that's too bad. Where is the puppy now?"

"Well, that's the thing, you know how selective we were last time we had puppies. We carefully screened the people because we didn't want the puppies to be abused. We wanted to make sure that the puppies went to a good home. So, a lady found out that we had puppies and when she arrived to pick one out, you guessed it, she had a bad leg, just like the puppy. The lady and the puppy needed each other. It was a sign from the Lord. I'm sure of it."

"Yep, I think it was God's way of letting you know that the puppy would go to a good home. I'm sure that the lady will take good care of that puppy. So, how are the young girls doing that live with you?"

"Oh they are doing fine. It's the Lord's way of helping us adjust to Nicky not being here. The girls and I do things together all the time. We have a lot of fun. We sit and laugh for hours, especially the youngest one. They cooked supper for us last night. The youngest one can't live at home with her own parents so we invited her to live with us."

"Oh that's nice Jan. Well, I just wanted to see how you were doing. I'll talk to you later, Okay?"

I hung up the telephone and sat on the front porch. I stared at the lake as I tried to figure out what was going on with Jan. Jan refused to talk about Nicky probably because it was such a painful experience. Did Kim see Nicky as a threat? There were several times when Jan said that Nicky was breaking down. She said that Nicky was coming home. Jan frequently told me that Nicky would soon see that she was following the wrong path. Each time, Kim's promises were left unfulfilled and Jan's heart was broken. Jan's heart seemed to be getting more and more callous from all the disappointment. Kim appeared to use Jan's vulnerable state of mind to his advantage. He convinced John and Jan that Nicky was rebellious, that the Bible said that they must chose the Lord over mother, daughter, sisters, and brothers. Kim promised Jan that she would have a new family.

I believed that Kim needed Jan happy, without Jan, there was no way that he could take control of John's money and all their assets. Kim kept Jan distracted from her problems and busy doing work for the Lord. Kim choreographed Jan's happiness, her family relationships, her finances, and her walk with God.

It wasn't long before Jan stopped calling me. I knew that if I wanted to talk to Jan I would have to initiate the call. I was determined to stay in Jan's life one way or another, something wasn't right.

I prayed that Jan would find happiness and get Nicky back in her life.

CHAPTER FORTY-THREE

▼

LAST TELEPHONE CALL

For a period of time I tried to call Jan on the telephone but she never picked up the receiver. I called the Ouray home and left messages. She was living the life of a nomad and was very difficult to find. If Jan was at home in Boulder or in Ouray when I called, She was screening her calls. Mom told me that Jan stopped talking to her and that Nicky didn't know where her mom was either. Finally, I decided to tell Jan what I thought. I called Jan's house and left a message, "Jan, I don't know what you are trying to prove. But I want you to know that you are acting just like our Aunt Lula. Remember Jan? Aunt Lula stopped talking to the family and now you are acting just like her. Well, if that's what you want…than that's fine." I hung up the telephone in disgust.

Within a few days I got a telephone call. "Hey Betty, this is Jan. I'm calling you from a very very far away land. I just picked up my messages. I haven't been in town that's why I haven't called. I can't stay on the telephone because I'm in a distant land. I can't tell you where I am but, I just wanted to say that we're okay and I love you."

"I love you too, Jan. When will you be home?"

"I really can't talk now. I have to go. I love you, good-bye."

I felt better because she called. At least she cared enough to call. I wondered where Jan was. Why was Jan so secretive all the time anyway? Something was just not right.

When Jan arrived home it was the same story. She never called on the telephone. I continued to call and leave messages, making sure that Jan knew that I wouldn't forget her.

Finally, I called the Boulder residence and John answered the telephone, "Hello."

"Hi John, how are you doing?"

"Not so good, you know I had a problem with my heart and ended up in the hospital a while ago."

"You're kidding! Are you okay?"

"I'm taking medication now, but it was scary."

"John, you need to take care of yourself. I just had a stress test for my heart too. I had a pain in my chest and then the pain went into my jaw and my arm. It really freaked me out, all I could think of is how Daddy must have felt when he had his heart attack. You know John, we just have to make sure we take care of ourselves."

"Yeah, you're right, and you better watch yourself, Betty."

"Hey, is Jan around?"

"Let me see. Hold on a minute Betty."

There was a long pause before I heard a reluctant "Hello."

"Hi Jan, I never hear from you anymore. How come you never talk to me?"

"I don't want to."

"You don't want to?"

"No, I just don't want to."

"Well okay, I guess I'll let you go then. Bye, Jan."

Tears filled my eyes as I hung up the telephone. I was dazed and started walking aimlessly out of the yard toward the lake, oblivious to my surroundings. I didn't remember walking past the petunias or the cars in the driveway. My mind was swimming with questions. I walked over to the park bench overlooking Standley Lake. I sat on the bench and cried. Why would Jan treat me so cold? I felt like I lost my best friend and a sister at the same time. What made Jan talk to me like that? How could she throw away a lifetime of friendship and sisterly love? I played back the whole conversation, over and over in my head looking for a clue why she treated me bad.

I decided that Jan was not going to get rid of me that easy. I'm not giving up on her. I will continue to call her even though she doesn't want to talk to me any more. Jan and I have never stayed mad at each other for very long. But this seemed different, Jan wasn't mad at me. Jan simply didn't care about our relationship anymore. She was emotionally detaching herself from me. I made up my mind and said softly, "I'm not giving up, I will continue to call Jan and be a pain in her butt. I will reach out to her no matter what she says. Something is just not right."

The red sun slowly disappeared behind the deep purple Rocky Mountains. It was getting dark and I needed to head home. I stumbled through the prairie dog village to the house. Nick and the boys would be worried about me.

When I got close enough to the house I noticed that Nick was sitting on the porch with his binoculars next to the rocking chair. He knew that I walked somewhere because the car was in the driveway. His attempt to spot me with binoculars was in vain. Nick was concerned. It wasn't like me to walk away from the house without leaving a note telling him where I was. As soon as he spotted me on the road, he yelled out, "There you are, where have you been, you had us worried?"

"I had to take a walk, Jan said that she didn't want to talk to me anymore."

"Why?"

I started to cry, "I don't know, I just asked her why she never talked to me and she responded by telling me that she just didn't want to talk to me."

"Jan's weird, don't call her anymore, you don't need that kind of shit in your life."

I choked on every word as I said, "She's still my sister. Something is wrong, I don't know what. I can't give up on her. You wouldn't give up on your brother Mike if he were in Jan's place. I think it's her religion. Jan is removing herself from any contact with the family. Jan doesn't even call Mom. Jan's been giving mom a monthly check to subsidize her fixed income since she left high school."

Nick was angry that Jan was so insensitive that she hurt my feelings, "Brother Mike isn't that stupid, but I understand what you're saying. Do what you need to do. I've never stood in your way before, I will support you in whatever you decide to do."

I wrapped my arms around Nick and held him close. "I know and I appreciate it, she really hurt my feelings this time."

I went into the house to start supper. I had to push the incident out of my mind so that I could function. There was nothing I could do at this point anyway. But I had a plan, I would let some time pass before I would call Jan again. But I didn't want to wait too long. Jan seemed to be getting deeper and deeper into this Kim Miller guy. He stopped her from going to court to gain custody of Nicky. Now, he was controlling whom she could talk to, even John was getting distant.

A few weeks later, Jan's words were cutting deep into my soul. Every day since my last telephone call to Jan's house, I had an urge to talk to her. I had come up with a plan. I had to figure out how to reach her. I wondered if Jan was mad that I didn't take the time to have lunch with her. It was usual for Jan to schedule a lunch date with me so far in advance. We were always more spontaneous than that. I should have picked up on the subtleties. Now that I think of it, there *was* a sense of urgency in Jan voice. This meeting was important enough to plan in advance so that nothing would interfere with our plans. If I only would have picked up on the clues, I would have realized that it was a now or never situation. But I figured Jan and I could simply reschedule lunch another time.

I kept running the scenario in my mind, questioning why I didn't meet with Jan that day. Did something come up, something so trivial that I forgot what it was? I told Jan I wouldn't be able to make it, work was keeping me busy. I must have had a deadline. Jan was undeniably perturbed with my priorities that day.

I couldn't stand it anymore. I had to call Jan and see how she was doing. Maybe she had time to cool off. I picked up the portable phone and walked over to the window facing the lake. As I pressed each number, I thought of what I would say if John answered and then what I would say if Jan answered. I pushed the last number and decided just to wing it. I didn't want my words to appear too well rehearsed. I would just talk from my heart.

"Hello." John answered in a cheerful voice.

He was always a pleasant person to talk to and rarely had a negative attitude. He sounded like the old John that I used to know. It was great to talk to him again.

"Hi, this is Betty, how are you doing John? I just wanted to call and see if you guys were okay. I haven't heard from you for a while."

"Jan and I are okay, Betty. You know Jan's been busy remodeling this house and I'm on the road to recovery, I think I'll be fine."

"You better watch out, John, heart disease is nothing to fool around with."

"Oh hey! I have to go…See-ya-bye!"

I heard a dial tone. What was that? What happened? Did Jan just walk into the room? I hung up the telephone. John's curious behavior captivated my imagination. What in the world just happened? I heard what sounded like paper grocery bags in the background. Had Jan surprised John? Why was John afraid of letting Jan know that he was talking to me? It was too mysterious, first Jan and now John. Something was wrong, very wrong.

CHAPTER FORTY-FOUR

▼

THE LAST VISIT, MAY 1998

Mom came to stay with us for a few days. As usual, she was in the kitchen baking bread when I told her, "I have a doctor's appointment in Boulder in a couple of hours. Do you want to go with me?"

"Oh, I don't know Betty."

"I'll take you to go get a beverage or something afterwards. You need to get out of the house a while."

"Okay, I'll go with you. What time is your appointment?"

"It's a 1:00, it shouldn't take long." In the back of my mind I knew that I was going to pop in on Jan. I was certain this time that Jan didn't want to see me but I thought to myself, our mother deserves to be treated better than this. I know that mom wonders what's going on with Jan, just like I do. Jan's not going to get rid of us that easy.

Mom and I rode to Boulder and talked about all the new buildings around the Superior and Broomfield area. We arrived at the medical center and while I was talking to the doctor, Mom waited patiently in the lobby.

Afterwards, Mom and I walked out of the medical building, "Well Mom, where do you want to go?"

"Oh I don't care Betty. We don't have to go anywhere. It was just nice to go for a ride."

"I know, let me surprise you."

As we drove down the familiar road toward Pinebrook Hills Mom realized where we were going. "Oh Betty, I don't want to bother Jan. You know Jan just wants to keep to herself."

"It's not right Mom, you deserve to see your daughter, you love Jan and miss her and so do I. We'll just pop in for a minute and then we will go back home."

Mom acted edgy about dropping in on Jan, but Mom was a captive passenger in my car, and I had to see Jan. I don't know why but I had a gut feeling that this visit could be the very last time that mom, Jan, and I would see each other. We drove up the winding driveway. I knocked on the door but the door was already opened. I stepped inside and announced our arrival. "Hello…anybody home?"

Jan met us at the door and saw that we were already inside. She asked us to come into the kitchen. Jan was uncomfortable and didn't act as hospitable as she normally did. Jan never warmed up to us. I remember walking through the living room and dining room to the kitchen. There was something very peculiar about the house but I couldn't figure out what it was. Jan and John were both very skittish. Finally, Jan said, "The place looks pretty bare, we've been remodeling you know."

I acknowledged the fact that I knew they were remodeling. "Yeah, you guys have been doing that for some time now haven't you?"

"It's taking a long time."

We stood and stared at each other. It wasn't the warm welcome that I was used to. I felt sorry for Mom because she didn't appear to know what to do or say. None of us did.

I rambled, "Well, I was at the doctor's office and I dragged Mom with me. You know Mom likes to get out once in a while. I thought it would be good for Mom to see you again." Sensing that Mom and I should not stay any longer, "I guess we should go now…Mom and I were just coming by to see how you both were doing."

John said, "We love you Mom."

"We love you," Jan said as she walked us both out the door.

"We love you, take care of yourselves." Mom and I echoed as we climbed back in the car. As I backed down the driveway I looked at Mom and said, "That was strange. I don't know what to think of those two."

Mom said sadly, "Jan and John just want to be left alone. We just have to let Jan and John live their life the way they want to live it,"

Of course Mom didn't want to make waves, she just wanted her children happy. The meeting left Mom and I with an empty feeling.

For the next several months, I tried to call Jan, but no one would answer the telephone. Instead the answering machine picked up, and I almost always left a message. Depending on how insecure, sensitive, or even angry I was, my message reflected my mood. But I never received a return call. I felt hurt, but I didn't quit calling. I wanted Jan and John to know that I cared about what was going on in their life.

The next time we heard anything about Jan and John was on the 6:00 News…

▼

PART IV

LOST BUT NOT FORGOTTEN

CHAPTER FORTY-FIVE

▼

MEDIA BLITZ

It was only a day after Mom and I watched the shocking news about Jan and John's mysterious disappearance. I woke up anxious to read the paper and to learn more about what was going on with the Concerned Christians. I walked out to the end of the driveway, picked up the morning paper, and as I walked back to the house I noticed Mom and Nick standing at the door waiting for me to bring the newspaper in. They followed me as I walked in the door and toward the kitchen table. I sat down and impatiently thumbed the rubber band off the newspaper. I didn't have to look far for information about the Concerned Christians. An article was on the front page. I quickly started reading. Mom and Nick hovered over me in desperation wanting to know more about Jan and John.

Nick said impatiently, "Read it to us, we don't want to wait for you to finish. Tell us what it says Betty!"

I read the article as Nick and Mom listened gravely. Mom's eyes looked moist and sad. The article left us feeling empty and wanting to know more.

"I didn't know Kim's real first name was Monte. Well, I guess Jan and John are gone. It's true. The paper confirmed last night's news report. No one seems to know the exact number of people in the Concerned Christian's that are missing. Last night the news said 80 people, today the news says there are 60 Concerned Christians who mysteriously left the Denver area."

I started to tear the article out of the paper as Mom and Nick sat down at the table. "Apparently a few cult experts in the area have been tracking the Concerned Christians actions for the past two years. I agreed that Kim's early teachings were on track and non-threatening, but later, the Concerned Christians started saying strange things about the American flag and the government. That is when I made the decision that the ministry was getting too weird for me."

Nick commented, "I guess I'm not surprised that Kim went to college and worked in marketing. He certainly knows how to market himself."

"I read somewhere that a study was done on people in leadership positions. More often than not, the leaders are tall. Kim had that going for him. His 6'6" stature probably added to his perceived charismatic character, but I never saw him as anything special. I saw Kim as a charlatan, not charismatic."

Nick shook his head in disgust, "How can Jan and John believe that a mere mortal with such a colorful past, is God's chosen voice? It's ridiculous. You would think that if God were going to pick someone to represent him, God would have picked a believable character not a divorcee who claimed bankruptcy. How could intelligent people like Jan and John believe that God picked Kim…of all people?"

I glanced over at mom. Her worried look made me angry again. Although Jan could be insensitive at times, I didn't think that she would ever do anything that would hurt Mom, certainly not this bad. I thought to myself, Kim must really have brainwashed Jan and John. How many people did Kim hurt? All the mothers, fathers, brothers, and sisters of the Concerned Christian disciples were victims. The loved ones of the

Concerned Christian's suffered and worried just like my family did. They were all innocent victims who were tormented by their loved ones, the media, and unintentional acquaintances."

Mom said, "Jan doesn't mean to hurt me, Betty."

"Shoot Mom, I'm sure Kim has hurt his own mother. The article said she was too distraught to talk to the media. And why should she? She didn't deserve the embarrassment or the pain caused by the thoughtless actions of her child. I wondered if Kim tried to save his own mother's soul, before the end of the world, or was Kim just out to scam the people whom he didn't have any emotional attachment to. He made sure that his wife and child were close to his side. How could Kim's actions be pleasing to the Lord? How are the Concerned Christians honoring God's commandment by causing their own family pain?"

Nick and I avoided talking around Mom about the part of the article that said that the Concerned Christians were reported to be a very dangerous group, in fact a doomsday cult that was unpredictable. No one could guess what the Concerned Christian's might do. There was speculation about whether the Concerned Christians would actually kill themselves.

"Nick, how many people do you think join a cult believing that they are going to kill themselves?"

"I doubt if very many do, Betty."

"My guess is, ordinarily cult followers don't believe they are in a cult. So without acknowledging the fact that they are in a cult, the Concerned Christians may believe that they may die because of some divine intervention. But I don't think any of the Concerned Christians would knowingly take their own life. I've seen Kim control every aspect of Jan and John's lives and I wouldn't be surprised to learn that Kim has tricked them into harming or maybe even killing themselves. You know the article in the paper said that Kim could simply order the group to become violent and they would follow his command, just to prove their devotion to God. I have watched Kim control Jan for some time. I find it interesting that Kim claimed bankruptcy within the last few years. Why could Kim go to court and file bankruptcy and not allow Jan to go to court and fight for custody of Nicky? I remember Jan telling me that the Lord didn't want her to go to court. Courts are for the unbelievers, people who did not put their faith in the Lord."

"Betty, I'll never understand why Jan didn't fight for Nicky. And now the Concerned Christian's are in some secret location. I wonder what makes people believe that the Concerned Christians are in Mexico or Jerusalem?"

"Who knows? I guess some of the relatives are afraid that the attention from the media would expedite their demise or that they will go deeper into hiding. From what I can tell, the Concerned Christians haven't broken any laws and as Americans, they have the right to choose where they want to live." I thought for a minute, these were the same freedom rights that the Concerned Christians were preaching against. "It seems like the Concerned Christians are living a contradiction to me."

CHAPTER FORTY-SIX

▼

DENVER APOCALYPSE

Monday, October 12, 1998, I continued my all too familiar routine. I had Jan on my mind the minute I woke up, I pulled on my jeans and hurried downstairs and out the front door in anticipation of what might be in the newspaper. I impatiently wrestled the damp plastic off the newspaper and quickly glanced at the front page as I walked back to the house. Thank God, there's nothing on the front page. I didn't have to look far before I found an article mocking Kim and his prediction that Denver would be wiped off the map on Saturday, October 10.

I walked into the house and saw Nick scurrying around getting ready for work. Curious, Nick looked at me to hear the news.

"You would think that all Kim's victims would leave him after they figured out that his predictions were bogus."

"Well, Betty, what does the article say?"

"It just says that Kim's prediction didn't come true and that the 30 to 60 members of the cult are still missing. It doesn't seem like they have a very good count of how many people were involved in the Concerned

Christian's departure. The news went from 80 to now 30 to 60. I wonder if anybody *really* knows."

"And…yeah, go on, Betty," Nick was impatient to hear more, tell me what else the newspaper says, I have to leave for work."

"Well, the article just reiterates what we've already heard. Kim claims he is the Earth's last prophet mentioned in Revelations. Apparently, Kim says that he will die on the streets of Jerusalem in December 1999. Afterward, he's supposed to be resurrected and appear three days later. Oh, give me a break!"

"Yeah right, Betty, that man is delusional."

Nick was searching in the kitchen, opening and closing the cupboard doors, "Have you seen my travel cup?"

"Look in the cupboard above the double ovens," I continued to read, "Anyway, it goes on to say that the cult members are in danger. No one knows where the Concerned Christians are and family members are afraid to talk about them."

Nick poured coffee in his travel cup, "They're acting too suspicious, something's up."

"I think so too. Hey, listen to this. I guess Kim had a home that is empty and up for sale. People knew as early as a few months ago that some of the Concerned Christians had applied for passports to Israel and that they were going to leave unexpectedly. Can you believe this, Nick? People knew this stuff three months ago. I wish we knew!"

"Well it was certainly a surprise," Nick shook his head, "I feel sorry for your Mom and Nicky."

"I do too, it makes me mad when I think about it. Anyway, we knew that Kim worked with people in New Age cults and counseled their relatives." Shaking my head I added, "Yeah, Kim knows what he's doing, all right. I think Kim's a calculated scam artist." I started skimming the article for more information. Alarmed, I gasped, "Oh my gosh, Nick. They are comparing the Concerned Christians with the Heaven's Gate victims of Marshall Applewhite!" I paused for a moment as I remembered not giving

Jan and John a chance to answer when I asked Jan and John if they were going to drink poison Kool-Aid. I scolded myself…sometimes I should just keep quiet and let others speak.

"Hey Nick, you know those tapes Jan always used to send me. I never found time to listen to one tape in its entirety, in fact, I think I discarded all of the tapes. The tapes reportedly contained a mixture of history, rhetoric, numerology, and anti-government beliefs. That's not surprising, Jan and I discussed that stuff for years. Jan once mentioned that a person's date of birth identified interesting facts about them. I always wondered if they had me figured as a patriot, especially since when I was young, I used to tell people that my birthday was the 4th of July, the 9th. Sounds pretty patriotic, don't you think? Kim's teachings gradually put a wedge between Jan and I, not to say what his teachings did to Jan's relationship with her own daughter and mother. Kim was filling Jan full of nonsense, he knew how to separate Jan from her family and even separate Jan from her country. I'll always resent Kim for what he's done to this family."

Nick patted me on the back as he walked over to his briefcase, "Well, I'm thankful that you didn't go along with Jan."

"Nick, I guess Kim used to preach on the radio but the radio stations discontinued his messages because Kim had the nerve to refuse to pay for the airtime."

Nick looked at his watch and grabbed his briefcase. He walked quickly toward the door. "Jeez Betty, I have to go or I'm going to be late for work. If you feel like you need to talk, give me a call at work. I should be in the office today. We'll talk more tonight when I get home."

CHAPTER FORTY-SEVEN

▼

FIRST E-MAIL

I remembered that Nicholas Shawn used to e-mail John. I searched in the computer for John's email address until I found it. I doubted that John would write back to me, but I had to try. I wanted John and Jan to know that I loved them and that we wanted them both to come home. I wondered if they were embarrassed that they believed Kim's prediction and followed him out of Denver. I offered Jan and John a place to live and told them that I wouldn't ask any questions and that I wouldn't tell the media if they would only come home. At the end of the email, I pleaded to Jan and John to get away from Kim.

I waited a few months and neither Jan nor John responded.

CHAPTER FORTY-EIGHT

▼

UNWANTED ATTENTION

The house was quiet after Nick went to work. I was depressed, just another day in the home office. Working at home was nice in many ways, but with no one to talk to, I had a hard time getting Jan off my mind. I couldn't talk to Mom about Jan. Mom had enough on her mind with Larry's frequent hospital stays and Carol's declining health. I worried about how Mom was handling the barrage of questions from well-meaning friends and relatives. Mom was distressed and embarrassed that her daughter was involved in such a bizarre religion. Now Mom had to deal with a bombardment of comments about Jan being on national news, and had to listen to people who didn't know Jan comment about how poor a mother Jan was for leaving her only daughter.

I wanted to protect Mom, so I made a few telephone calls and asked our relatives not to mention the Concerned Christians to Mom. To reinforce the message I said that I would be sure to contact anyone that gives Mom a bad time. Deep inside, I really couldn't blame our relatives for being inquisitive about Jan.

Chapter Forty-nine

▼

Invisible Chains

One of the biggest tragedies that resulted from the Concerned Christian's actions was the separation of a young daughter from her mother. At a very young age, Nicky was wise enough to escape the invisible chains of the Concerned Christians ministry. I'm thankful that Nicky had the courage and intelligence to leave Kim or we would have lost her too.

News about the Concerned Christians became commonplace and I was angered by comments criticizing Jan for deserting her only daughter. Jan was an exceptional mother, it didn't seem reasonable that the world would hold Jan accountable for her actions when historically cult victims are brainwashed and coerced into action. I compared Jan's situation to that of a prisoner of war. When a prisoner of war is brainwashed, they are not held responsible for their actions. Should a mother be punished and persecuted as if she left her child out of malice instead of under involuntary mind-control?

Jan's actions were controlled long before she left Nicky. I know that Jan loved Nicky more than she loved anything on earth. But, when I watched the news on television, it occurred to me that all the time, energy, and love that Jan put into raising her beautiful baby girl were lost, when rumors of Jan wanting to kill her only daughter surfaced.

The idea of Jan wanting to kill Nicky was absurd. Many years before Jan left Denver, we talked on the telephone about Hebrews 11:19, "Abraham reasoned that God could raise the dead, and figuratively speaking, he did receive Isaac back from death." Jan figuratively spoke of the verse. I never believed that Jan would intentionally hurt her daughter. Jan loved her daughter but due to Jan's strange behavior, it was impossible to convince anyone how good a mother Jan was. Unfortunately, the world didn't get to hear about the countless hours of love, and devotion Jan gave her and that it was the endless hours that Jan spent home-schooling Nicky that enabled Nicky to advance beyond the level of other children her age. The world would never understand why a mother who loved her daughter could intentionally leave her motherless.

I wanted to shout at the top of my lungs, to set the world straight that it was Jan who was there for Nicky in every aspect of her life…her life was destroyed along with those of her loved ones. Jan was a victim, someone who was coerced away from her home, family, and country. Jan's daughter was victimized and robbed of a fairy-tale childhood. The cult leader who did this to Jan reportedly spent many years studying the behavior of cult leaders and cult victims. But the people listening to the story about the religious doomsday cult who left in the middle of the night didn't know Jan. The world didn't know what a truly good mother Jan *was*…. That is, before the destruction of a mother and daughter relationship, a special bonding that they both loved and cherished.

CHAPTER FIFTY

▼

E-MAIL PLEAD

I was obsessed with trying to figure out the answers to the multitude of questions that Jan and John left behind. I read every news article, and watched every television special about the cult. I decided to write Jan and John another e-mail. I pleaded with Jan to give me an answer as to why she left me to perish in Denver. I wanted to know why they determined that I should die instead of joining them. I asked Jan and John what gave the Concerned Christians the right to play God and damn the rest of us to Hell.

I decided that if nothing else, I would feel better. I needed to get the question off my chest, to move on with my life, even if Jan or John didn't respond.

After I hit send, the email didn't come back to me as undeliverable. I knew that the message was received...by someone.

CHAPTER FIFTY-ONE

▼

SURPRISE RESPONSE

The next morning, it was cold outside…seasonal for December. Instead of reading the news, I hurried downstairs to check my e-mail. Did Jan respond? I could feel my heart beat faster as I got closer to my office. I sat down in front of my computer and clicked on the icon that dialed my server. I noticed that I was short of breath. I didn't like the feeling of antic-ipation. Was Jan going to answer? Did she care? I heard the electronic handshake of the computer. I clicked on "send/receive" and waited. Good, three messages. I waited. Finally, the messages were received. I clicked on my "inbox." Oh my God! Jan wrote back! I quickly clicked on the message.

I couldn't believe it, Jan not only wrote back but she actually acted like she cared enough about me to see if there was a possibility that I would come join her. Then I wondered if the email was really from Jan, anyone who had her computer and her password could answer an email. It wouldn't be out of the realm of possibilities for Kim to know Jan's pass-word and have access to her email. I proceeded with caution.

Jan said that she didn't realize that I might be interested in joining them. She asked me if I was willing and able to do what I needed to do to join them. She challenged me with snide remarks about me loving my life and predicted that I would not be willing to sacrifice everything to join them.

I wanted to learn more. I wanted her back. I needed to keep the dialogue going. I told Jan that I love the Lord and that material things were not important to me. I asked Jan who her God was? I told Jan that she didn't need to prove her love to the Lord, the Lord accepted her the way she was. I ended by telling Jan that Nicky needed her home and signed the email, In Jesus Christ Our Lord's Name, Love, Betty.

I hit "send" and checked to make sure that it didn't come back.

A week went by before I heard back from Jan. I checked my email several times a day, each time my anxiety was building. Finally, I had a message from her. I impatiently waited for the message to open. I read the message and felt bad. The message was mean. Jan was telling me that I loved my life and did not love the Lord. She was pushing me away.

I responded by telling Jan that I didn't love my life and that there has been so much heartache in our family that I didn't think life was all that great anyway. I had nothing to lose and I was not going to give up on her because, I loved her and John and wanted them back.

I hit "send" and checked again to make sure they didn't block my message. The message was received.

Another week passed before I heard back from Jan. The message spoke of hell and dying and they said that I only contacted them so that I could tell the newspapers and media. I couldn't understand what they were saying to me. The message was threatening and said that the authorities were going to get me and she called me a liar.

Not to be intimidated, I shot back an email telling Jan that I didn't believe that the threatening email was from her. I told Jan that I knew and suspected that someone else was writing to me. I told Jan that I was not interested in the newspapers that I only wanted her to come home. I believed that I was corresponding with a group of Concerned Christians and not just Jan. I told them that I wasn't afraid of dying, and that I loved the Lord, and was not worried about where I would go when I die. I asked Jan and John to please pray quietly so that Kim did not know that they were searching for answers directly from the Lord. I ended the email pleading with Jan and John to come home and I closed the usually way, telling them that I loved them and wanted them to come home.

I hit "send."

I didn't hear back from Jan or John within a reasonable timeframe. It wasn't long before I found out why. I read it in the news.

CHAPTER FIFTY-TWO

▼

ARREST IN ISRAEL

The Concerned Christians made the front page again, the newspapers reported that fourteen Concerned Christians were arrested in Israel. Jan did not respond to my last email. I read the newspapers looking for hints of whether Jan would be deported from Israel. The newspaper said that the Concerned Christians were planning to commit some "violent act" to hasten the return of Christ. The contradictory information in the article left me feeling even more confused. One person said that the Concerned Christians were dangerous, and in the same article, another person said that the members of the group were peaceful.

I read with interest in the article that boxes of files were taken from the house during the arrest. It frightened me when I read that quotes from Charles Manson, and information about the earthquake in Los Angeles in 1971 and Hurricane Andrew were found among the documents confiscated in the Israeli apartment building.

I imagined that the Concerned Christians believed that the information was in some way connected to the end of the world. I thought for a moment and concluded that if the Concerned Christians did their home-work, they would realize that it only appears that there is an increase in earthquakes. The reason that there seems to be an increasing number of earthquakes is largely due to the fact that modern man can actually meas-ure earthquakes with sophisticated seismographs that constantly take measurements. I wondered why the documents found mentioned Hurricane Andrew and not the 1969 hurricane called Camille, which was ranked second in severity of all time. I guessed Camille didn't serve Kim's purpose.

As I read in the article that the Israeli government was preparing for the assumed anniversary of the Christian millenium, I remembered that Jan told me that Christians never celebrated holidays on the actual day of the Christian event. I thought back to a conversation Jan and I had, when she reminded me that Christmas wasn't really on December 25, and Easter wasn't celebrated on the right day either. With this in mind, I wondered when the Concerned Christians believed the millenium would end. Since traditional dates meant nothing to the Concerned Christians, it appeared that Kim was free to change the date of his predictions at a whim. I was concerned that there was no possible way to predict the Concerned Christian's actions based on the calendar.

I read the second article and shook my head in disgust. The article said that Jan didn't have any particular religious upbringing. Jan was not raised an agnostic. Jan was primarily raised as a Baptist. Although our family didn't always go to church, Jan was raised in a Christian environment. Our family always had the Lord in our life. I wondered who fed the news-paper reporter such bogus information. Perturbed, I read on...

Jan and John were identified as high-ranking members who were financing the doomsday cult and were planning a disturbance in the streets of Israel. I agreed that Jan and John most likely financed most of the cult's activities, and I was pretty sure that Kim was salivating for the rest of Jan and John's assets. Fortunately, Jan and John's houses had to be sold before Kim could consume the rest of their assets. I was convinced that Kim held a special place in his heart and pocket for Jan and John, but it was clear to me that both Jan and John were victimized by Kim and that Jan and John were not cult leaders themselves.

I was troubled with the prophecy that the Concerned Christians were plotting to riot in Israel. The prediction reminded me of Patty Hearst when she was brainwashed into participating in an armed robbery. It was obvious to me that Kim controlled Jan and John's mind. I wondered if Kim could possibly make the Concerned Christians open fire on Israeli police. The whole idea of the Concerned Christians carrying weapons contradicted their early teachings of resisting evil. I was skeptical about whether the newspaper article contained any truth.

I had heard the message before, directly from Jan and Nicky. Nicky was taught that Kim was a prophet and that God spoke through Kim. Kim controlled the Concerned Christian's lives and insisted that they home school their children, and discouraged women from working outside the home. Kim packaged the Concerned Christians into a neat little box totally isolating them from society.

Each news report presented various reiterations of the Concerned Christians lives. Upon further investigation, there was evidence that the mortgage papers indicated that Monte Kim Miller owned the Israeli apartment building. Kim Miller was the same man who reportedly claimed bankruptcy and couldn't pay for radio advertisements. I watched national television and I joined millions of people witness Kim using spiritual extortion by threatening a woman to pay him thousands of dollars. The woman reportedly didn't pay Kim but she lived in fear that Kim would retaliate.

Our family was anxious to find out if Jan and John would be among the deported. Still there was no indication that they were among the fourteen Concerned Christians that were deported from Israel and would soon arrive back in Colorado.

Nick asked me, "Would you go meet Jan at the airport if she was among those deported?"

Disheartened, I responded, "No, I don't think so, it's clear from Jan's email that she is not the same person. She doesn't want anything to do with anyone. I don't think I would meet her, but it will be interesting to see how the relatives and the government handle the Concerned Christian's when they arrive in Denver."

CHAPTER FIFTY-THREE

▼

CONSTITUTIONAL PROTECTION

The day came when the deported Concerned Christians landed in Denver. The year 1999 was certainly the year of paranoia for cults and the end of the world. The media covered every hint of a story concerning cults. Many people were asking questions about what the government would do to protect victimized cult followers. Many relatives of Concerned Christians were looking for someone to intervene and to free their captive loved ones.

It was clear that there were changes in protocol since the incident in Waco, Texas in 1993, when FBI seized the Branch Davidian cult's compound that resulted in the deaths of more than 80 people. The FBI was forbidden to place any religious groups under surveillance.

The deported Concerned Christians arrived in Denver and many relatives gathered at the airport to get a glimpse of their loved ones, hoping to meet them and to convince them to return home. The media swarmed around to capture the emotions of the crowd hoping to get the best representation of the pain felt by each one. Finally, the plane landed and the crowd became restless. Their expressions went from anticipation to antag-onizing depression as they watched the fourteen people shuffle from the airplane to a bus. The bus drove away.

The crowd stood helpless, abandoning their hopes of talking to their loved ones and trying to persuade them to come home. The authorities were mysteriously quiet. No one would say where the bus took the deported cult members. The only people that knew where the Concerned Christians were staying were sworn to secrecy.

I couldn't believe that government officials protected the deported Concerned Christians from the media and from their families. Maybe one of the relatives in the crowd could have reached one of the cult members and convinced them to stay. I wondered how much money the taxpayers paid for the Concerned Christians protection. I became angry and I wondered what governmental funds were designated to protect deported citizens of the United States from meeting their concerned tax paying loved ones. I couldn't help wondering, if the government author-ities misappropriated funds.

Kim Miller preached that the Constitution of America was evil written by Satan, but the American Constitution was also the same Constitution that allowed Kim Miller to establish his own religious group. It is the same Constitution that allowed Kim Miller to become a prophet and a spiritual leader of his own doctrine, the same Constitution of America that Kim Miller condemned in his ministry.

I shook my head. "Nick, I can't believe the irony of the situation. The government that the Concerned Christians dislike so much, landed up helping them hide from their loved ones. On one hand, the people in the United States were afraid that there was an anti-government movement, a potential mass suicide, and God knows what else. And on the other hand, the American government protected the cult from the very people who stood the best chance of saving the victimized loved ones lives and theo-retically could prevent an anti government movement. I'll never in my life understand this crazy world."

The subject was wearing the family down, Nick said, "Don't get yourself all worked up, and just forget about it. Jan and John are doing what they want and there's nothing we can do about it. See Betty, even if you thought you had a chance to rescue Jan, someone would have foiled your plan anyway. Don't even try, Betty, it's simply not worth it."

"I guess you're right. But if I don't try, I know what I'll accomplish...nothing, and I'll never know for sure if I could have done any good. There must be a way to get Jan to see what's going on. What do I have to lose?"

"Betty. Promise me that you won't make yourself crazy over this."

CHAPTER FIFTY-FOUR

▼

MASTER SWINDLER

Nick and I sat at the table reading the paper on the morning of January 8, 1999. Tears swelled in my eyes as I read the headlines. John, a handsome man who possessed a wonderful combination of intelligence and sensitivity was the focus of an unkind article. The author obviously did not know John. The author didn't know that John was a computer genius and could talk intelligently about nearly any current or historic topic. Even if John wasn't already rich, he could have earned a handsome living based solely on his brilliant mind. The author did not know that John cared for injured animals and nursed them back to health, and after John was attached to the wild animal, he loved the animal enough to set it free.

"Nick, this really aggravates me."

"What Betty?"

"The article leads the reader to believe that John could not be trusted to handle his own finances. I don't think it's fair to say that John cannot handle his own finances without making it clear that John was victimized...wronged by a con artist posing as a spiritual prophet. This is the sort of press that perpetuates the cult's bondage. The victim, John in this case, sees that he is being criticized for being incompetent. The accusations reinforce the cult's teachings that John doesn't fit in society and can never return to the life he once knew. The end result is that the victim remains in the cult because it is the only place that the victim is accepted and respected."

Nick shook his head and said, "John is certainly not stupid or incompetent. John is merely a victim with a kind heart."

"That's right, I guess falling prey to an extortionist is akin to falling prey to a rapist. Uneducated people seem to believe that somehow the victims in either case deserved to be victimized. The petition for conservatorship was filed to thwart Kim's scheme to coerce more money from John. The person who petitioned the courts acted out of love, a step to protect John from the master defrauder. John didn't deserve the way the news presented the information to the world and neither did the loved one who was forced to protect his assets."

"Unfortunately, Betty, the article actually mislead thousands of people into thinking that John was an incompetent man. It's ironic but the people who believed that John was actually incompetent were also deceived, but it was deception in a lesser degree."

"Well, at least the article explained that Kim used spiritual blackmail to get to our brother-in-law."

CHAPTER FIFTY-FIVE

▼

BATTLE OF THE E-MAIL

It dawned on me that the cult members must have communicated via email long before the Concerned Christians left Denver. Email provided an international vehicle for the reputed heavenly kingdom of Concerned Christians to correspond with one another and maintain unity away from the so-called secular world.

I was not surprised that Kim was not among the Concerned Christians who were arrested in Israel. Distance adds to Kim's mystique and enhances the Concerned Christian desire to see and learn from their fearless leader. E-mail correspondence was the perfect tool for Kim to maintain an electronic leash that allowed him to keep a distance from his victims. E-mail also enabled Kim to communicate his orders and control the Concerned Christian's correspondence with the outside world. As an extra bonus, distance protected Kim from making mistakes in front of his victims, mistakes that could signal to the Concerned Christians that Kim was just an ordinary con man.

On Tuesday, March 23, 1999, I woke up at 6:00 and walked downstairs to work. As I waited for the email to be received I realized that it had been a long time since I heard from Jan. I could feel my anxiety escalate when I saw John's return address in my "inbox." I quickly clicked the message. On the subject line were the words: Mark 10:28-31. I read the message several times. I wondered why John and Jan wanted me to ask people I knew if I served the Lord with my heart, soul and my entire mind.

The message gave me the creeps as I read the last line. The last five words said to listen to the people laugh. A terrible feeling came over me, a feeling that something was dreadfully wrong with the author of the email. The words were not from a compassionate Christian looking to save souls. Instead the author appeared to be a condemning stranger. Who was the Concerned Christian's god anyway? Would the message ever make sense? I wrote back:

Tuesday, March 23, 1999
To: John
From: Betty

Watch them laugh? Are you sick or something? It is not the way of the Lord to laugh at someone who is supposedly going to go to Hell. Mark 10:45 is an example of why you should minister to sinners and not hide from them. Are you hiding from sinners to consume your time with self and only saving self, and then laughing at the condemned? Where would you be if we did not have a forgiving Lord? Why should you be forgiven and the rest of us left to go to Hell?

John 3:16 "For God so loved the world that he gave his one and only son, that whoever believes in him shall not perish but have eternal life.

John 14:21 "Whoever has my commands and obeys them, he is the one who loves me. He who loves me will be loved by my Father, and I too will love him and show myself to him."

If you think I am going to persecute you and turn my back on you, you are wrong. I love you and I care about you. I want you to live in Heaven for eternity. Our Lord Jesus is a teacher, someone who is among the sick to guide them *to be healed not someone who is sitting…passing judgment. Think about it. Do **you** serve the **Lord, or** is he a false prophet? My Lord healed the sick…show me a place in the Bible where He turned his back on the sick. Concerned Christian's left the sick to save their selves when they thought Denver was going to vanish. Your Lord brought his wife and children with him…where is his sacrifice? Why could he bring his child and you, Jan, couldn't?*

*Nicky is a child…the Lord would not condemn her to die in Hell. You and I both know that He has forgiven you for sins of greater magnitude, greater than anything that your daughter has done in her short life. Convince me that your Lord is **the** Lord.*

*You mentioned Mark 10:28-30 and asked me if I would could leave my family, or remain with my family and persecute you. I will follow the Lord Jesus Christ to eternity. I love the Lord and he is not going to condemn me for staying with my children and for teaching them to love the Lord. I personally am not looking for a "hundredfold" of anything. I simply want to serve the Lord Jesus Christ. Mark 10:28-30 does not say this is the **only** way to get to heaven…but says that this is one way to get many rewards in Heaven. So tell me whom **your** focus is on. Serving the Lord or the rewards? I'm not interested in rewards…I'm **only** interested in serving the Lord and I'm interested in bringing the Lord's children to Him.*

You know your sacrifice is not unusual. Monks, nuns, and many others have sacrificed more than you and are not being critical of innocent people. Loving the Lord throughout eternity is enough for me.

I love you and always will throughout eternity.

Love
Betty

I clicked on send/receive and checked to make sure that the message was sent. Satisfied that the message was received I knew that it would be days before I heard back from Jan and John.

CHAPTER FIFTY-SIX

▼

COMMUNITY E-MAIL

I received a telephone call from Nicky. She told me that she sent her mom an email and she received it back along with the addresses of all the other cult members. Apparently, the Concerned Christians collaborated on the how to respond to email they receive from family or friends.

I thought about the logistics of managing a cult that was dispersed around the world. It made sense to me that Kim could gain a lot by passing email around to all the Concerned Christians. Controlling e-mail was a well thought out tactic to shield any one particular member from emotional trauma and to control their response. Passing the email around allowed Kim and other member to identify if a member was breaking down. Kim protected his dynasty by using email as an early warning sign to identify if a member was in danger of defecting back to reality. I had to admit that the master of deceit thought of everything to protect his reign.

Kim certainly did his homework and it suddenly made sense to me, the email didn't sound like Jan or John because the email came from all of the Concerned Christians. I believe that the sarcastic email came from Kim.

Lost But not Forgotten   199

Although Kim lacked intelligence in his response, Kim's message was filled with demonic cruelty. I likened my correspondence with Kim as if it were a battle of spiritual proportions with the devil himself.

The next morning was Saturday, March 27 and everyone in the house was still asleep, and as usual, Jan was on my mind. I needed to know if she responded to my last email. I walked down stairs. Darn, someone shut off my computer. I hate waiting for the computer to boot up. I reached over and pushed the button on the tower. Great, an error message. I read the error and followed the instructions.

Finally, my computer desktop displayed the icon to call up the server. I clicked on the icon and listened for the computers to handshake. I hit send/receive and waited. Good, Jan and John responded. With the subject of Jesus Christ's Love, the message was not unlike the last one. The message said that they were laughing at me because I was sleeping with liars. Do they think that I am talking to the media when they say that the media loves my lies? This is insane! I haven't talked to the media. The email ended with a message saying that the author knows that I am embarrassed to be caught in the lies. No one signed the email.

The words in the email did not sound like John and it certainly did not sound like Jan. The author was a stranger…someone foreign to the grace of God. It seemed obvious to me that my email correspondence was a Concerned Christian community discussion. It wasn't going to be easy tolerating the Concerned Christian's stupid abstract communication and the frequent threats from the "authorities." I accepted the challenge to try to reach Jan even through the intervention of the entire cult. I decided that I would have to try tough love to reach Jan's heart and I would have to use the Bible to reach Jan's soul. I started typing:

Date: Saturday, March 27, 1999
To: Jan and whoever "we" are:
From: Betty
Subject: Love through Jesus Christ

*I don't know what you're talking about. If your reference is in the "world"
and you think that the Concerned Christian's behavior is newsworthy, you are
sadly mistaken. There is only a hand full of people that even care about what
is going on with your little group, and they care only because they miss their
loved ones. Furthermore, the only Authority worthy of my attention is Our
Lord, Jesus Christ Our Savior. There is no embarrassment in serving Jesus.
Ephesians 5:4, "Nor should there be obscenity, foolish talk or coarse joking,
which are out of place, but rather thanksgiving."*

*I will not quarrel with any of you and I will continue to focus on Our Lord
Jesus Christ Our Savior. I will continue to love you and pray that you may see
Truth. Proverbs 17:19 reminds me of you and your propensity to quarrel. Your
words to me are wicked and not from Our Lord Jesus Christ Our Savior. Your
words do not convince me that your Lord is Jesus. In Psalm 37:12 we are
warned about the wicked who gnash their teeth.*

*Pray quietly for the Lord Jesus' Truth. The Lord Jesus loves you and wants
you to worship Him and only Him. I will continue to pray for you and will
love you through eternity. I love you enough to say these things. Please pray for
Truth and save your soul. Find happiness in celebrating our Lord Jesus Christ.
He has given us much in which to rejoice! There is nothing to fear when your
faith is in Jesus. I Love You Forever.*

Eternal Love Through Jesus Christ Our Savior,
Betty

I hit send. That email will give them something to think about, I
thought, it will be a while before I hear from them again.

The next day while researching information on the Internet, I received
an email. As the email was downloading on to my computer I thought it

was unusual to receive email on a Sunday. Surely the email wasn't from Jan, I didn't think that the Concerned Christians had time to make route the email and poll their response.

I clicked on my "inbox." Sure enough, I had a message from Jan or John and they were trying to tell me what love is. They wanted me to know that love is not lying about the innocent. The author believed that I was persecuting all of the Concerned Christians and said that the Concerned Christians are the ones who truly love. The email threatened me with the wrath of God. As usual, the message was not signed.

I wondered who had John and Jan's computers. I couldn't be sure that the author of the messages was either one of them. The messages did not sound like anyone I knew. I believed that either someone had taken control of their computers or someone had taken control of their will, maybe both.

Okay, I thought sarcastically, here come the loving threats from those who truly love. Don't they see how silly this is? I get it. I'm persecuting that little innocent lamb, Kim. The author had given me a taste of his all too familiar infamous threats. I wondered how dangerous they were. After all, the authorities did find Charles Manson quotes in a manila folder when the Israeli police arrested the fourteen-cult members in Israel. I prayed to the Lord for guidance and strength and I prayed that Jan would have the strength to search for answers that could save her life and her soul. Then I proceeded to respond to the email.

Sunday, March 28, 1999
To: John
From: Betty
Subject: None

Jan,

I have not lied about anyone. WHO are you referring to? If it is your mortal friend Kim Miller, I'm afraid you are the one among liars. Guard your soul. Pray that you may see the Truth. Jan, pray in silence. You are Jesus' child and He loves you and would not put you in this world only to destroy you. Do not fear any God but Jesus Christ. Serve only Jesus Christ Our Savior. I will continue to pray for you, Jan. I love you and will never persecute you.

You are lost and must find Jesus once again. I never hear you mention Jesus. What God are you serving? Jesus Christ is your Savior; He died for your sins, Jan. God gave his only begotten Son to die for your sins. It's not rocket science! Pray to the Lord Jesus Christ. Read the Bible, His saving grace is in this Great Book.

I wrote to you to see if you were serving Jesus Christ Our Lord or some other master. Answer the question, who is your master? I will continue to pray that your true master is Jesus Christ.

Love,
Your sister who loves you enough to come face to face with one of many false prophets,
Betty

I clicked on send/receive. This time I was sure that they would receive the email so I didn't check. I could feel my heart pounding. I walked up stairs to the kitchen and Nick immediately noticed that I was irritable.

"What's wrong with you?"

"Oh nothing, I'm just thinking about Jan and John."

"I wouldn't even write to them Betty. Jan and John are old enough to make their own decisions, even stupid decisions. Just let them!"

"No, I want to reach Jan and John. I want to help them see what's going on."

CHAPTER FIFTY-SEVEN

▼

THREATS AND LIES

I checked my email every hour. Finally I was receiving a message. It had to be from Jan and John, I thought. As soon as I read the first line, I had a strong feeling that the author was Kim and not Jan or John. No one talks like this, I thought. "Your wickedness is before me?" The email was the most threatening that I had received to date. The author said that I was covering up my wretchedness by quoting the Bible. I don't know anyone who uses the word wretchedness! Again the author did not sign the email but said that my coming judgement would be more severe.

This email concerned me. I called the police and asked the police to place my house under surveillance. I told them that I felt that I was threatened by a cult called the Concerned Christians. Then I wrote the following email:

Sunday, March 28, 1999
To: John
From: Betty
Subject: Re: (no subject)

Jan or John (whoever is not brave enough to identify oneself),
   That amazes me, I did not quote scripture in the last e-mail I sent you. I thought you would be able to identify a true scripture quote. This is evidence that you are not who you claim to be. Your foolish threats are meaningless for the Lord Jesus Christ knows my heart and I do not have to prove anything to you.
   This is scripture:
   Matthew 12:35 "The good man brings good things out of the good stored up in him, and the evil man brings evil things out of the evil stored up in him."
   You are spending too much time dwelling on the dark and evil while the rest of us rejoice in the glory of Jesus Christ Our Savior! We have nothing to fear in our walk with Jesus. Praise Jesus Christ Our Lord for He is the True God. Life is wonderful in Jesus and we are receiving the rewards of His good grace!
   Jan, although we all have moved into new homes and continue our lives in Jesus, we still hope that someday you will come home to us. Also, you may go back to Denver since it was not destroyed as has been predicted. Send an e-mail to me when you are ready to come home since we are now living in New York. I will not continue this dialogue with you because I believe that you have turned this conversation over to your master Kim Miller, whom I will never recognize. Please pray to the Lord Jesus Christ in silence.
   I love you, Jan, through eternity and will continue to pray for you. Kim Miller, this is the end of my dialogue with you; you are a crazy man.

In Blessed Jesus Christ's name,
I love you Jan and John, Pray for your souls.
Betty (I will not respond to future correspondence. May Jesus Christ Be With You.)

   I didn't bother re-reading my email. As soon as I hit send I realized that I shouldn't have responded as I did. I believed that the last email was from

Kim and I was surprised by my reaction to his message. Afraid that cult members were going to harm my family, I told them that I had moved. After I hit send I immediately regretted saying what I did. It was a stupid thing to lie and certainly not a godly thing to do. But I lied and it was done. I tried to justify my actions because we *were* looking for a new home at the time and after all, I did work out of a New York office. But those facts did not make my lie right in eyes of the Lord. Kim was successful in making me fear for my family's welfare.

It seemed as though Kim Miller's Concerned Christians was sending me increasingly more threatening email. I did not fear them on a spiritual level, but I thought that some of them might just be crazy enough act out their own version of "Helter Skelter." It seemed as if the Concerned Christian's were blindly following Kim Miller and would do anything Kim asked so that the followers could prove to the Lord that they were devoted to Him. Would Kim make the cult followers prove that they deserved to be in the heavenly kingdom church called the Concerned Christians? I didn't know and I was not anxious to find out.

The next day I hoped that I wouldn't receive a response from the Concerned Christian's again. But I turned on my computer and checked my email. Sure enough, I received an email from the cult. My heart raced as I opened the correspondence. Again the author of the message was unidentified. I read the first line and thought of the childish mind that was behind the words. I had heard that Kim often spoke in threes. The first line only said "excuses" three times followed by laughter, and said that I tell lies and can't handle the truth. It seemed obvious to be that they accomplished what they had set out to do. The author of the emails wanted to break me down so that I would quit writing to Jan and John. I figured that somehow they felt victorious in their senseless talk. The Concerned Christian's were just playing a game with me. The author seemed to get some sort of sick and perverse pleasure from ridiculing my efforts to convince Jan and John to leave the cult. I was so sick of hearing the Concerned Christian's nonsense. I had to stop the craziness.

At my wits end I responded in an equally childlike manner. I lost my composure. I did not feel that I was speaking to Jan or John. I was speaking to a demented soul to which I could not reason.

Monday, March 29, 1999
From: Betty
To: John

My God, Jesus Christ, is more powerful than yours! You, Kim, are a Freak! *I will continue to pray for you, for you are Lost. Do Not Bother Writing Back for I will not respond…only pray for your souls.*

In Jesus Christ Our Lord's Name
Betty

I admitted that I had stooped to a new low in responding to the author's email. The author's threats were childish and senseless. I was not talking to Jan or John. There was another force present and I couldn't take the stress any more. I blocked the Concerned Christian's email from coming back to me. The Concerned Christians won the email battle, but the war wasn't over.

CHAPTER FIFTY-EIGHT

▼

REACHING OUT AGAIN

Everywhere I looked I saw knick-knacks, books, and pictures around my house that reminded me that Jan and John were gone. Time was quickly changing everything that Jan once knew. Not only did our children grow and become adults. But Nicholas Shawn would soon have a child of his own.

I wondered if Jan, Carol, and I would ever enjoy the loving seasoned relationship that my mother shared with her sisters. I prayed that Jan, Carol, and I might someday experience an occasional loving spat. Carol used to say, "God bless the irritation." I longed for the days that my sisters and I could bicker again…on a lighter note, of course. I had to try to reach Jan again. Giving up was the easy way out, I wanted Jan and John home.

May 18, 1999
Celebrating Life and Love

Dearest Jan and John,
    I am sending you this picture of Mom so that you can see that Mom is happier than ever. We are celebrating life and love for each other through our love

for Jesus Christ. You see, nothing is more important to us than Jesus and our loved ones.

How could you desert everyone? You surely are not so self absorbed to only care about your own salvation? We would like you and John to come back and find out what true happiness is. Your children deserve stable parents.... That's all they really want.

I read a book the other day that reminded me of Kim Miller. I'm sure he read the book. There appears to be many common practices adopted by most cult leaders. Remember when Kim "transformed" during the time that he fasted? You told me that God spoke through him after Kim starved himself and lost a tremendous amount of weight...I remember. Kim's reference to the "authorities" is another example of the tactics of cult leaders. The "authorities" is an example of vague language. Who the Hell are the authorities anyway?

Can't you see that Kim is nothing but a charlatan, a fraud, and a fake? It's not uncommon for the cult leader to give followers rituals to perform...what "Kim Miller" rituals are you performing?

Kim preached against cults at one time! You have a real pro on your hands, Jan. Kim Miller is not about salvation but power and greed. You claim that you have left all your "material" possessions. Well, why is it that you want more "money?" Maybe you have sacrificed everything by giving your money and all your worldly possessions to Kim Miller...but Kim Miller is playing you for a fool. There is laughter but it comes from deep inside Kim Miller...not anyone else! I know that it is Kim Miller that wants all your money, he has everything in his name right? Remember the lady that he threatened on television if she did not give him thousands of dollars? Wake up! Or are you too afraid to leave?

I am attending Nicky's graduation soon. Sometimes a person has to make sacrifices for what is right. I love you all enough to take care of you. I pray that the Lord Jesus will show you Kim Miller's true greed. May the Lord Jesus Christ watch over you and let you see the light. You **have** to open your minds to the fact that Kim Miller is not as he seems. I love you, but will not respond to any e-mail filled with hate from you.

My thoughts, prayers, and actions are in your best interest. I love you very much. We will find a way to bring you home if you just let us.

Love,
Betty

CHAPTER FIFTY-NINE

▼

EXTRAORODINARY CHARACTER

It was the end of the school year 1999, and Jan's beautiful svelte sixteen-year old daughter Nicky was graduating from Wentworth Military Academy. I was thankful that Nicky spent a couple of days with Nick, Kristopher, and I during the school year. Nicky lived a life of conditioning and discipline that was peculiar to the average person but normal to structured military training.

Nicky often talked about how different her relationships with her military school friends was compared to some of the friends she had in public schools. Nicky said that when her military friends got together they were very focused and knew what they wanted to do. Her public school friends spent most of the evening trying to decide what to do and where to go. Nicky seemed impatient with their indecisiveness.

In April, Nicky called me on the telephone and gave me the details about her graduation. I could tell that Nicky didn't want to impose on us when she mentioned that she hoped that we would come to Missouri to watch her graduation.

I knew that Nicky needed her Uncle Nick, Kristopher, and I to watch her graduation. She missed her Mom and I realized that it would mean a lot to Nicky if we were there for her.

"Nicky, we'll do everything in our power to be there for you. We are very proud of you Nicky."

"Oh, thank you Aunt Betty. I would really like you guys to be there…if you can."

"We'll try. Do you want to talk to Kristopher?"

"Yes I want to talk to my Kristopher."

"Okay, hold on a minute."

I turned the telephone over to Kristopher and a short while later I could hear him laughing in the other room. I thanked the Lord for the blessings He had given both Kristopher and Nicky. I walked outside to talk to Nick about traveling to Missouri to watch Nicky's graduation.

"Nick, I just talked to Nicky. You know she'll be graduating pretty soon. Do you think you could get off work so we can drive to Lexington, Missouri? I have some award points so we can stay in a hotel pretty cheap. It would mean so much to Nicky." My eyes started to feel warm as my vision blurred with tears, "Her Mom won't be at her graduation, but at least we can be there for her. It has been very difficult for Nicky to focus on school, but she has turned a negative into a positive and now she's graduating."

"Betty, I wouldn't miss Nicky's graduation for anything. She's as close to my heart as a daughter could be. We'll be there."

The tears rolled down my cheeks as I went back in the house.

CHAPTER SIXTY

▼

HONORS

Nick loaded the car the night before we left for Missouri. "All we have to do in the morning is grab a breakfast burrito and our coffee, Betty. We'll wake Kristopher up just long enough so that he can crawl into the car with his pillow and go back to sleep on the way, when he wakes up he can eat a breakfast burrito."

"Sounds like a good plan to me. I guess there's some festivities on the night we arrive, Nick."

I don't want to leave our house any later than 5:00 a.m. We will try to make it to the evening festivities if we can."

"Okay, Nick."

It was hard to sleep that night, I stayed awake and waited for Kristopher to come home. Finally, I heard the front door open at 12:40 a.m. Kristopher walked quietly into our bedroom and kissed Nick and I goodnight.

"Kristopher, it's going to be tough getting up in a couple of hours."

"I know, Mom. Goodnight."

With Kristopher finally home I could sleep. It seemed like only a few minutes later when the 4:20 a.m. alarm sounded.

"Time to get up, Betty. We have to get out of here in less than an hour."

"Nick, our plans to wake up early sounded better last night. This is rough." My mind fought the urge to sleep. I sat up in bed and forced my eyes open. "Okay...I'm ready! I'm looking forward to seeing my Nicky."

"Me too, Betty. I'll turn on the coffee pot."

An hour later we were on the road. Kristopher was sprawled out in the back seat asleep, while Nick and I enjoying the early morning hours with our travel cups full of fresh morning coffee. As we drove east toward Kansas I remembered how much I enjoyed watching the sunrise. "Look at that horizon, Nick. The good Lord can sure paint a beautiful horizon."

I was disappointed by the time we arrived in Kansas. "It's too late to try to drive to Lexington. I guess we'll miss the festivities tonight, Nick."

"Our timing was off, Betty. There's nothing we can do about it. We'll be there for Nicky tomorrow."

The hotel staff gave us directions to Lexington the next morning. The remote town was further than Nick and I previously thought and I began to worry that we would miss Nicky's graduation ceremony. We hurried to the car, determined that we would not disappoint Nicky.

Finally we arrived at Nicky's school and quietly walked into the large gym shortly after the graduation procession began. Nick, Kristopher, and I climbed up the bleachers and sat down as we searched for Nicky in the crowd of graduates. With their backs turned toward us, the cadets all looked alike in their wool military uniforms, short hair, and military hats. "This is impossible, we'll just have to listen when they call Nicky's name," I whispered.

We patiently listened as one by one each cadet was called by name. The master of ceremonies was at the end of the list and called a young man's name. The muscular cadet weighted down with shiny gold medals on his chest, walked majestically to the podium. Nick raised his eyebrows in awe,

"Wow, look at that guy. He must be their best student and athlete. Look at all those medals."

Impressed with the square shouldered young man's appearance, we watched as he accepted his diploma and proudly walked from the podium I whispered, "He received a different medal than the rest of them. I bet you're right, he must be their star student. Hey, I didn't see Nicky, did you?"

"No, I can't find her, Betty. Everybody looks the same from here."

The master of ceremonies moved on to another part of the program. He began to announce someone very important, someone who broke several school records, the first in the school's one hundred-year history. We listened while we continued to search for Nicky. This is impossible, I thought, we would just have to try to find her after the ceremony.

After a long dissertation, I noticed that the master of ceremonies was wrapping up his introduction as I heard him say "…an exemplary example of a citizen and student with a remarkable 4.25 grade point average. It is my honor to present to you our cadet who has achieved Wentworth Military Academy's Highest Honors, Nicolette LeVee…."

I didn't hear anymore. Nick, Kristopher, and I simultaneously looked at each other with our eyebrows raised and shouted in unison, "That's Nicky!"

I continued, "Nicky received the highest honors! Wow, Nick…!" My eyes filled with tears of joy. "I wish Jan could see Nicky. Jan raised an exceptional daughter. I am so mad at Kim for robbing Jan from sharing this happy event with Nicky. Well, at least Nicky's dad is here. Look at him, he's so proud of her. He has done what he could to support Nicky. I'm thankful for that!"

Nick agreed, "Yeah, I admire Nicky's dad for being here for Nicky."

We followed the crowd out to the football field to watch the cadets march and fire the canon. I was proud of Nicky as I watched her lead her company of cadets. We watched the inspiring ceremony and a suitable grand finale complete with the cadets firing the one hundred-year old canon and throwing their graduation caps in the air.

When the ceremony was over, Nick, Kristopher, and I walked to the sleeping quarters to find Nicky. Nicky's eyes glistened when she saw us, "Aunt Betty and Uncle Nick, I cant' tell you how happy I am that you came. I was kind of...uh...hoping that mom would come, but I knew that she wouldn't. I couldn't help but hope. I wish Mom could be here and see me graduate."

"I wish your Mom could be here too. I was hoping that she would come. But hey, we're very happy to be here, Nicky. We are so proud of the work and effort you put into achieving what you have at this school. I had no idea that you were doing so well. Not that I doubted you could, I guess I just didn't understand the structure here."

"The Lord helped me to focus on my school work, Aunt Betty. All my friends here at Wentworth are like family. We're going to be friends long after we all leave this school."

"You should hold on to your friendships Nicky. I think they're lucky to have you for a friend. Your time will be freed up a little now and you know that you are welcome to come to our house any time you want. We have your room ready for you. We just want you to know that we love you very much and our home is your home."

Nicky gave me a quick hug and said, "Oh, thank you Aunt Betty and Uncle Nick." She touched Kristopher on the arm, "Hey Kristopher, want to help me move my stuff out of my room? I'll introduce you to my roommate."

We waited outside and talked to Nicky's dad and realized the sacrifice he made putting Nicky through school. It was the first time I looked at the situation from his perspective and for the first time I realized the sacrifice Nicky's dad made to place Nicky in a safe and productive environment.

Like most teenagers, Nicky and Kristopher were hungry so we headed for the nearest fast food restaurant. After getting our food, we sat and praised Nicky for her efforts in school and listened to a young lady with purpose and unbridled enthusiasm. It was obvious that Nicky was going places...I wish Jan could see her daughter now....

CHAPTER SIXTY-ONE

▼

CARRYING CROSSES

When I arrived home from Lexington, Missouri, I placed my luggage in the doorway and walked to my computer to check my email. I clicked on my inbox and noticed an email from Jan. The message was puzzling. Jan said that there were two types of Christians; one type of Christian will go to Hell. This type of Christian uses weapons to hold on to their worldly possessions and does not care about the souls of individuals. The other type of Christian understands the Bible and carries their cross for Jesus.

Jan didn't mind telling me that I was among the first group of Christians.

My heart ached for Jan, I wanted to grab her by the shoulders and shake her. I wanted to awaken some kind of emotion, something that would reach to the core of her soul so that she could see what was going on.

Maybe if Nicky were older I would not be trying so hard to get Jan out of the cult. My thoughts were in conflict between allowing Jan to worship the way she wanted and trying to protect Jan from missing her only child grow up in a happy home. I wanted to protect Jan from financial ruin, and to save her from someone I thought was a con.

Other family members were trying equally hard to reach Jan and John by pleading with them to come back home and talking about daily events. I did not see any reason to join their plea, so I tried to reach Jan a different way. I wanted Jan to see a different perspective. I kept telling myself that I had to use "tough love" if I hoped to be successful. I believed that Kim Miller was involved in Jan and my email correspondence. The emotional approach would not work with Kim Miller; besides, Kim Miller had his immediate family with him. He had to protect his livelihood.

Sunday, May 23, 1999
To: Jan
From: Betty

Jan,

You are wrong; Lord Jesus gave us much to glory in. All of my life is surrounded by God's glory. Only He can make a human being, only He can make Heaven and Earth. Our Lord Jesus Christ is wonderful and has created everything on Earth plus a place for those who believe in Heaven. Why can't I glorify the Lord in all that He has done? I'm sorry that your lord Kim Miller has deceived you. Believe what your prophet tells you and you will be condemned to Hell. Jesus wants you to love only Him. I am sorry if these are hurtful words because I do not want to hurt you and I feel that you truly believe what Kim Miller is telling you. I have warned you against your false prophet. Kim Miller values your earthly things or he wouldn't want you to sell them and give him the profits! Your sacrifice is Kim Miller's rewards!

I love you and I do also love your daughter. I will become the mother that you cannot. You care only for yourself and your own salvation and have abandoned your only daughter to save yourself.

*I do love you and hope that you get well. I will continue to pray that Jesus will enter your heart and be the **only** Lord in your life. I will continue to love you and we will look forward to the days when we will see you again. I pray* *that you will glorify in **all** that the Lord has done. I love you while I also love the Lord. You Can Do Both!*

*Love from your sister who will always Love **you**, (and John)*
Love,
Betty

I quickly proofread my message. I didn't like what I said. I had joined in with the rest of the world and criticized Jan for the mother that she had become. I didn't feel good about telling Jan that I would replace her in Nicky's life. I knew that I couldn't possibly replace Jan in any way but yet I told her that I would be the mother that she couldn't. It hurt me to write the message but I felt I had to, I had to reach Jan's soul.

I leaned back in my chair and stared at the computer screen and reflected on the past. I had loved my sister all my life, I remembered our silly childhood quarrels and longed to battle Jan face to face instead of writing sinister email.

The battle of words didn't seem to accomplish anything, but instead, tear us further apart. I realized that I did not have the luxury of talking to Jan in person, I didn't even know if Jan was living on the same continent as me. The cult had built an indestructible shield around Jan and I did not have any other choice but to try to reach Jan's inner feelings. I felt I had to reach Jan where she was most vulnerable. I knew that Jan loved Nicky as only a mother could love her daughter. After I convinced myself that I had to send Jan the message I leaned forward and with my hand on the mouse I clicked on "send."

In retrospect, it was too easy to send cruel messages through email, just say what is on your mind and hit "send." I prayed that Jan would receive the message and understand that she needed to change her life. I waited for a response.

Monday, May 24, 1999, Jan replied. Unfortunately, I underestimated Jan's loyalty to Kim. Jan told me that she could not agree with me. Jan said that she has known both Kim and I for a long time and she knew who really loved the Lord. Jan also told me that she knew which one of us God loved and who knew God's Truth. She called me a liar, a servant of Satan, and a pitiful judge of doctrine. Jan said that she was telling me this in love and that I was going to go to Hell but she would be going to Heaven. She ended her message with Love, Jan.

I was surprised that Jan did not mention Nicky in her email. Maybe she was avoiding talking about Nicky so that she could remain strong. Or did Kim tell Jan what to say in the email? It was obvious that Jan was battling with me by comparing me to Kim. I cringed at the thought.

CHAPTER SIXTY-TWO

▼

DEATH OF FAMILY

I was torn between telling Jan what was going on in the family and not sharing any information with her. I resented the fact that Jan chose not to ask about her loved ones and that Jan elected to desert all of us. I decided to try to arouse her curiosity. I began writing what I hoped would be a mysterious message. I wanted Jan to realize that time was running out and that Jan might not see some family members if she didn't come back soon. Time was rapidly changing the world that Jan once knew.

Maybe I said the wrong thing, but I had to try, so far, nothing seemed to work. It was clear that Jan simply wasn't going to come home without any coaching. I had nothing to lose, I had to find a way to remain on Jan's mind.

Tuesday, May 25, 1999
To: *Jan*
From: *Betty*

Jan,

I went to a funeral yesterday. I will not tell you who died because you do not care. But the reason that I bring it up is because I talked to our cousin Donnie from Oregon. Did you know that his daughter is also named Jan, and she too, joined a cult? She was saved from destruction and she was able to get out of the cult early enough to turn to Jesus and not her cult leader. I wish that I could save you from your cult leader, but you are following him blindly.

*Jan, you do not send a message of love. Your messages to me are of blind righteousness. You are a typical example of a person in a cult and of course you think that you are doing right. I love you so much that I cannot stand back and let Kim Miller destroy you and John. I know that at one time you loved Our Lord Jesus and I know that you have taken the wrong road and that Satan has been able to penetrate into your faith. You know that Satan attacks Christians and he came at you with all the power he had. I wish that you could see that whom you are following is a leader of the lost. Satan is counting on you blindly following him and **not** questioning what is going on.*

I am confident that I will go to Heaven. I am not following a mere mortal to try to get to Heaven. Kim Miller has taken away your family and your money. He still has his family with him and he has control of your money. When it's all over, Satan will win if you do not wake up and see what's going on. You have helped Kim Miller recover from being bankrupt and Kim Miller was able to defend himself in court, yet you could not even go to court to try to get your only daughter. Jan, you have to ask yourself... "Where's the logic in following Kim Miller's direction when he has a separate set of rules for himself." Kim Miller does not follow the Lord Jesus.

I'm afraid that you cannot see the forest through the trees. Kim Miller's master is powerful, all right. His name is Satan. I only ask you to please see what Kim Miller really is. Satan is a master of disguises. Satan has fooled you for fourteen years. Think about what I am saying, Jan. You are in a deep, deep sleep. You told me yourself, Satan comes into your life gradually and after he has gotten in, Satan then takes full control of your life. You have lost your ability to think for yourself...Satan is doing all your thinking.

(It bothers me you never mention Jesus. You know there has been many, many gods throughout time, but only one Jesus. I feel you should always mention Jesus when you speak of God so that there is no mistaking whom you are worshipping. I suppose Satan hates the word Jesus.)

I know you think you are doing right, Jan, but you are not. Please pray to Jesus so that you may see what is happening. You and John can come home to Jesus. Our Lord Jesus Christ loves you forever. Come home, Jan and John. Please do not follow this false prophet. I love you very much and want you to re-establish your relationship with the Lord Jesus.

In Jesus Christ Our Lord's Name,
Love,
Betty

I realized that my message would probably torture her into knowing who died. Did she think it was her daughter Nicky, her elderly mother, her dear sister with cancer or her brother with heart trouble? Did Jan think that maybe someone else died in an accident. It was mean, but I felt the mind trip would reach her soul. I wanted Jan to ask me who died. Then I would know that Jan cared and loved her family. I waited.

CHAPTER SIXTY-THREE

▼

THE CHALLENGE

I was anxious to hear a message back from Jan. I woke up at 5:00 and walked downstairs to check my email. As I read the message it was obvious to me that I had a reaction. I tried not to think about the cruel tactics I used.

I once heard that a person should not say hurtful things, because once said, it was impossible to undo the damage. I felt I had no other recourse. I hoped that my constant plea to return home would convince Jan to see the truth, and to forget the lies that the cult placed in her mind.

Judging from John's return email on Wednesday, May 26, 1999, I not only succeeded in the objective of reaching Jan but unfortunately, it appeared that I shut the door on our communication, unless I accepted a challenge.

John told me that he was responding on behalf of Jan because I was reckless and irresponsible in my email to Jan. John wanted me to make sure that Nick participated in all my correspondence to the Concerned Christians. John told me that negligent accusations such as mine have caused the Concerned Christians a lot of pain. Lies like mine even caused the Concerned Christians to be falsely arrested and their personal property destroyed.

John said that he refused to allow me to abuse Jan with my false accusations and would not tolerate my revolting behavior. The Concerned Christians would not communicate with me unless I listened to Kim Miller's tapes and tell them what exactly was wrong with them. John offered to send the tapes to me and said that he acted on Kim's teachings. John wanted me to review the tapes and justify my position. If I could not give the Concerned Christians a logical explanation as to why the tapes were wrong then John and Jan would know that I was intentionally trying to deceive them.

John closed his message by saying that Nick needed to be involved so that Nick can take some responsibility for my disgusting conduct. John signed the message.

I read John's email several times. At least Jan and John were still trying to talk to me. The Concerned Christians were giving me an opportunity to get to know them a little better. I was interested to find out if the package that John was sending would have a return address so that I would know where Jan and John were living.

Date: Wednesday, May 26, 1999
To: John
From: Betty

I am happy to hear from you. I do love you and Jan and want to save you from what I believe is going to send you both to Hell! I am not coming to you to be mean or hateful, I am much too busy. My mission is not to upset you both.

I will listen to your tapes and I will stay in contact with you to discuss the tapes. Identify the order in which you want me to listen to the tapes. I expect that there will be some truth in the tapes laced with lies. I will be your "critical thinker" for this project. I hope that you and Jan will remain open to my comments...if you cannot be objective, then I should not waste my time. Let

*me know if you are going to be open-minded or if you are going to use my mes-
sages to twist the truth. We must remain civil and objective. I will listen to
your logic if you listen to mine. We must base ALL of the discussions on the
Bible literally and the center of our discussions must be on Jesus Christ Our
Savior. Jesus is the only God and Kim Miller is not God! I expect to grow with
this discussion as I hope you and Jan will. Kim Miller is not to be involved. I
believe Kim Miller has other motives.*

*As far as Nick is concerned, he (like most everyone) doesn't really care about
what any of you are doing. Although he cares for you personally, he does not
want to waste time on what he thinks is inevitable. He has told me to leave
you alone and that he thinks that it is unfortunate, but you are both bound for
Hell. Also, I do not know what happened to your group, any invasions of privacy or anything else. Since I am not privy to the events, I cannot comment. As
for me, I cannot sit back and let you destroy yourselves. I am strong enough to
fight Satan to save your souls. I will do whatever is in my power to save you
from destruction. And I do not fear death or dying so there is no stopping me.
If I should choose to stop trying to reach you, it is because I feel that you both
are totally lost. Then I will not waste my time.*

*You know Jesus allows you to make a choice. If you are not following his book
literally, then you are not following Jesus. So let's start with John 3:16 and
Ephesians 2:8-9. Explain to me why you cannot be saved by grace. (Remember,
I'm not interested in talking to Kim Miller, I believe he is distorted. Our discussion must be from only you and Jan. I love you and Jan very much.*

*By the way, Nicky will be here later. We look forward to seeing her. Praise
the Lord Jesus that she is able to spent time with her family.*

I look forward to receiving the tapes.

Love,
Betty

I was happy to have the opportunity to openly discuss what Jan and
John were doing and to try to make them both understand what Kim was
doing. Of course, I realized that the Concerned Christians were trying to

get me to join the cult. Since John requested Nick's input, I asked Nick if he was willing to discuss with Jan and John the Concerned Christian theology. Nick responded in a resounding "no".

By the end of the day, Wednesday, May 26, 1999, another unread message was in my inbox. I clicked on my email icon and waited to download the message from Jan and John. They insisted that I involve Nick in my correspondence and said that if I wasn't ashamed of my message that I wouldn't be afraid to let Nick know what I was writing. They said that if Nick knows what I have said, Nick was also persecuting them. They promised to explain Ephesians 2:8-9 to me in a few days and promised to send the tapes and charts soon.

Now Jan and John were signing their correspondence. I was aware that the Concerned Christians request to have Nick join our discussion had a much larger purpose than to keep my tongue civil. Jan and John had everything before they fell under Kim's control. I was convinced that Kim was interested in our assets, not Jan and John. I knew I wouldn't be able to reach Jan or John while Kim was present in our discussions.

I took a deep breath. Nick was in the other room so I walked up to him and said, "Jan and John want you to be involved in our correspondence. They say I'm too reckless with my accusations. Jan and John want your participation or they say you too are persecuting them. So, do you want to respond to Jan and John with me?"

"Betty, you know how I feel about those two. I don't give a damn what either Jan or John do with their lives." I want you to tell them exactly what I have to say, Betty. Don't leave out any of the words."

"Nick, I don't want to talk to them like that. Besides, they think they are serving the Lord. I don't care if you talk to Jan and John, but, I have to continue to try to get them home."

"Well, I want them to know how I feel. Tell Jan and John what I said, Betty."

Reluctantly, I walked over to the typewriter and began writing as Nick looked over my shoulder:

Date: Wednesday, May 26, 1999
To: Jan
From: Betty
Subject: *Nick's response... it is not pretty*

John and Jan,

Alright, you asked for it, Nick told me not to leave anything out of what he has to say to you, and I don't want to write this but I also do not want to go against Nick's wishes either. I read all our correspondence to Nick and he told me to tell you in quotes, "I don't give a damn what either Jan or you do, you've given up your family and deserted everyone, so I couldn't care less what the two of you do." Nick also says that he doesn't care if I continue our conversation and furthermore, Nick has no problem with what I've already said to you. You see, Nick and I have known each other for more than 30 years, I know Nick and I know how he feels about what you two are doing. Nick says "Jesus did not abandon his family and even Mary was able to attend Jesus' funeral. God did not ask Jesus to be away from his family."

About family, Nicky is here. Kristopher and Nicky just left to buy some shorts for the summer. Nicky said, "You know Aunt Betty, I don't even own a pair of shorts." Nicky is just a little girl. She deserves better than what she has and I'm not talking about money or possessions. I'm talking about love from her Mom and the dad she loved so much. I hurt for Nicky and that is why I am spending my time with the two of you. I want to learn what you know and to understand how you can do what you do, and not care. So let's get on with what we have to do....

I guess we have an agreement that we will maintain our discussions based solely on the Bible and on Jesus Christ. Is that correct?

I look forward to receiving the tapes. Pray with me so that we all understand the Bible and can discern between right and wrong on the tapes. Remember that the Bible is the only Truth. I will listen to the tapes and discuss with you what is said and both of us must remain objective.

Take care of yourselves.

Love in Jesus Christ Our Lord's Name,
Betty

CHAPTER SIXTY-FOUR

▼

CHILD'S BASIC NEED

The next morning, I was looking out the kitchen window watching the birds eating seeds out of the birdfeeder. Birds always reminded me of John's kind heart. I heard a stir upstairs, it couldn't be Kristopher, he never wakes up until at least 10:00 during the summer. A perky head poked down from the top of the stairs.

"Oh, Good morning Nicky."

She smiled sweetly, "Good morning Aunt Betty."

"You're up early."

"No, I'm not, Aunt Betty. I'm going back to bed."

"Okay sweetie, I'll see you in a few hours." I watched as she turned and walked to her room. She was a beautiful girl, tall and thin. I think she could have been a successful model. But she was doing what she wanted to do. Nicky has received a lot of personal satisfaction from being in the military. It was obvious to me that Nicky liked the structure and the discipline that the military school brought into her life.

It was refreshing to have Nicky visit and nice to finally have a female perspective around the house. Nicky and I had something in common. I worked in the male dominated field of nondestructive testing and Nicky was in a military school. We talked about hairstyles and make up and Nicky's future career. I bowed my head and thanked God that Nicky was strong enough to focus her energy on something positive in her life. I prayed that Nicky realized that I was here for her if she ever needed me.

An hour later, I heard someone shut the bathroom door. A few minutes later Nicky walked down the stairs. "Good morning, Aunt Betty."

"Good morning Nicky. Do you want some pancakes for breakfast?"

"Umm, pancakes sound good."

"I was wondering, Nicky, were you able to take anything with you when you left your mother's house?"

"Aunt Betty, I didn't think I was leaving forever. I only took two outfits with me."

"You've grown so much since you were fourteen-years old. I'm sure you outgrew those two outfits within six months. You had so many nice things. Here, follow me, Nicky."

I walked Nicky around the house and showed her all the things that her Mom had given me. "All the things that your Mom gave me have tremendous sentimental value to me. In addition to my memories of your Mom, these things are all I have left from her. But, I want you to have them when you are ready. I realize that you don't have any place to keep them while you are in military school. But let me know when you want them and they are yours. It would mean a lot to me if you had something to remember your Mom by."

Tears swelled up in Nicky's eyes as I said to her, "Your Mom loved you very much and know that she still loves you. I am sorry that you had to suffer so much pain. I want you to know that I am here for you when you need someone to talk to. I'm here for you no matter what the circumstances."

Nicky reached and hugged me and said, "Oh thank you, Aunt Betty."

"You know, I've been writing to your Mother, Nicky."

"Is she writing back to you, Aunt Betty?"

"Yeah, but our emails are all about the Concerned Christians. I try to convince your Mom to come home. But…well, you know…she's not listening."

"Do you mind if I write to my mom on your computer?"

"I don't mind Nicky, but I don't want you to get hurt."

"I just want to tell her what's going on in my life, maybe she'll write back."

"Okay, Nicky, I hope your mom writes back to you, I don't want her to break your heart again."

"Oh, I really don't expect mom to write. But I just want to let her know that I love her."

"Here you go, the computer is dialed in."

Thursday, May 27, 1999
To: Mom
From: Nicky
Subject: Hi Mom

Dear Mom,

How are you, Mom? I guess I really don't expect you to respond to this message, but I'll go ahead and tell you what is happening in my life. Somewhere in my heart, I think you are still interested in me. Last Saturday I graduated from high school as Valedictorian and I accepted a United States Marine Corp scholarship and will attend VMI this fall. After graduation I will be commissioned as a 2LT, flight navigator in the Marine Corps. My plans are to be the rio or "back seater" on a FA/18 fighter jet and then I hope to be in military intelligence.

There has been so much that has happened during the past two years. I would love to share all the memories with you as well as hear about your life. I will send you my mailing address and my email address in college when I get it.

I just wanted you to know how much I love you and miss you. There is nothing I want more than to see you at least one more time in my life. I don't believe that anything will happen at the end of the millenium as Kim Miller predicted. I do worry about what you and all the others might do when Kim's prophecy is left unfulfilled.

I will be staying with Aunt Betty this summer. I'm working a few hours a day with her. You can reply to this email address or you can call me on the telephone. Mom, I love you no matter what happens and I will always be here for you. I wish we could spend time together. I love you. Please tell daddy that I love him and that I miss him very much…my puppies Peaches and Bitt too.

Love,
Nicky

"I sent the email Aunt Betty. Let me know if you hear back from Mom."

"I will Nicky. I pray that your Mom will write back to you." I watched Nicky walk up the stairs and wished that I could ease her pain.

As the day progressed, I was very busy working on the computer and talking to my business colleagues. During the course of the next few hours Nicky checked with me three times to see if her Mom replied to her email message. Each time I had to tell her "no." On one hand, I was anxious for Jan to respond, but on the other hand, I was worried that Jan may say something mean and hurt Nicky.

Finally on Thursday, May 27, 1999 I received an email message from Jan. Unfortunately the message was not to Nicky, but to me. The one-line message only asked me if I believed in eternal security. The message was signed by Jan and John.

I read the email and it made me angry. Jan loved Nicky so much…she used to *live* for Nicky. And now Jan couldn't even acknowledge that Nicky wrote to her. It seemed as though Kim removed Jan's ability to be sensitive and to show her only daughter that she loved her. But I knew that Jan loved Nicky because of one comment Jan made the last time I saw her. "I want to know about Nicky, Betty. After all, she is my daughter."

I was immediately reminded that that Jan was just obeying Kim.

CHAPTER SIXTY-FIVE

▼

ETERNAL SALVATION

Date: *Thursday, May 27, 1999*
To: *John and Jan*
From: *Betty*

John and Jan,

I believe in what the Bible tells me. Before you read the rest of this pray that you will understand my intent (as I respond to your e-mail) and I realize that all that I say to you, I say in love for our Lord and for his creation in both of you. 1 Thessalonians 5:9-11, "For God did not appoint us to suffer wrath but to receive salvation through our Lord Jesus Christ."

*John, Jan, we have all been sinners and we are not Jesus Christ so we will continue to sin, that is why the Lord sent his only son to die on the cross for us, so that we may have eternal life through Jesus Christ. My personal favorite verses are John 3:16 and Ephesians 2:8-9. Throughout the Bible we are taught that Jesus died for us and he did this as a **gift**. That means you do not have to pay for salvation in any way, shape, or form. And it is because of this that we* *live to serve the Lord and to act in a way in which he would want us to act, not because we are trying to pay Him for dying for us, but because we love Him. How could you possibly repay the Lord for dying for you or sending His only child to die for you?*

You simply cannot repay the Lord, and to try would de-value His gift. Simply live your life to please the Lord, not as payment, but because you Love the Lord. Titus 3:3-11, "At one time we too were foolish, disobedient, deceived and enslaved by all kinds of passions and pleasures. We lived in malice and envy, being hated and hating one another. But when the kindness and love of god our Savior appears, he saved us not because of righteous things we had done, but because of his mercy. He saved us through the washing of rebirth and renewal by the Holy Spirit, whom he poured out on us generously thought Jesus Christ our Savior, so that, having been justified by his grace, we might become heirs having the hope of eternal life. This is a trustworthy saying. And I want you to stress these things, so that those who have trusted in God may be careful to devote themselves to doing what is good. These things are excellent and profitable for everyone."

John and Jan, you are trying to get to Heaven the hard way and Kim Miller is the benefactor. You do not have to leave your families or responsibilities and you do not have to pay your way to Heaven. John, I understand that it is your money that is funding the new lifestyle for many of the Concerned Christians.

I'm sure that you have been told that it is harder for a rich man to get to Heaven. That is because many rich men worship their money instead of the Lord. A rich man actually can have money and still only worship the Lord and gain eternal life through Jesus. The rich man must only worship the Lord Jesus Christ! Of course, if someone wanted your money, they would tell you different. The Lord loves you and only wants you to love Him back. Love must be totally free. Have you ever tried to pay for love? Money cheapens love and "paid for love" is not genuine love.

Please, I plead with you, read the Bible and learn that you do not have to pay to get to Heaven. Through God's Grace, all you need to do is to accept Jesus Christ as your Savior. Yes, I believe in Jesus Christ's eternal grace, why should I

doubt the Bible. I am not able to repay the Lord anyway, but through my love
and devotion to Jesus Christ and by bringing others to Him so that they may
experience what He has done for us all.

  I love you both. Take care of yourselves.

Love,
Betty

There was no way of determining whether I was reaching Jan with my message or if I was making her angry. I remembered the many discussions that I have had with Jan over the telephone. I was never comfortable preaching about Jesus and I never considered myself an expert on the Bible. Jan was the only person that I ever had these discussions with. Before I wrote my messages to Jan, I always prayed for guidance. I thought about calling the pastor of my church to get direction on how to approach Jan, but I decided to just pray that God would show me the right words to say to Jan.

That evening, I reflected on our email correspondence, and was filled with peace and hope. Maybe I could reach Jan through the Bible. I couldn't imagine that Jan and John would continue to choose to suffer when given an option. I prayed that my message would also give Jan and John peace.

On May 28, 1999 Jan began her return email by thanking me for the message and asked me to read her message carefully. She told me that people frequently do not read all the necessary passages when referring to Ephesians 2:8, 9. She insisted that I include verse 10. Without verse 10 the meaning of Ephesians 2:8 and 9 are skewed. Jan said that although God wants us to accept Him as the Savior and verse 10 explains that good works are required to do His will.

Jan said that she sent the tapes and that the Concerned Christians welcomed my critique and told me that they will be judging my ability to analyze good doctrine. Jan said that if I could not find fault in the tapes that I should be prepared to follow the true Jesus Christ. She said that I needed to be prepared to leave any family members who refuse to follow me. She referenced Matthew 19:29, "And everyone who has left houses or brothers or sisters or father or mother or children or fields for my sake will receive a hundred times as much and will inherit eternal life."

Jan said that the Concerned Christians were of the Lord because they were willing to leave their family and all the people who are uneducated about God's will and who are not worthy of the kingdom. Jan supported her position by quoting Matthew 10:35-39, "For I have come to turn a man against his father, a daughter against her mother, daughter-in-law against her mother-in-law, a man's enemies will be the members of his own household. Anyone who loves his father or mother more than me is not worthy of me; anyone who loves his son or daughter more than me is not worthy of me; and anyone who does not take his cross and follow me is not worthy of me. Whosoever finds his life will lose it, and whoever loses his life for my sake will find it."

Jan said that if I agree with the doctrine that I must leave my family and worldly possessions, then all we had to discuss was whether the tapes were from man or a true gospel of Jesus Christ. She said that I should let their daughters go so that they may receive the truth. Jan closed her message by telling me that Jan and John had a higher love for their daughters, a love that would last an eternity and not simply selfish human love. Her message was signed, "Willing to lose our reputations, Jan and John."

I knew all along that Jan still loved Nicky and I was sure that John still loved his daughter and his son. Their unorthodox approach in saving their daughter's eternal souls was the only way Jan and John could express their love for them. I was convinced that Kim told Jan and John that I was keeping their daughters from joining the Concerned Christians. If Kim was so powerful, why didn't he just make Jan and John's daughters join them? I was an easy patsy for all the things Kim couldn't do, I became Kim's excuse and a model sinner.

I wondered how many people feel doomed to hell because they are not willing to make the sacrifice of leaving their families, jobs, friends, and possessions. How many Christians have lost hope of going to Heaven because the Concerned Christians told them that they must make unreasonable sacrifices before they can enter Heaven? I was sickened by the Concerned Christian's elusion of divine knowledge. Did the Concerned Christians expect me to believe that I too, could have divine knowledge if I joined them?

I prayed for guidance and decided to respond later.

Date: Monday, May 31, 1999
To: Jan and John
From: Betty

I guess I should have quoted the entire Bible. Again, please pray that you understand the message that I am sending and that my intent is not to insult or hurt you. I do love you and pray for your souls.

I am not convinced that your interpretation of "works" is the same as Jesus Christ Our Savior's. The Bible was written for us…to us. To try to bend the words to mean something that it does not say is wrong. The good Lord knew that He was writing to sinners and to non-believers when He wrote the Bible, He does not want you to try to misrepresent His message as "Gods interpretation," this is a common tactic of cult leaders. The Lord does not care about your worldly possessions, the Lord wants you to bring praise and glory to Him, and does not want you to worship anyone other than Jesus and never worship your possessions. If you focus on Ephesians 2:10 as an explanation of why the Lord has saved our souls, please read the rest of Ephesians and specifically Ephesians 4:22-6:9 to determine what "good works" really are in the eyes of our Lord Jesus Christ. Do not take "good works" out of context. The Bible does not tell you to literally leave your family. His message in Ephesians and in Matthew boils down to: placing the Lord before everything in your heart, mind, and soul.

A powerful verse in the Bible for your cult is Matthew 19:29 which was written because the rich man covets his riches. This is the rich man's main problem and prevents him from entering eternal life. Jesus is telling you not to covet your riches. You have taken Matthew 19:29 out of context.

Jesus wants you to love Him over all others, and it's simpler than you think. If the Lord only wanted you to leave your family why would the Lord have your honor your father and mother and love your neighbor in the Ten Commandments?

In Matthew 22:37-40 "Jesus replied: Love the Lord your God with all your heart and with all your soul and with all your mind. This is the first and greatest commandment. And the second is like it: 'Love your neighbor as yourself.' All the Law and the Prophets hang on these two commandments."

My heart, mind, and soul have already been given to the Lord Jesus. I do not need to prove anything to your lord Kim Miller. Do not suggest that I am controlled by any earthly possession. My faith in my Lord, Jesus Christ is not bound by walls or by mere mortals. I place my faith fully on my Lord Jesus Christ and what He tells me in the Bible. My possessions are the Lord's and are not possession that I deserve, but possessions given to me by the Lord. My family and possessions already belong to my Lord Jesus.

I praise the Lord in everything that happens, good, bad or indifferent. It is foolish to even suggest that I do it for your Kim Miller since my Lord Jesus Christ already has my heart. As for whether the tapes and charts that you send me are from the mind of a man, I believe they are of man. Remember Jan, I've heard some of the tapes already. And I don't believe that you can win souls to Jesus Christ by leaving everyone and talking amongst yourselves.

Your reputations are the least of your problems. Your reputation is only a concern of yours, why do you care? You must recognize that your lord Kim Miller is not as you believe. Take care of yourselves, I am afraid that Kim Miller will have you kill yourselves for him. I love you and pray to Jesus that you can see the Truth.

Love,
Betty

CHAPTER SIXTY-SIX

▼

FREEDOM TO SPEND

It was late in the afternoon, my workday was over and I had time to reflect on Jan and John. My frustration level was high due to the lack of progress I was making in convincing Jan and John to leave the cult. I guess this is the Lord's way of helping me become more patient. I stood by the sink in the kitchen taking skin off the chicken before placing it in a pot to boil. The telephone rang. "Can somebody get the phone? My hands are oozing with chicken fat."

The telephone rang the fourth time. "Darn!" I dried my hands on the tea towel as I walked over to the telephone and said, "Hello," just as Nick bolted through the garage door. I listened to the voice on the other end without saying a word. Finally I said, "Well, I don't know. I'll really have to think about it. Give me some time."

"Who was that Betty? I was working on my bike in the garage or I would have picked up the phone. Whom were you talking to?"

"It was a relative who was concerned about the upcoming sale of Jan and John's Boulder home. They are concerned that the proceeds from the house will be funneled to Kim and never seen again…and from what I can tell, I think the relatives have a reason to be concerned. You know Nick, if Jan or John needed medical care or if they return from the cult, they might not have a dime to their name."

Nick walked over to see what was cooking on the stove, "So? That's Jan and John's money, Betty, their finances are none of our business."

"Well, my initial reaction was that I did not want to get involved in Jan and John's finances. I really need to do what is right. By the way, we're having chicken mole tonight and I'll make some home made tortillas," I said as I added the chicken bouillon cube and chile molido puro to the pot."

"Yum, one of my favorite meals," Nick said with a smile. His smile disappeared as he added, "That money is John's and we have no business getting involved. If Jan and John want to throw their money away…let them."

"I don't know, I'm really torn about what to do. You know, Nicky needs things and if something happened, the money would be lost, and Nicky could be without financial support. Hopefully, Jan and John will come back someday and if we protect some of the money, they will have some funds to start all over." I sighed as I thought about the Constitution, and the fundamental rights of freedom of religion. How can I step in and interfere with Jan and John's right to worship the way they want? But then again, how can I just sit around and not intervene and help prevent Jan and John from what I believe to be spiritual coercion?"

"I would rather you not get involved, Betty."

After supper, I wanted to be alone so I walked upstairs and shut the door to my bedroom to quietly reflect on Jan and John's circumstances. I changed into my nightshirt and knelt beside my bed and prayed to God for guidance and the courage to do the right thing. That night I dreamed of Jan and woke up missing her more than usual. But I didn't have the answer. I didn't know whether to petition the courts for a conservator based on her competency. What kind of sister would take her sister to court and say that she was incompetent? How could I live with myself?

CHAPTER SIXTY-SEVEN

▼

PETITION OR NOT

The following week I returned from the post office to find a package on the doorstep. I quickly picked up the package and read the return address hoping that I would see where Jan and John were living. I sighed heavily as I read the post office box number from Boulder, Colorado. Jan and John have thought of everything.

I opened the package and saw a series of audiotapes that were labeled in Jan's beautiful handwriting and dated 1993. Included in the package were pages and pages of charts that were filled out by someone other than Jan. I immediately came into the house and placed the first tape in the tape recorder. The sound of Kim's voice sickened me. I realized that it would be very difficult for me to listen to the tapes objectively. The innermost core of my soul churned as I listened. Finally, I gave up and placed the tapes to the side promising to get back to them later.

My thoughts were in turmoil, should petition the courts for a conservator for Jan's half of John's estate and the proceeds from the sale of their homes in Boulder and Ouray. Judging from what I knew about the

Concerned Christians and how Jan was held captive from her family, I rationalized that the cult leader robbed Jan and John of their civil rights. I was not taking away Jan's freedom, but I did have an opportunity to protect Jan and John from further coercion. I was beginning to formulate the rationale behind the action to petition a conservator for Jan.

By the end of the week, I had processed an assortment of feelings. I felt resentment and occasionally I felt selfish. My selfish moments made me want to turn my head and run from making a decision. I asked myself, why do I have to make the decision anyway? I never thought that I would have to make a decision based on a religious doomsday cult, for crying-out-loud? This sort of thing only happens to other people, not me, not in my family. I love Jan so much, how could I publicly declare Jan incompetent? Then again, how could I not protect her?

The easy way out of the dilemma would be to run away from the problem. My first reaction was to pass the problem off to one of my brothers or my other sister. I didn't need to deal with this, I was busy raising my own family. I certainly had enough of my own problems. I began to look at each of our family members to decide who would be the most likely candidate. I thought about the lives of each of my siblings with objective rationale.

I considered my sister, Carol. I immediately ruled her out. Carol and I were suddenly having trouble communicating. In my forty-five years of life I never fought with Carol, well, except when she fired me on my birthday from my job at the corner grocery store. Carol didn't see the humor in using the store's paint shaker to shake soda pop minutes before two cute guys came in for their routine afternoon beverage. It was funny…for a while…I don't imagine Carol laughed too much when she was cleaning the soda off the merchandise in the store though.

Carol surely was not happy about me petitioning the courts. Lately, when Carol and I talked we strained to relate to one another. Everything I said came out wrong. Carol was disappointed in me and disgusted that I would even consider freezing Jan's money. Her deteriorating condition frustrated her because she wanted to fight the petition in court. Carol scolded me, "Jan's money is none of your business and please do not interfere, if you do I will never speak to you again."

I was surprised at my persistence in protecting Jan considering Carol was the person I admired more than anyone in the world. I respected Carol's values, her devotion to her family, and I loved Carol like she was my other mother. I needed to think this whole thing out. I needed to decide what would be right for Jan by objectively reviewing the situation.

My thoughts turned to our younger brother Lenn. Lenn was always smart enough to stay out of everyone's business. Lenn lived in Utah and would not be a likely candidate to petition a Colorado court, he was off the hook.

Larry was the only local Colorado resident who could actually make it to court in less than two hours. Larry and Jan were never crazy about one another. I sighed as I thought; Larry just had surgery, no, Larry certainly didn't need another problem.

The only one left was Mom. I would never even consider Mom as a possible petitioner. She was the epitome of selflessness and fairness. Mom wouldn't want to interfere and would never bring the courts into a family matter anyway. She was already broken hearted with the national news about her daughter's affiliation with a "doomsday cult." Her life was painful enough, I decided that the least Mom had to get involved the better it would be for her.

That left me with the decision. My head was already starting to pound with stress. I needed to clear my thoughts. Even though I would have preferred to turn my head and go about my business, I decided to focus all my attention to the options and once I made my decision, I never looked back.

I walked over to the sink and turned on the faucet as I looked out the kitchen window. There were a few raindrops falling from the sky. Mom used to tell us when we were young that when it rained, the angels in Heaven were crying. I thought of Jan and how Jan was trying to please the Lord by devoting everything to Him. Jan sacrificed everything.

I struggled to open the childproof cap on the aspirin bottle. How do they expect someone with a migraine to open these things? I finally opened the bottle and dropped two aspirins in my hand. Maybe if I just lie down for a while I will be able to think more clearly. This decision doesn't have to be made today. I have time.

I walked up to my bedroom, turned down the covers and kneeled by the bed and began to pray. I prayed to our sweet Lord Jesus to guide me to do the right thing. I crawled into bed.

I woke up after 40 minutes. Jan was on my mind. Over the past fifteen years, Jan and I grew closer than ever. I considered her my best friend. I figured that I probably knew what was going on in Jan's life more than anyone else in the family. I wanted to protect Jan, to keep her from destroying her life. Before Kim entered Jan's life she had everything. The Lord blessed Jan with good health, an intelligent daughter, a lovely husband, and several beautiful homes. Now, Jan was giving it all away. I wanted to reach out to Jan and tell her she didn't have to sacrifice everything to earn the Lord's love.

As soon as the thought entered my mind, I wondered how I could be objective when my own religious beliefs were so strong.

CHAPTER SIXTY-EIGHT

▼

UNTIL PROVEN INNOCENT

I thought about Jan's ability to manage her money. Jan certainly managed her finances in the past and she lived a frugal life even though Jan and John's riches lie in their bank account. Before Kim was in the picture, Jan was a conscientious spender. Jan rarely spent money on herself but when she did, she enjoyed a bargain at a local thrift shop. Jan always got her husband's approval first, because she was a dutiful Christian and subservient to her husband.

Jan once told me that there were some people in her life that criticized her for her conservative lifestyle. They equated her thriftiness to lack of class or style. To Jan, their comments were insignificant and reinforced her focus on godly principles. Her perceived childhood status was irrelevant because Jan said that she knew that she was from a good family that earned an honest living. The only thing that mattered to Jan was the Lord Jesus, her husband, her daughter, and other family members.

It was Jan who introduced me to her tax consultant, Judy. Judy prepared my taxes from that year on and every time I sat in Judy's office, I heard nothing but praise about Jan's ability to keep meticulous financial records. I knew Judy must have wondered why there was such a contrast between my tax records and Jan's. Maybe Judy was hoping that she could instill a little competition between Jan and I. It wasn't ever going to happen. I knew I was out of my league when it came to competing with Jan's organization skills.

Ironically, the petition I was considering would state that Jan was incapable of handling her finances because there was reason to fear that Jan would give all her money to Kim Miller. I knew that my actions would enrage Jan and the pain in the pit of my soul would ach forever longing for the day that I could visit with Jan and talk of the good times. I wished that I could go to Jan for advice and guidance. Oh, how I wish I could see her happy little family enjoying the simple life of the obscure rich.

I heard a car door slam shut following by several giggles. I glanced out the window as Nicky and Kristopher walked up the sidewalk. What were Nicky and Kristopher up to now? I figured the facts would remain a mystery so I didn't bother asking, I was just happy to see the two sixteen-year olds enjoying each other again.

"Nicky, Kristopher, come here. I want to talk to you about something."

Both of them walked in and plopped themselves on the couch, giggling as they slouched deeper into their seats.

"I have a serious subject for both of you. I will take full responsibility for the decision that I make but I want the opportunity to listen to anything you may have to say about the subject. Nicky, I am afraid that your Mom and John have either given all their money to Kim Miller and are funding the activities of the cult. It will only be a matter of time before they are out of money. I am considering petitioning the courts to have your mothers half of the money controlled by a conservator so that she cannot give her money away. This may save her from complete financial ruin. What are your thoughts about what I am proposing to do?"

"I don't know Aunt Betty, Mom's going to be real mad."

"I realize that she's going to be real mad. But I'm afraid that Kim Miller will take all their money. No one will be able to touch your mom and John's money. Except you, of course, as Jan's underage daughter some of the money would be available to you if you need money while you are in college or something. Shoot Nicky, you are a growing girl and you still outgrow your clothes. If she were able to make the decision, I know that your mom would make sure that you had what you needed.

"Aunt Betty, I don't want her money."

"I know you don't honey, but I would rather Kim Miller not get Jan's money either. Besides, it's my understanding that if Jan needed some money to live on that Jan would just have to approach the conservator and ask for the money. The conservator would make sure the request was legitimate and based on the amount of money in the account, your Mom would have the money she needs. Besides, your mom and John have the money from the sale of the Connecticut estate and maybe even the yacht that was sold a couple of years ago. The money that is currently tied up in assets will be saved for Jan and John. I assure you, it's still their money. If I petition for a conservator, the money would just be in a safe place...away from Kim."

"Whatever you think, Aunt Betty. I just want my Mom back."

"Well, I don't want to burden you with this decision. I just wanted to hear what you had to say about it. I will take full responsibility for doing this to your mother. It is a terrible thing to do. It's my decision, no one else needs to feel responsible. I feel an overwhelming need to protect Jan. Besides, I know this sounds bizarre, but someone mentioned that John's life could be in danger since his money is already under conservatorship, the cult could actually kill John in order to have all the money go to Jan. Not that your Mom would kill John of course, but there's a motive for murder right there. I do not understand the whole cult mentality. I really don't know what they might do, and I quite frankly do not trust Kim. I don't think he's in his right mind."

Kristopher sat up and adjusted his shirt. "Jan and John still have some money, right?"

"Well, as far as we know they do, but how much and where? I don't know, nobody knows."

"I guess if you were in the cult Mom, and had money to live on, I would want someone to make sure that you had some money to live on, if and when you got out of the cult."

"I agree, Kristopher, I would hope that someone loved us enough to step in and protect our assets from a shyster. I truly believe that I should protect Jan from having all her money swindled away from her. Jan is so kindhearted that she would give her last dime to someone in need."

"I see what you mean, Mom. You're trying to protect Aunt Jan from financial ruin, but she will hate you for it though. Aunt Jan has been sending you sarcastic email for some time now. I've read some of the messages. U-g-l-y!"

I anguished over the decision. In the meantime, I was in communication with Jan and John through e-mail. Their email to me was harsh and mean and convinced me that they were drifting further from reality. If Jan and John only knew the decision I was trying to make.

The answer to my dilemma was suddenly clear. I decided that the only way to help my dear sister and her husband was to go ahead and petition for a conservator. Petitioning for a conservator was not going to be a pleasant experience by any stretch of the imagination.

As the evening progressed I felt more and more depressed. The only time I felt this bad was when Daddy died. Now instead of going to a funeral, I was going to court. Overwhelmed with sorrow, I cried. I cried for the pain that my dear sister would feel as she thinks of me as Judas, a trader, and an enemy. I cried for the pain that our mother would endure as I opened up a nasty wound that reminded her that Jan was gone. I cried because of the wedge that would separate Carol and I. I cried for the pain suffered by every family member who has a loved one in the Concerned Christians cult. I cried myself to sleep.

CHAPTER SIXTY-NINE

▼

MATERIAL POSSESSIONS

Awakened by the aroma of hazelnut coffee, I climbed out of bed and walked into the kitchen just in time to talk to Nick before he left for work. As I poured coffee in my cup, I said, "Umm, there's nothing like a fresh cup of coffee in the morning. I would be hard pressed to give up coffee."

"Why would you give up coffee, Betty?"

"I guess I said that because of the messages I've been getting from the Concerned Christians. I think that Kim is trying to produce some level of guilt in me for my behavior. The Concerned Christians have suggested that my attachment to my material possessions is a flaw in my willingness to devote my life to the Lord and will prevent me from entering heaven."

"But isn't that consistent with most cults?"

"Yes, from what I've read it is. The Concerned Christians criticized me harshly about my attitude and behavior and they frequently speak in plural to strengthen their argument. The Concerned Christians let me know that they disapproved of my behavior and threatened that I would go to

Hell if I did not conform to their way of thinking. They are threatening to socially ostracize me if I do not agree with Kim."

"What do you mean "they?" Are you talking to more than Jan and John?"

"Yes, from what I understand, my email is routed to all the Concerned Christians for their input. I think that sending each email correspondence to all the members serves several purposes for the cult leader. It enables the cult leader to pulse what is going on within his group and to use my message as a lesson plan for the group. Also, it prevents Jan or John from responding to me emotionally. I think that is why Jan didn't respond to Nicky or maybe Jan never saw Nicky's email. Some of the messages I've seen are too threatening to be from Jan or John."

"Betty, you should just leave them alone," Nick sighed heavily, "But I know that when you set your mind to do something there is no stopping you. I guess stubbornness runs in your family."

"It's crazy, the Concerned Christians continue to bombard me with criticism about my loyalty to my country and serving Satan. They think that Satan is the god of America. I guess they're trying to make me feel guilty hoping to spawn a desire to be accepted by their Lord and give up everything I own. In my new environment, I would feel worthless and undeserving unless I followed the acceptable behavior patterns of the Concerned Christians. My normal social status would be erased and I would be an outcast to society. The classic cult tactic of coercive persuasion would effectively gain one more victim." I poured another cup of coffee and added, "I only wish that Jan and John could have seen how calculated Kim was. If only Jan and John could see…Well Nick, I'm going to check my email and get to work. I'll see you when you get home."

"Okay, don't let yourself get too stressed out over this thing, Betty. We'll go out for Chinese tonight so don't make supper."

"Sounds good to me. Be careful. You know I worry when you ride your motorcycle to work. Watch out for those crazies on the road." I gave Nick a quick kiss on the lips.

As I walked down into the basement I could feel my stress level build. Maybe if I show Jan what the Concerned Christians did to Carol, maybe Jan will see that Kim is just after her money.

I started typing:

Date: *Tuesday, June 1, 1999*
To: *Jan and John*
From: *Betty*

Jan and John,

I talked to your sister, Carol, about 8 months ago concerning Kim Miller's teachings. She believes that Kim Miller left her because she is not a wealthy person and could gain little from her "salvation." Your focus on me leaving what I have already given up to the Lord re-enforces what Carol and I thought back in November, that Kim Miller is just after material possessions…maybe for his own personal gain, or maybe to perpetuate his glory in having people worship him.

I know all too well that the material possessions that I am using in this life are really nothing and can be taken away at any time. They are not important. Do not focus on material possessions because it is souls that Jesus wants. We must nurture souls in God's grace, to bring others to know the Lord Jesus Christ, and to focus on Him and only Him. There are two fallacies in Kim Miller's doctrine. 1) Christians in Jesus Christ do not have to pay for salvation through material things, Ephesians 4:22-6:9. 2) Christians in Jesus Christ do not have to leave (the Lord does not say body in Matthew 22:37) their family to show that they place Him above all others.

I do not understand what you are doing. You have traded your possessions for another rich life, I am interested in souls not my own salvation…. (I already have the Lord's Grace). At least the Amish and monks live a life of poverty to focus solely on their Lord. As you know, that some Amish live without electricity or modern conveniences. I have seen where some of you live and it looks like paradise! Please see that Kim Miller is leading you down the wrong road. *Kim Miller will lead you to destruction if you do not realize soon who Kim Miller really is.*

*Read the Bible completely. It's not difficult to see that what the Lord wants is pure and simple...your unconditional love and devotion and to place him above everything and everyone. Come home to show your daughters and mothers that they too can get to Heaven and that Jesus died for their sins as a **gift**, and they too will want to please the Lord by glorifying Him.*

I love you and want you to come home,
Love,
Betty

I hit "send" and checked to make sure that the message was received. Afterwards, I re-read the message and felt a pang of desperation.

A few hours went by before I received Jan's reply. I read the message again and began to cry. The Concerned Christians were turning the tables on me. How could I reach Jan and John's heart if the Concerned Christians collaborate on each and every one of my emails? The Concerned Christians made sure that I was the bad guy.

Although the message on Tuesday, June 1, 1999 was supposed to be from Jan, I was not surprised to hear the Concerned Christians say that I was hopeless and that I did not have God in my life. The Concerned Christians told me that I was trying to use human reasoning to understand scripture. They challenged me to discuss "once saved always saved" verse by verse. They told me to give up my will and release their daughters so that their daughters may know Truth.

The Concerned Christians predicted that my analysis of the tapes would be a pathetic joke and that I would insist that the tapes are from man and not of God. They told me that I was not a worthy opponent for a discussion on doctrine. I was threatened that I would experience hotter fires in Hell because of my wicked agenda to lead people astray. The Concerned Christians ended the email by agreeing to play my game a while longer as they sarcastically told me that they expect me to make plenty of mistakes with my immense knowledge of scripture. Without comment about Carol, they signed the email, Jan and John.

Callused by their caustic squabbling, I walked upstairs and made a salad for lunch and carried it back downstairs so that I could reply to Jan's message. I bowed my head and talked to God. I thanked Him for the food and prayed for my family's health, and prayed for guidance to reach Jan and John through the evil clutches of the cult. The words filled my head as I placed my hands on the keyboard.

Tuesday, June 1, 1999
To: Jan
From: Betty

I have quoted the Bible just as you. Tell me where the Bible is lying. You believe that you must include your body with your heart, mind, and soul. The Bible does not say body. Where does one's body come into this specific Scripture?

I am handling Scripture just as any fundamental Christian would. And I am giving you my heart and my time so that you may see things differently. Open your mind to accept what the Bible is really saying…no one said this was going to be easy.

I have only two objections to your doctrine (so far) and I have given you scripture as the basis for the discussion. Show me where the Lord says that you must, as a requirement to go to Heaven (one of the Ten Commandments would be nice) that you must use your body in addition to your heart, mind, and soul to dedicate yourself to Jesus. I couldn't find it in the Bible, maybe you can.

*And no, I have not spent my life studying and preaching about cults to tell you everything you need to know. You are **with** the master of this subject.*

Did I say "once saved, always saved?" I believe that you must follow the commandments, and do those works that are discussed specifically in Ephesians. I am following the Lord Jesus and He knows that I am. I am not convinced you are with Jesus. This is the main topic of our debate. I believe that we are saved through the grace of Jesus Christ and that we must continue to walk in the Lord to please Him.

*You do not know how close I am to God. I have not seen you for a long time and you do not know what has gone on in my life to come to this conclusion. I'm sorry, but this is an area that you **do not** know anything about.*

My will is the Lord's will. I gave up my will when I accepted Christ as my Savior. I know that I am not perfect just as you, John, and yes, Kim Miller is not perfect. (What's this about Denver being destroyed anyway?)

It is not necessary to become a martyr. Maybe it feels good to you to be a martyr, but you don't have to. You have read Scripture. You have read John 3:16 and Ephesians 2:8,9& 10, and you know the Ten Commandments. You know that you need not make Kim Miller rich in wealth or ego to get to Heaven.

Our discussion is only between John and you and myself. I have not shared your views with anyone. I am not convinced that you are of sound judgement. The way to bring your daughters to the Lord is to talk to them, nurture them, to care for them, answer questions, and become their conduit to the Lord Jesus Christ. You cannot do this through e-mail, we both know that this is one of the most difficult ways to win someone to the Lord. There is too much to say and too much to explain, you need to present the Lord's message to the non-believer in person.

I told you that I would be objective. I have heard some of Kim's tapes. I know that you now regret sending them to me. I am sorry.

*I took on that responsibility of judging doctrine when I started writing to you. One of us is definitely wrong. Of course, I believe it's you and you believe it's me. I think we must **all** keep our minds open. I think **all** of us have already taken on the immense responsibility but we have time to recover if we find True doctrine.*

Its true, Kim Miller is a professional. I am just one of God's children, and maybe an infant in Christ, but I know the Lord Jesus Christ and Kim Miller is an imposter. My reasoning may not be totally flawless, but there are two areas of Kim Miller's doctrine that I cannot find in Scripture. I cannot find where you have to physically be with Kim in order to give your heart, mind, and soul to the Lord Jesus. Nor can I find that in order to prove that you do not love your possessions more than you love Jesus that you must give your possessions to Kim Miller. What if I give my house, car, and money to the poor? That works too, right? If not, it is clear, that my material possessions are important and not my soul.

It seems that every time I want answers, you want to leave me without answering the question…I really want to know the answers!

I have not led anyone astray. You are the one that is following someone who claims that God speaks through him. I am asking only that you see the Truth in the Bible. Yes, I would gladly take full responsibility for your souls if you see things as they should be and Praise the Lord! And yes, I am not perfect and will make mistakes, but I am making honest mistakes, with nothing to gain (I am not after your money nor am I asking you to worship me.) My words to you are from my heart reaching out to try to save you from eternal damnation. I find no satisfaction in spending my time trying to keep you from destroying your lives when you both are bent on following your chosen path.

I am not playing a game. I do not consider spiritual warfare a game. I take my discussions with you very seriously and I know that Satan does too. Satan is involved in our little "game" whether you like it or not. I realize this and you should too. It is important that we remain objective. And I know I need to heed this advice too.

I only told you what I perceive to be true. Why did your group abandon Carol? We both know that she has few possessions to give, was it because she would not leave her family…did she get a chance to make the decision herself?

Jan and John, you never say anything about love. The Bible is full of love, is Kim Miller afraid that you would be weakened by such sentiments? I'm not asking you to love me more than Jesus. (You do not have to comment…it's just an observation.) Do you realize that if you sent a message to your daughters and mothers, a message that says that you love them, your mothers and daughters would open their hearts to you and what you are saying? It could be your only opportunity. (Honor your Mom and father and love your neighbor as you love yourselves.)

I love you both and will continue to pray for our salvation in Jesus Christ Our Lord's Name.

Love,
Betty

I hit "send" and looked over at my uneaten salad, I wasn't hungry any-more. Satisfied that I made an effort to reach Jan, I made a conscious effort to push any thought of Jan out of my mind. I was not interested in writing another email to Jan until morning. I've had enough of the Concerned Christians for the day.

It was over twenty-four hours since my last email to Jan and I still felt like avoiding her. I had too much work to do to be distracted by the Concerned Christians. At one o'clock in the afternoon, my curiosity about Jan was building. Finally, I decided to check my email. I turned toward my desktop computer and dialed into the Internet. I watched as the computer accepted three messages. I clicked on the inbox and noticed one from John. I avoided John's email as I answered the other two mes-sages. Finally, I read John and Jan's message. I wasn't surprised. The Concerned Christians found "body" in the Bible. I figured they would but I was sure that the reference would have nothing to do with God demand-ing that the Christian remove their "body" from their family.

I smirked at the predictable message and began to type:

Date: Wednesday, June 2, 1999
To: Jan
From: Betty

In reference Romans 12:1-2 where you suggest that scripture includes the idea of the body with the heart, soul and mind…Okay, so you found a passage with "body" in it and you are now applying it to your verse in Matthew. But read the rest of Romans 12. I feel that you are not seeing what is meant to see. I believe you have only a portion of the picture. Romans 12 says that we have one body with many members and every member of the body does not have the same function. We also have different gifts according to the grace given to us. We do not all share the same gifts, right? Why then would we all follow the same pattern and go isolate ourselves from society and as a result, prevents us from saving souls? How do the Concerned Christians share their gift of prophecy, teaching, encouraging, or contributing to the needs of others when the Concerned Christians isolate themselves? It's nice that you have your fellowship but you are a closed society, I do not think this is what Jesus had in mind as "good works."

So in summary, this verse does not apply to leaving your family and friends. You must love our Lord Jesus with all your heart, mind, and soul...and dedicate your body to pleasing the Lord in the way he has asked in Romans 12:3-8.

You say that the tapes teach about loving your enemies and picking up weapons against enemies. You predict that I will be soon be talking about picking up weapons against my enemies and how that is what God wants. You call me a hypocrite and say that I will be talking out of both sides of my mouth. You think that I will be defending the position of killing my enemies and you will defend loving your enemies. You say that my hypocrisy has not been fully exposed because I haven't addressed the tapes.

Well, time will tell, I know that I am not perfect. I also know that I have no reason to call my earthly brothers or sisters, sons, daughters, or mother spiritual enemies. You see I love them and forgive them for their shortcomings and do not know their spiritual shortcomings...as they do not know mine. Do not think that you are perfect, because you too are growing in Christ. When was the last time you spoke to your brother Larry? It is more difficult to stay and fight for souls for Jesus than to seclude yourself among those who are like you and live a life of luxury. I'm sorry but I cannot see where you walk your talk.

I understand that you have offered to pay the expenses for our sister Carol to depart Babylon. I am not suggesting that you spend your money on anything. I do not care about your money. But since you brought it up. Romans 13 talks about taxes, I know that you took care of things before you left, but are you current now? (You do not need to answer this, it's not my business and I am just saying this so that you may think about it.)

I am also concerned about your minor, Nicky. I would think that you would have a moral obligation to be sure that Nicky's basic needs are fulfilled...I know that Nicky does not because I am doing what I can to help her. What you have done concerning Nicky is wrong. This is the true tragedy in following the doctrine of "body" leaving mother, father, brethren, daughters, etc, *and does not say much about Christians when a non-believer looks at Kim Miller's Concerned Christians as a "model."*

About Carol, I have talked to her and I know that she has seen some truth in Kim Miller's teachings. I do not know her spirit and without hearing all the tapes, I couldn't discuss much with her. She related to me that she felt that she was "dropped." And just to let you know what's going on with her now, Carol has moved to another home and is undergoing numerous medical treatments. Obviously, she is not physically well. She has not been open to talk to me about the Concerned Christians. Because of the volatile nature of Carol's and my last conversation, I have not talked to Carol about you or John in several months. I cannot tell you whether she is willing to "leave Babylon" or not and I do not see me asking her at this time.

Take care of yourselves, In Jesus Christ Our Savior's Name.

Love,
Betty

I didn't bother reading the message again. I hit "send" and continued to do my daily job. I allowed my mind to reflect back to the first email that I received from Jan. We were squabbling back and forth like children on a playground. It was obvious that neither Jan nor I was going to give in. Obviously, my strategy was not working. Jan couldn't see that I was trying to help her. I prayed that Jan would act on something...anything that I said to get her to move in the right direction.

CHAPTER SEVENTY

▼

THE NEXT STEP

It was almost 4:00 in the afternoon and I had an appointment with an attorney in Boulder at 4:30. It takes more than a half an hour to get to the 16th Street Mall in Boulder so I put on my shoes, grabbed my purse, and ran out the door. It felt good to get out of the house but I hated the circumstances. I needed to disclose my decision to my attorney soon. The decision was made more difficult because it was tearing apart my relationship with Carol and some of her children.

When I arrived at the attorney's office he asked me several questions about Jan. I understood that if I petitioned the courts for a conservator that only Jan and her minor child could get to the money. I weighed the facts as I saw them against the wretched emotional feeling I had inside. I wanted Nicky taken care of and I wanted to prevent Kim and the Concerned Christians from getting more of Jan and John's money.

I remembered my Daddy and how he hated for anyone to butt into his business. How could I make a decision about how Jan was going to spend her money? I was in turmoil. I had no right acting on my opinion that a couple of million dollars was enough to give away to a religion. But I rationalized that a "doomsday cult" was not an ordinary religion. It would be much easier to mind my own business and turn my head but I likened the action to that of someone witnessing a armed robbery in the back of an alley and nonchalantly continuing to read the evening news. No, I couldn't be passive. I had to help Jan even though Jan and John will hate me for it. I wanted them both to have a fresh start when they return.

"And you say that Jan can get some money if she wants for her daily expenses or medical expenses, is that right."

My attorney nodded his head.

"Well, it's a terrible thing to have to do, but I don't want Kim to get anymore money. Besides, I'm concerned for John. Jan is his beneficiary and if he dies, all John's money will go to Jan. I think Jan would give the money to Kim to prove her love for the Lord and that she doesn't worship money. I don't see another alternative."

I signed the petition and slid the form across the table to my attorney. "I guess the court date will be pretty soon, huh?"

"Yes, we'll be doing it sometime in July or August. I'll keep in touch with you, Betty"

"Okay, thank you for explaining the process to me. I'll talk to you later."

I walked out of the attorney's office feeling relieved that I at least formalized my decision, but I still felt a heaviness in my chest. I began to dream that I could still reach Jan before we went to court. Maybe I've been more effective than Jan has led me to believe.

CHAPTER SEVENTY-ONE

▼

POSSESSIONS BE MINE

As soon as I got home, I checked my email. I took a deep breath when I saw that the message was from the Concerned Christians. I clicked on the message from Jan and started to read. Jan insisted on convincing me that Mark 10:28-30, Matthew 19:29, Luke 9:59-62, and Luke 18:28-30 were justification to leave my family and my possessions and follow Jesus. The Concerned Christians trusted the Lord and gave up their permanent homes.

I felt the burden of Jan's pain when I read that the Concerned Christians encourage and help one another while they are under immense persecution by phonies, and because of their beliefs, maliciously called a doomsday cult. She explained that some of the Concerned Christians honored the Lord's request to provide for those who truly serve Jesus Christ. They demonstrated their love for the Lord through good works by placing their loving children in God's hands, some of the Concerned Christians had their children taken away through the courts.

The Concerned Christians have suffered tremendously and did not retaliate when they were thrown in jail because of their beliefs. They were wrongly accused of plotting to kill with guns. Jan insisted that the Concerned Christians are opposed to violence and have proven their civility by treating their captors with love. Their suffering was their good works for Jesus Christ. They were carrying their crosses for Jesus Christ.

Jan told me numerous times that I couldn't begin to teach scripture because I didn't even know that each Christian needed to present their body as a living sacrifice, something that the Concerned Christians have known for a long time.

Jan was very noticeably upset by my comment about her taxes and called me a meddler, saying that I accuse them of one thing after another while at the same time preaching love and Jesus. She closed the email by telling me that I clearly did not know what I was talking about satisfied that she had sufficiently told me off, Jan signed her name in love.

My frustration level reached a new high. I realized the intensity of Jan and John's conviction. I saw how deeply rooted their determination was to honor the verses that they quoted. Didn't the Concerned Christians know that these are the verses that a majority of the cults throughout the ages have used to place their members in bondage and make them leave their happy families? I wished that Jan and John had studied cults and knew that they were falling for the same lines that have worked for literally centuries.

All the "good works" Jan and John suffered were self-inflicted painful sacrifices they endured while the cult leader enjoyed the spoils. Kim convinced the Concerned Christians that they must suffer these things to be worthy of the "heavenly kingdom church." Christ carried his cross, the Concerned Christians must carry their crosses.

I detected contradictions between what I learned in the news, what Jan communicated to me, and what I heard on the tapes. Again, I wondered about the email threats and the quotes from Charles Manson with the words Helter Skelter. I reflected on the tapes that said that the "heavenly kingdom church" was not to revenge their enemies…at *this* point in time.

Kim seemed to be eluding that at some time the Concerned Christians would be able to avenge their enemies.

Oh that's just wonderful, I thought, since I've been so vocal about my feelings for Kim, I'm sure that the Concerned Christian's think I'm one of their worst enemies. In a few days Jan will learn through the mail that I have petitioned the courts to appoint her a conservator.

As I picked up the telephone to call the county sheriff to patrol my house again, I thought, there is no way of telling how the Concerned Christians may react. But, I was convinced that whatever the Concerned Christians did would be at the hands of their leader as he plays each member like a pawn in a chess game...

CHAPTER SEVENTY-TWO

▼

PAIN

I arrived at Boulder Community Hospital dreading the unknown and wondered if mammograms hurt as much as people said they did. I decided that I could tolerate a little pain for a short while. Then I remembered something that I read about how cult victims endure the pain of being without their family because they believe that the pain will last only a short time.

My experience in x-ray was over, and although the mammogram was uncomfortable, it was not unbearable. The medical assistant said that I would have the results in a few days. I didn't suspect that there would be a problem so I smiled and thanked her as I walked out of the hospital and climbed into my car. I immediately hit the heavy evening traffic. By the time I arrived home Nick and Kristopher were already eating supper.

That evening I checked my email. I was trying to remove myself from Jan. I didn't see how I could do anything for her. The computer began to download five messages. Two were from Jan. I read the message and realized that Jan knew that I had petitioned for a conservator. The message was not signed and that usually indicated that the message was not from Jan or John. The author wanted me to know that they thought that I was intentionally trying to deceive them.

I clicked on the next message dated June 3, 1999. I glanced down at the bottom of the message and noticed that it was signed Love Jan. The no-nonsense message told me that I loved my life too much to change it and that I wanted things my way not God's way. She suggested that I should give up and remain silent because I clearly lost the battle that I was fighting. She warned me that I would pay for my actions on the day of my judgement. Jan feared that her and John's daughters and other individuals who love their lives believed me and regarded me as their hero. She was afraid that they would all follow me instead of hearing the true gospel. Jan pleaded to me to let their daughters go and not take them to hell with me. Jan ended the message telling me that I was an intentional sinner.

Once again I felt the hopeless feeling of watching someone fade away into an endless pit of quicksand. Was there any way that I could rescue Jan from the middle of the oozing muck of lies? What better way to seal Jan's hate for me than to hold me responsible for the salvation of her only daughter? I was tired of fighting and I knew that my reaction was exactly how the cult leader would want me to act. I wanted to walk away from my computer and never write again, but I couldn't walk away from Jan. She was my sister and she was in the middle of the pit of deceit. I wanted my sister back. I wrote a quick message to tell Jan that I would pray for her and asked her to pray that she could see what was happening to her. I shut down my computer and went to bed.

The next morning a nurse from the hospital called and said, "Betty, the doctor saw something in the radiograph that he would like to monitor your condition for the next few months. You will have to come in and have some follow-up mammograms. We want to make sure that we have some good baseline measurements of the indication we see in your left breast."

Anticipating the worse I asked, "Is there anything else the doctor can tell me at this time?"

"No, not at this time. We will have to just monitor you for a while."

"Okay, I appreciate the telephone call. I'll make an appointment with X-ray. Thank you."

I walked downstairs Saturday, June 5, 1999. Life is full of mixed blessings, I thought as I checked my email for messages. Disappointed, I realized that Jan was refusing to talk to me as I read her email. Jan told me that the audiotapes explained her beliefs. Jan ended the message with the same message as she sent me a few days earlier.

I was frustrated and second-guessed my actions again. Maybe I should have sought professional help from a cult expert when contacting Jan. But I really didn't know where to go. Who could I confide in to get advice? How could I help Jan if I didn't know where she was? If only I could help Jan help her self. I started typing.

Sunday, June 5, 1999
To: Jan
From: Betty

Jan,

You must think I'm stupid or something. You do not need to send the same e-mail three times. It appears that you do not have the ability to look at what is going on objectively. I am simply trying to ask you to be objective and to read the Bible as it is written. From what I can tell, you are worshipping tapes not the Bible. This is just an observation, Jan. As for my purpose in spending my time writing to you…my purpose is to simply show you and John that I love you and that I care for you and your salvation. I hope the tapes answer the questions that I am asking. There is no underlying reason here. You may say that I am wicked, but you are wrong, you have a powerful force among you that wants you to believe that I am the enemy. Your actions have caused me to have many emotions about your ability to reason, and I am concerned only because I love you.

As far as loving my life, I have a life in Jesus Christ, and He has not given me a message to do anything else with my life. He asks only that I read the

Bible and follow the Bible as it is written. This is not a defeated action, but a triumphant one, and to worship only the Bible is what I WILL do. I love the Lord Jesus Christ that I've come to know through the Bible. This is what I will not change.

I will be sending you a gift within a couple of months. I love you and John, in Jesus Christ Our Lord's Name.

In Jesus,
Love,
Betty

I wondered if I should tell Jan that I was sending her a picture of Nicky through her post office address. It was hard to resist the urge to be mysterious, I hoped that she would be curious and think about her family a little longer.

I figured that if Jan and the rest of the Concerned Christian's announced their intentions to move to a foreign country, the Concerned Christians would not have received the unwanted attention or the persecutions. But because of their cult like actions, the cult leader gained the necessary attention that he needed convince the Concerned Christians that they were the "chosen" few that would rule on the right hand of God. I imagined that Kim relished the media attention as he affirmed to the Concerned Christians that they must suffer the persecutions as "good works" while he convinced them not to belong with the rest of the so-called secular world.

The fact that Jan never acknowledged Mom or Nicky made me cynical toward Jan. Our Mom and Nicky were naturally tormented daily about Jan's absence. I tried to control my hostility towards Jan. She was still a victim and was not the person that I once knew.

I wished I had a digital version of Nicky's picture. If I could only attach the picture to an email, Jan would get it sooner. I wasn't sure how Jan's post office box worked. Apparently Jan's mail was received by a service that forwarded the mail on to Jan's location. I wondered how Jan learned about the post office service. Kim thought of everything. But, I couldn't be sure that Jan was even the person that I was talking to. So, I wasn't sure of anything anymore. I shook the thought out of my head. E-mail was all that was left between Jan and I. I had to assume that I was communicating with Jan.

I hit "send" and checked to make sure the message did not come back.

CHAPTER SEVENTY-THREE

▼

CHOICES

Jan sent me the exact same message again. John wrote me a message to try to convince me that I would sleep better if I did not petition the courts. I responded to John telling him that I slept fine and that I didn't want Kim to get any more of their money. John let me know that it was none of my business and that the money was his to do with whatever he wanted.

I knew that I was placing a larger wedge between the three of us. The court date was nearing and I was pretty sure that I was going to follow through with the petition for conservator. But I continued to question whether I was doing the right thing and for the right reasons. The emotional decision to appoint a conservator for someone that you love is difficult. In Jan's situation, there were no clear answers.

Tired of receiving the same email over and over again, I scornfully responded:

Date: *Monday, June 7, 1999*
To: *Jan*
From: *Betty*

Jan,
   Hello Jan, how's your mental health now a days? I think you have gone off the deep-end. But, not to worry, Jesus can heal you if you just come to Him. Read the Bible as it is written, you will see a lot of happiness in God's glory. I'm afraid you are focusing on a very dark side, there is no dark side when you have Jesus in your heart. You see, I do not fear the Second Coming because I know Jesus Christ. I know that you want to believe that your little message is true. I'm sorry honey, by repeating your message over and over, you cannot make the message true. You know that I love you and if it helps you, I really don't mind seeing this message, you may send it a hundred times. I will try to console you.
   Remember that you only have to read the Bible in the order in which it is written and follow what the Bible says…No one else, Jan. But, I'm sure that whatever you are doing "In the Name of the Lord" will benefit you in the end. Just make sure that your Lord is the right one. God wants you to have no idols before Him. Read the Bible…straight and simple.
   I love you and hope that you are doing well, please don't cause yourself stress by writing to me. If you are stressed out, just send me the message again. It's ok. I love you and pray for your salvation.

In Jesus Christ Our Lord's Name,
Love,
Betty

   I hit "send." I didn't like talking to Jan that way but I wanted her to communicate with me. Maybe Jan's e-mail correspondence to me was just another routine duty that Kim had her do to keep Jan's mind off real issues? Jan didn't have to think or even read my messages, all she had to do is hit forward and type in my email address.

As if to shout at me, Jan tried to bold the entire redundant email. I responded:

Date: Wednesday, June 9, 1999
To: Jan
From: Betty

Jan,

Your bolding didn't work, I guess that should be expected since the message you sent me didn't work either. Jan, I love you and I always will. You might want to remember this someday since I am currently undergoing tests for cancer. I know you really do not care, but life (and death) goes on. Praise the Lord in All that He has done and will do.

Love,
Betty

Once again Jan sent me the same message. Discouraged and exhausted from trying to reach Jan's emotionally and spiritually, I admitted that I had exhausted my efforts to communicate with Jan. I knew that as a Christian, I was just an infant and I didn't stand a chance to combat Kim's deception. I suspected that Kim used my words to strengthen his position and leadership and further separate his flock from the rest of the world.

I began to type:

Date: Thursday, June 10, 1999
To: Jan
From: Betty

Jan,

*You have an **evil** force behind you. You are afraid to admit that you are wrong, the prophecy that you are following is in error. You are taking the Bible **out of context** and the mystic knowledge that you are taught is not divine but serves another purpose.*

*I grieve for your lost souls. I do not believe that you can reason with the unreasonable or the insane, so I will not even try. I told you that I would try to work with you until I am convinced that there is no use. You must find the strength within yourselves to save your souls. I will continue to pray for you and John so that you may see the Light of Jesus Christ. **I love you both and pray that you read the Bible as it is written.** You will see that the prophecy you are given will not come true (again) but Jesus Christ's Word will! Take care of yourselves.*

I love you and always will.

In Jesus Christ Our Savior's Name,
Love Forever,
Betty

CHAPTER SEVENTY-FOUR

▼

E-MAIL BLOCK

I searched through my computer to block Jan and John's email from coming back to me. I did not want to see the same email again. I was looking forward to a long needed break from the stress of trying to convince Jan and John to come home. I knew that I was only talking to myself and I was worn down. I had done what I could to try to reach Jan and John. At least I could still try to foil Kim from scamming Jan and John out of any more money.

I wondered if anyone would come to the court to stop the petition…

▼

CHAPTER SEVENTY-FIVE

THE CONSERVATOR

It was already August 1999 and the dreaded day had arrived. My stomach churned as I drove to Boulder. It would not be long before Jan and John's home in Pinebrook Hills was sold, and Jan's half of the estate would be available. It was important that a conservator be appointed soon. Like others in the family, I feared that Kim would coerce Jan into giving him the proceeds of the sale.

I walked toward the Boulder County Courthouse and felt a familiar ache. My body grieved with each step. I walked through the door and through the metal detection. Aimlessly I walked down the hall reading the bulletin boards looking for the list of court hearings. Finally, I looked on the wall and saw Jan's name, opposite her name was mine. The gut wrenching feeling grew stronger and tears began to stream down my cheeks.

Jan is my sister, I rationalized, its only money,…filthy, stinking money. I just wanted my sister, I didn't care about her money. Am I foolish to believe that I might be able to get to my sister through her money? Would

Jan care enough to be in the courtroom today or would Kim send some unfamiliar person to take care of business?

I walked toward the courtroom and noticed my attorney standing outside the door. He greeted me in a soft voice, "I know this is hard. You should keep an eye out for anyone who looks suspicious. Let me know if you get any bad vibes from anyone."

I nodded my head as we walked in the courtroom, I sat down toward to middle of the courtroom and scanned the crowd to see if I could see anyone suspicious. I looked at each person wondering if he or she could be a member of the cult or possibly a newspaper reporter. After a few minutes I whispered to my attorney, "I feel strange about the guy in the back of the room. There's something about him."

"Really, I'll tell the officer at the door." I watched as my attorney whispered to the officer and walked back to sit down. "He'll keep an eye on him."

As the judge entered the room and individuals systematically presented their case. After a while, the courtroom was emptied leaving only the man in the back of the room and the people involved in petitioning a conservator for Jan. The man in the back of the room noticed that I was keeping my eye on him. He stopped writing. It was my turn to take the podium. I felt uneasy, the last thing in the world I wanted to do was hurt my sister and damage her credibility.

The judge asked a few questions about Jan, but was familiar with the case. After some discussion, the judge appointed Jan a conservator. In spite of the verdict, I felt defeated. Although Kim would not be able to get any more of John and Jan's money, the world would look at Jan and see a weak-minded patsy instead of the strong-willed Christian. The public didn't know Jan. They didn't know how incredible she really was.

I turned and slowly walked away from the podium, there was no turning back now. I would have to suffer the consequences of my actions. Through my glazed eyes I could see that the strange man in the back of the room was talking to my attorney. Depressed, I slowly gathered my purse and my notes and drifted out of the courtroom.

My attorney followed me out of the door and said, "The guy in the back of the room was a newspaper reporter for the Boulder Daily Camera. He just asked me some innocuous questions…nothing really. I don't think you'll hear anything more from him. There will probably be just a short article in the paper tomorrow. I don't expect it will amount to anything."

"I kind of thought he was a reporter. I think he could tell by the way that I glared at him that I was unapproachable. I'm not interested in talking to anyone and less interested in being quoted. You know, most of my family didn't want me to do petition the courts for a conservator. I've made enemies out of some of my dearest loved ones. But I feel strongly about Kim not taking all of Jan's and John's money. I think Kim has received enough of John's money."

I climbed into my car and drove out of the parking lot, I just wanted to spend some time alone to reflect on what just happened. I was emotionally drained and felt as if I was living in another dimension. The traffic was streaming by my car as I drove down the Boulder streets. I cried and hoped that the tears would erase my sorrow. When I pulled in my driveway, I realized that I had no memory of the ride home but somehow the pain remained. Jan would surely distance herself from me even more now. I grimaced as I thought of Kim's loving ministry and all the heartache that his teachings caused. I knew my pain was nothing compared to our mother's pain and little Nicky's pain…and even Jan's.

I had to move on. There were positive things happening in my life. I had a grandchild coming into the world soon, a blessing from above. I had to change my focus.

CHAPTER SEVENTY-SIX

▼

A SIGN

September 6, 1999 was the fifteenth day in a row that the temperature soured above 100 degrees in Houston, Texas. It was time. Nicholas Shawn, Lynn and I were at the hospital, waiting for the new baby to arrive. I realized that Nicholas Shawn and Lynn needed some time alone, so I excused myself from the room.

I stepped out of the elevator into a dark lobby. I noticed that the hospital gift shop was closed so I sat down in the dimly lit waiting area. I glanced down at the coffee table in front of me and on top of the pile of recent periodicals. My eyes caught the words CULTS on the cover of the magazine on the top of the pile. I couldn't believe what I was seeing. For the past few years, my job had taken too much of my time and I hadn't researched cults. Now, I had time and the information presented itself to me.

I picked up the magazine hoping that it would provide possible answers to the questions that haunting me. Maybe this article would give me some insight about how Jan became so involved with the over zealous religion of the Concerned Christians. Is this about the Concerned Christians? No, the article was about Waco, Texas. But Waco happened years ago. My heart started racing when I noticed the magazine was over five years old. The date of the publication was June 1994. The magazine survived for more than five years! Why would this magazine be on top of a pile of recent publications? I couldn't help thinking that the magazine was destined to be read by me.

I was surprised to find out that in 1994, there was reportedly between 2,000 and 5,000 cults in the United States that comprised of 3 to 5 million cult members. I was astounded to learn that 10 to 20 million people in America were affected by cults! I concluded that with the end of 1999 approaching, the number was likely to increase.

I learned that it wasn't uncommon for cult leaders to target the aging population, people who focus more on illness and their own mortality. It thought it made sense…the mature population had assets, home equity, retirement benefits, 401K accounts, savings, and all the spoils of working hard for twenty years or more.

There were so many similarities between Jan and the woman in the article. Like Jan, the woman had a personality change and mysteriously left her home. And similarly, Jan's affection and warmth to her family was gone. Where there used to be love and understanding, Jan replaced it with condemnation, hate, and ridicule…at least toward me. E-mail and "snail mail" letters to others, including myself, were filled with accusations that caused a deep pain which was directed to the people that loved her the most, the same people who would have always loved her no matter what she said or did.

I think that Jan believed that she could save all the people she loved by making sacrifices to the Lord. Jan was willing to sacrifice her happiness, her wealth, her love for her only daughter, and her love for her Mom and sisters and brother in order to protect us. Jan was a headstrong person and I think that initially she "took up her cross" to save not only herself, but to save all of us from eternal damnation. Jan believed that once a Christian knows God's Truth, the Christian has the burden to accept the Truth and obey the Truth, or openly reject it. I realize now that she was telling me that rejecting the enlightened doctrine of Kim Miller was the same as sentencing myself to Hell.

Satisfied that I made the right decision to fight for Jan's freedom. I placed the article back on the pile of magazines and rode the elevator back to Lynn's room. When I arrived, Lynn was ready to have the baby. Nicholas said that he would come out to the waiting room to get me once the baby arrives.

I waited patiently for an hour before I was invited back into the room. There I saw the beautiful miracle of life and met my first grandchild.

CHAPTER SEVENTY-SEVEN

▼

DEPORTED FROM GREECE

It was late Friday, December 3, 1999 and I was busy going through my clothes deciding what to pack in my luggage. I always tried to get a cheap airfare when traveling back to the office in New York, which meant a Saturday night stay. I glanced at my ticket to see what time I would leave. Darn, a 6:00 a.m. flight! It takes all day to get to the East Coast. I guess I don't have a choice. I'll take plenty of reading material. My luggage was heavy, clothes for five days, a laptop computer, and written examinations for the class that I was scheduled to audit.

I knew some good people in New York. My business associates usually tried to include me in their weekend. I hoped that I would have an opportunity to get a little Christmas shopping done and to spend some time with my friend Nancy on Sunday. I looked forward to seeing everyone and of course I always looked forward to shopping.

My daydreaming was interrupted as Kristopher shouted upstairs, "Mom, I just picked up the telephone to call Johnny and you had a message from Jennifer. She said that her Dad and Aunt Jan are being deported from Greece!"

"You're kidding? What's Jennifer's number?"

"I don't know Mom, listen to the message again."

I listened to the message and jotted down the number. I quickly dialed the telephone. "Hello Jennifer?"

"Hello Betty! They are deporting Dad and Jan! No one knows what state or airport Dad and Jan are arriving at. It could be Atlanta or New York."

"You're kidding! I leave for New York first thing tomorrow morning!"

"Really? If Dad and Jan land in New York, do you think you can meet me at the airport? I'll give you more information when I get more of the details, okay?"

"That sounds good, it's worth a try. Call my house and let me know if you made it to New York or what happened. Leave a number and I'll call you back."

"Okay, I hope we can get together Betty."

"Me too. I'll talk to you tomorrow."

I hung up the telephone and shook my head. "Nick, this is so weird. Jan and John were arrested in Greece and may be deported this weekend. They may actually arrive in New York just hours after my plane arrives in New York. What are the chances of Jan arriving in New York from Greece the very same weekend that I arrive in New York?"

"That's pretty bizarre, Betty."

"Well, if it's meant to be, I'll connect with Jan. You know, I made my plane reservations in September. The last time I was in New York was seven months ago. I had nothing to do with the scheduling of the class that I'm auditing. I believe that my being in New York the same time Jan arrives is more than a coincidence. I believe that it's a sign that I needed to be there when Jan arrives. I've got to call Nicky and tell her that her mom is coming back to America."

I didn't have any numbers to reach Nicky at school. I usually just communicated with Nicky through email. I called information and got the number for the Virginia Military Institute (VMI). I left a message for Nicky to call her Uncle Nick.

I hung up the telephone and felt a sinking feeling. Somehow I knew that Nicky would not hear the message in time to see her mother. I prayed that I was wrong.

I arrived in New York about mid-afternoon. I immediately called Nick, "Hey, I'm just calling to let you know I'm here and just settling down in the hotel room."

"Good, I'm glad your safe. Hey, John's daughter, Jennifer called, she wants you to call her. She left a New York number. Sounds like Jan will be arriving from Greece through JFK Airport. There's an article about their arrest in the paper today."

"I wonder if the government will protect them like they did the last group that was deported to Denver from Israel? The Colorado authorities totally screwed up any chance for the relatives to reach there loved ones and persuade them to come home."

"It's hard to say, Nick, maybe Jennifer knows. I can just tell you what I have read in the Denver paper. There are eleven adults and five children who were arrested by the police in Rafina, Greece. I guess that's about fifteen miles from Athens, and closer to the sea."

I said impatiently, "Okay Nick, I am dying to hear about Jan and John!"

"Well, relatives are hoping that by arresting the group of Concerned Christians from Greece, that the plans to commit violent acts or suicide will be disrupted."

"Why did they get arrested?

"Wait a minute, I'm still reading the article, Betty. Do you know what they got arrested for? Expired resident permits! Can you believe it? They are going to deport them for expired resident permits."

"You would have thought the Concerned Christians would have made sure they had current residency permits."

"Apparently, the Concerned Christian's have been in Greece long before the fourteen members being thrown out of Jerusalem but they don't know where the cult leader is."

"I'm not surprised, Nick. With email, he could be anywhere in the world."

"The locals in Greece are afraid that the Concerned Christians will do something violent or maybe commit suicide on the eve of the millennium."

"I don't know, Nick, everyone thinks that the date that Kim is planning all this stuff is on New Year's Eve. For the past ten years, all I've heard from Jan is how Christian holidays are never celebrated on the actual historical date. I don't think anyone can second-guess what Kim has told his victims. I think Kim just told his followers that the end would be soon."

"So, are you saying that they think the end of the world will be New Year's Eve 2000?"

"No, I would never attempt to second guess a crazy man."

"Yeah Betty, you never know. Besides if what we've read is true, Kim can predict something that doesn't come true and the Concerned Christians still believe him. That's because God supposedly talks to Kim, Betty. As God's messenger, Kim can always say that God changed His mind. As a result, Kim is not accountable for any errors in his predictions, it is always God who changes His mind, not Kim."

"That's what I think too. Well Nick, I'm going to call Jennifer now and see what she has found out. I'll talk to you later."

"Okay, let me know, Betty. I love you."

"I love you, tell Kristopher I love him and will talk to him later."

Not wanting to waste anytime, I called Jennifer in New York City. The telephone rang several times before the answering machine picked up. "I'm sorry, the person in the room that you have dialed is not available. Please leave a message after the tone."

"Hello Jennifer, This is Betty. I'm here in New York…." I left my telephone number and told Jennifer that I would be in my room waiting for her call.

I strained to lift my suitcase on the bed and unzipped the garment bag. Judging by the weight of my suitcase, I figured that I should have everything that I needed for this trip. I should coordinate my clothing better, four pairs of shoes for five days is a little ridiculous. I walked into the bathroom to place my cosmetics by the sink when the telephone rang. I stumbled over my empty luggage in an attempt to answer the telephone. "Hello?"

"Hey this is Jennifer, I'm glad you made it. I guess Dad and Jan will arrive at JFK Airport tomorrow. How far are you from JFK Airport? Actually, I'm in New York City, how far are you from New York City?"

"Well, I think I'm pretty far from JFK Airport and New York City is probably 30 minutes away. If the Concerned Christians are going to arrive at JFK Airport do you think that the government will step in and escort the Concerned Christians away like the authorities did in Denver?"

"This is New York, Betty! I don't think anyone in New York cares about the Concerned Christians. I really don't think the Concerned Christians are going to be whisked off like the group that came to Denver from Israel. I think that the Concerned Christians will be on their own." Jennifer paused, "Do you think that you can meet me at the airport? I could use the moral support."

"Sure Jennifer. I'm sure Jan doesn't want to see me, but I'll be there for you."

"Good. I'll meet you by customs. Hey, can you get in touch with Nicky?"

"I left an email message at VMI, but it's the weekend and I'm not sure Nicky's going to get the message in time. I wish I could have reached her but I don't know any other way to contact her. But, I'll catch a taxi and be at JFK Airport for you, Jennifer."

As soon as I hung up the telephone I called my friend Nancy. "Hi Nancy, I'm afraid I'm going to have to miss our shopping trip tomorrow. I guess my sister is among the cult members who were deported from Greece. Jan is going to arrive tomorrow at JFK Airport.

"I understand Betty, don't worry about it, we'll do it another time."

"I'd much rather be shopping with you, Nancy. I don't think this is going to be a pleasant experience. But I have to try to talk to my sister."

"I understand. Let me know if I can do anything to help you. You know Betty, I'm here if you need me."

"I appreciate it. I better go and take care of the logistics for tomorrow. I'll talk to you sometime Monday. See ya."

I hung up the telephone and sat on the edge of the bed wondering what I should say to Jan. I played out all the scenarios that I could think of. I thought, if only I could have reached Nicky. Maybe Nicky would have a better chance pulling Jan away. It would be awful if Nicky missed the only chance to see her mom again. Maybe the Lord is sparing Nicky from additional pain.

I walked down to talk to the hotel staff to find the best way to get to JFK Airport. On the way down the elevator I eliminated the possibilities of riding a train or subway. As a Colorado native, I grew up thinking that any city with a skyline that consisted of more than thirty buildings was filled with drug lords and underworld criminals. I saw too many movies with robbers, perverts, and murders who did nothing all day but commute from one place to another using public transportation, searching for their next victim. I just didn't need the additional stress of feeling paranoid.

"Excuse me," I asked the hotel staff, "what is the best way to get to JFK Airport. I am not interested in the subway or a train."

"We can call a cab for you about a half an hour before you leave the hotel. That would probably be the best way."

"Thank you. About how much will it cost?"

The hotel staff pulled out a notebook and ran her finger down the list. "It looks like the price is $70.00, one way."

I resisted the impulse to gulp at the price. "Oh good, I guess I will see you in the morning then. Thank you very much."

Ouch, I thought as I turned to go back to my room, there goes my Christmas money.

The next morning the hotel staff called a cab. When the cab arrived I asked the cab driver, "You do take credit cards, right?"

"Yes, I have to call it in before we leave. And how much are you charging. The trip to JFK is $70.00."

I thought for a moment. Of course, if I don't give this guy at least a fifteen-percent tip I could end up with cement shoes or something. After reading a book from James Patterson about a psychotic serial killer that posed as a taxi driver I decided that a person could never be too cautious. "I'll be charging $85.00 to the card, you know, to cover the tip for the nice *safe* ride."

The 20% tip didn't seem to impress the cab driver. He was kind of cold, I guess that's the way it is here in New York, I thought.

The ride was long and boring. After a while, the taxi cab driver said a few words about the weather. I was happy that he wasn't a *jabberwalkie*. I didn't want to spend my time on small talk anyway. I was grieving deep inside. I prayed to God that somehow He would give me the words and the courage and strength to reach Jan. I prayed that Jan would come home.

▼

CHAPTER SEVENTY-EIGHT

JFK AIRPORT

I finally arrived at JFK Airport. I approached the information desk to locate customs. I glanced at the arrival board to determine when Jan and the rest of the Concerned Christians were arriving. I looked into the crowd to find Jennifer and her dad's brother, Dave, but I couldn't see either of them. It was times like these that I was thankful that I was tall. Since there were few blondes in the crowd I thought that it would be easy for Jennifer to spot me in the drove of people. I continued to search the concourse. Suddenly, I saw Jennifer walking very quickly toward the double doors. She wouldn't be able to hear me call out her name from where I was, so I quickened my pace to catch up with her.

"Jennifer!"

Jennifer spun around quickly and walked toward me, "Oh, I was afraid we wouldn't find each other."

"I know, I've been waiting here for a while."

"The television crew for *Dateline* is waiting on the other side of customs with Uncle Dave and I. They are keeping us informed of Dad and Jan's whereabouts."

"You know, Jennifer, I don't want to speak to anyone, I'll just stand in the background."

"I know, I'm just glad you're here."

We waited for Jan and John to get out of customs. One of the television crewmembers periodically reported the status of Jan's plane. After everyone disembarked the plane, the reporter informed us where Jan and John were in customs. I watched as Jennifer paced nervously with anticipation, anxious to talk to her dad. I felt bad for Jennifer as I imagined her pain. I knew what it was like to miss someone. Daughters never stop being their daddy's little girls.

Finally, the sliding glass doors that separated customs from the rest of the world, opened wide. Bewildered, Jan and John took about three steps out the door and stopped and turned toward an outside door. Jennifer immediately thought that her dad was going through the exit door and ran outside the terminal to catch him. Confused, Jan and John suddenly turned and walked the opposite direction and walked down the roped path.

I tried to get Jennifer's attention so she would not miss her dad. Fortunately, Jennifer realized her dad's change in direction soon.

Dave met John halfway down the path and immediately started to talk to John. Dave helped John carry his bags and was rapidly trying to make the most of the short amount of time that he had with his brother. I couldn't hear what Dave and John were saying. My focus went immediately toward Jan. I approached Jan and reached to walk arm and arm with her. She took one stone cold look at me and looked away. She felt my hand reach for her arm. I was surprised at her reaction. She lifted her entire arm over her head to get away from me. I tried again and she threw her arm in the air and kept it high in the air to prevent me from touching her. There was no mistaking that she wanted nothing to do with me.

Jan repeatedly said, "John, I'm having a problem over here…John!"

The thought occurred to me to use force on Jan, to grab her, and whisk her away from captivity, but I didn't want to cause a scene in the midst of national media. I did not have a well-thought out plan about how I could successfully rescue Jan. The whole situation was too foreign to me. I thought, maybe I could get through to Jan emotionally by telling her the strange circumstances that brought us together and telling Jan how much everyone missed her.

I glanced over at Jennifer. It appeared that Dave and Jennifer were having a friendly exchange with John. I turned my attention back to Jan. Jan was walking fast and with purpose as she moved through the crowd of travelers and media. I felt defeated as I dropped back in the crowd. Then it occurred to me that I couldn't give up. I needed to talk to Jan while I had the chance. For some reason I was in New York and so was Jan. I needed to take advantage of this rare opportunity. I had to be the voice for Nicky, Mom, Carol, and myself. With renewed purpose, I sped up in front of the film crew and walked next to Jan telling her that Nicky needed her to come home and be a mom.

"Jan, you know that Mom is getting old and she needs you. Please come home. Don't follow Kim, he is a professional cult expert. He knows what he's doing. You know I had this trip to New York planned months ago and I had not been at the New York office since April. Don't you see, Jan? What are the odds of me being in New York the same weekend that you arrive from Greece? I leave on Thursday. If you were deported any other time…I wouldn't be here to talk to you. I think that God wanted me here. I think that God wanted me to reach out to you. You need to come home! Please, please come home and be Nicky's mom and Mom's daughter. Jan, please listen to me."

I talked fast but with each word I felt more and more discouraged. I've never had to beg for anything. I wanted Jan to come home and stop being a victim of a cult leader's dementia. I wanted Jan to come home to enjoy her family once again.

My heart sank as I realized that Jan's expression did not change with any thing that I said to her. It was as if Jan's soul was gone, her eyes were glossed over and vacant. As we stood in the bus line, I noticed that Jan's eyes were glued to the street in front of her as she searched desperately to find an escape vehicle. Occasionally Jan turned her head to glare at John who was still talking to Dave and Jennifer as the media swarmed around the conversation.

I felt defeated. Jan was not the person that I used to know. She was cold and heartless. Jan didn't say anything, she didn't have an emotional reaction to anything that I said. Finally I said, "Jan, you have no soul. You are an empty shell. You haven't displayed any emotion for the people who love you and are suffering because you are gone. I don't know what else I can do. All I can do is pray for you."

I walked out of the bus line and leaned against the wall as I listened to John talk about the ordeal in Greece. In spite of the circumstances and Jan's watchful eye, John was busy talking and explaining how the Greek police arrested them and only gave the Concerned Christians a few minutes to gather some belongings before being taken to jail. Each of the Concerned Christians left valuables behind. Their jail cell was filthy with human feces and infested with bugs. There were no beds, even for the tiny baby that was arrested with them.

I knew that John harbored the same resentful feelings towards me as Jan. In spite of the fact, I walked up to John. He saw me approaching him and gave me a look that said, don't even bother, just get away. But I didn't care. I stood on my tiptoes and kissed him on the cheek. "I love you, John. I only wanted to protect you."

John responded with a look that told me that he wanted to believe me but he just couldn't. I stepped back away from him. It was obvious that John did not want anything to do with me. As I watched him, I wondered if he would have talked to me if Jan were not watching him. I imagined that Jan and John had a pact not to talk to me again.

I stood up against the wall and watched as Jan finally flagged down a taxi. Jan quickly shouted something to John. John moved quickly toward the taxi. I noticed that the taxi driver wore a white turban on his head. Jan and John's image disappeared as they climbed in the darkened back seat of the taxi. My heart ached as I watched as the white turbaned taxi driver pull away from the curb and drove away.

Jennifer walked up to me with tears in her eyes and her arms open wide. She laid her head on my shoulder and began to cry and thanked me again for being at the airport with her. Then we both noticed that the group of relatives from New Jersey was trying to speak to their beloved cult victims. We observed a grandmother trying to convince her son-in-law to let her hold her new grandbaby, a grandchild that she had apparently never seen before.

I overheard the son-in-law sympathetically tell the grandmother, "You understand, under the circumstances, we can't let you do that." I heard the cult victim say as he shook his head in sympathy. I watched as the grandmother looked at him and appeared to be so choked up that she couldn't respond. All she could do is nod her head as if she understood why she couldn't hold her new grandbaby. The expression on her face broke my heart, you could tell she was devastated.

My thoughts turned to Kim. I looked at all the sadness that was created by one selfish, crazy man. My eyes narrowed as I shook my head in anger. There is enough pain in the world without this. The Concerned Christians are supposed to be full of love. They are breaking this poor grandmother's heart. How can the Concerned Christians say that they are following God's word, when they are not even honoring God's Commandments?

The crowd watched as the last of the Concerned Christians loaded on a bus and drove away. The media dispersed among the crowd. With tears in her eyes, Jennifer walked up to me, thanked me again for being at the airport with her, and invited me to her hotel to have dinner. I needed to talk to Jennifer. Our emotions were ripping at our hearts and we needed to try to piece together the meaning of the last twenty minutes.

Dave, Jennifer, and I flagged down a taxi. Once inside, I noticed a taxi driver with the white turban in the taxi next to us. I was sure that he was the same taxi driver that drove Jan and John away a few minutes earlier. I wanted to talk to the taxi driver to find out where he took my sister, but it was too late as our taxi quickly accelerated down the street.

Discouraged, the three of us commiserated about our experience. Dave mentioned that John's luggage was extremely heavy. We figured that the reason why John's luggage was heavy was because of the computer hardware that he must have rescued in the raid. Computer hardware was the most important thing they could bring with them. It was important to make sure that the cult's lifeline was not cut. The Concerned Christian's needed to communicate through email. I don't believe the Concerned Christian's could have maintained their cohesive bond without email…they needed the computers to survive.

We arrived at the hotel and sat in the corner of the restaurant where we continued to speculate what the deported Concerned Christians were going to do. The three of us shared our strategy in making the most of the fleeting moments that we had with our loved ones. We had to believe that we did the best we could do, but we each wondered if there wasn't something else we could have done to bring Jan and John home.

It was 10:30 in the evening, and I had an early morning meeting scheduled so I excused myself to go back to Tarrytown. Jennifer walked me out to the lobby and said good-bye.

I walked out of the hotel and flagged down a taxi, "Do you accept credit cards?"

"No I don't. You'll only find one out of a hundred taxis in New York City that will accept a credit card. Where are you going?"

"Tarrytown."

"Where's Tarrytown? I only drive in New York City. I don't leave the city."

"You're kidding me. You don't drive out of the city?"

"No, I'm sorry. None of the taxis in the city do. You're going to have to catch the train or call a limousine."

"Great. Well, thank you anyway." I climbed out of the taxi and walked up to the bellman. I asked him if he had any suggestions.

Following the bellman's suggestion, I walked up to the concierge, "Excuse me, could you help me get a ride to Tarrytown."

"I'm sorry madam. It is very late and I'm afraid if we could find you a ride it would cost a lot of money."

I looked at the lobby sofa thinking that I may have to stay there for the night. No, that would be loitering. I guess this is how some people end up becoming vagrants. "Well, I guess I really don't have any other options. Would you please try to find a limousine or taxi service that can take me to Tarrytown? I have already called several limousine services in town. None of them operate this late at night without a reservation."

"Sure." Two and a half minutes later, "Madam, I found you a ride but it will cost you $130.00."

I choked, "$130.00? And the service takes credit cards, right?"

"Yes, madam. You have to pay here and we will reimburse the car company."

"Okay, fine." I searched through my purse until I found my credit card and handed it to him. A few minutes later, the limousine arrived and I climbed in the back seat.

I grinned at the thought, if Jan only knew the day I was having. I'm sure that my misfortune would have brought a smile to her face.

CHAPTER SEVENTY-NINE

▼

GOOD MORNING!

Less than one week later, I received a message on my answering machine that said, "Hello, this message is for Betty, this is Yael calling from New York-ABC News, Good Morning America and I would appreciate if you could call me today."

I casually wrote down the number thinking that I probably would not call. But I eventually gave in to my curiosity and dialed the number.

"Oh Betty, thank you for returning my call."

"I was curious, Yael, how you got through my telephone block."

"Well, I thought it was pretty clever how you blocked the telephone. I've never run across that before. I understand your sister in the Concerned Christian's cult."

"Yes, how did you get my name."

"A relative of Jan's gave it to me and said that you might have a different perspective about what is going on with the Concerned Christians."

"Well, actually I do. My sister has gotten a bad name through this whole thing. I don't think that people understand that she really was a good mother. Her daughter and I are very close and I know what kind of mother Jan was."

"Do you have contact with Nicky?"

"Sometimes. Nicky's in school right now. She's about ready to go on Christmas Break."

"Is there a way we can interview the two of you."

"I don't know, I've avoided the media. I would rather not, unless I would have an opportunity to tell people what a good mother Jan was."

"I want you to say what you think needs to be said. What do you think? Can we do this sometime this week?"

"Let me try to reach Nicky. We could probably both meet in New York since she's already on the East Coast.

I contacted Nicky and explained to her my motive for agreeing to an interview. Although Nicky was skeptical that we would be able to accomplish anything, Nicky agreed to meet in New York. Good Morning America arranged for Nicky and I to arrive at Newark Airport. Nicky's plane was late and she arrived in Newark the same time that I landed. Nicky and I rode in a limousine to *Hotel Lucern* in Manhattan. In order to maximize the amount of time that we could visit, Nicky and I stayed in the same room at the hotel.

Since Nicky only had a few articles of civilian clothes, I bought Nicky a few items. The long black skirt and a red sleeveless sweater with matching long sleeve cardigan complemented Nicky's slim figure. Her big blue eyes even looked bigger and bluer than ever with her military haircut.

Our lovely hostess from Good Morning America, Yael invited Nicky and I for supper. Yael was in the military and from Israel, she was very interested in what was going on with the Concerned Christians. She and Nicky had a lot to talk about. Nicky and I told her that we just wanted to send a message to the world that Jan was not a bad person and that she raised Nicky with a lot of love and devotion. Yael said it is obvious that Jan did a good job raising Nicky and commented that for a seventeen-year old, Nicky was very sophisticated and mature.

After supper Nicky and I left Yael and went to the corner drug store. I bought a camera and some make-up and other girly items for Nicky. We walked out of the drugstore and into the rain. The night was young and Nicky and I had never been in New York together. We wanted to take in some of the sites but after walking a short distance, we decided to go back to our room so we didn't miss the call from the writer from Good Morning America.

While in the room, Nicky and I talked about her mom and what had happened in the two years since Nicky left home. Eric, the writer from Good Morning America, called us at 9:30 p.m. to prepare the story for the next day. Eric typed as Nicky and I talked. He would give the information to either one of the star anchors in the morning, and that anchors would base their 5-minute live interview on the information that we gave him.

The next morning I woke up at 4:30 a.m. to get ready for the interview. I was out of the bathroom by 5:00. "Nicky, honey, time to wake up. Too bad you just can't sleep in today."

"Okay Aunt Betty. Do you need in the bathroom for a while?"

"Nope, it's all yours Nicky. Feel free to use any of the cosmetics and cleansers in the bathroom that you need."

Although we would have preferred better circumstances, Nicky and I enjoyed a special time together that morning. Nicky was a little shy about going on national television with her hair short. We both laughed as I tried to punk Nicky's military haircut with temporary blonde highlights.

"Aunt Betty, I've never had closure with my Mom yet. I haven't been able to concentrate at school since Mom was deported from Greece. I really hated that I missed her at the airport last week."

"Nicky, I hope that we can reach your mom by talking on Good Morning America. I want the world to know that Jan is not a bad person."

"Me too, Aunt Betty. I want people to know that my mom was a wonderful mother."

"Hey, it's after 6:00 a.m. I guess we should go downstairs and wait for the limousine, Nicky. You ready?"

"Yes I am, let's go."

The limousine picked up Nicky and I at the Hotel at 6:30 a.m. and took us to the studio. As we approached the side of the building, we could see where the studio's sign caught on fire and burned the night before. We walked past the crowd of people in the front of the studio and entered the side door. Once inside, security checked to see if we were on the approved list to enter the building. After verifying the list, Nicky and I rode in a large production elevator to the waiting area. The guest waiting area was filled with the smell of fresh coffee. Nicky and I walked over to the complimentary fruit and rolls and talked to the staff as we poured fruit juice and coffee. Yael entered the room fresh and cheery. It occurred to me that the glamour of television, although rewarding, was not easy and filled with long hours at the studio. Yet Yael managed to look like she had a full night's rest.

When it was time for the television interview, Nicky and I sat on the sofa facing Charley as the cameras filmed our discussion. Charley asked us each a series of questions and before we knew it, our five-minute interview was over. I had hoped to say more to Jan, and to tell the world that Jan was a good person, but there wasn't enough time. I realized that it would take a book to say everything that I needed to say.

Nicky and I thanked Yael for her hospitality and as we climbed into the limousine. When Nicky and I arrived at the airport we were pleased that Nicky's plane was delayed and was scheduled to leave for Virginia at the same time as my plane was leaving for Denver. We couldn't help but feel that God had a hand in allowing us more time together.

CHAPTER EIGHTY

▼

MOM'S STROKE

When I returned from New York I found out that Mom had a slight stroke. Mom's health was deteriorating. She was having a tough time getting around the house. I thought that I could reach Jan by telling her what was going on with her biological family. I rationalized that I would want Jan to do the same for me if the situation were reversed.

Date: December 17, 1999
To: Jan
From: Betty

Jan,

   I thought you should know that Mom had a slight stroke the other day. Mom's health is failing. You should come to your senses and be the daughter that Mom deserves. You will not get another chance, Jan. Each day can never be replaced. You are missing valuable time with your Mom and your only daughter. Nicky has missed out on her childhood. You know that Nicky doesn't have any money and that she earns very little at school. It is not meant for a *mom to leave her only child. I just spent the last two days with Nicky. Nicky misses John and you so much, there are some days that I really resent what you have done to Mom and Nicky's innocent hearts. Mom and Nicky are the persecuted. You have chosen to act bizarre and draw attention to yourself. You call this persecution. You are all fooling yourselves.*

God would never pick the likes of Kim Miller to represent him in the end days.

I'm sorry we did not get to talk the other day. You looked and acted as if your soul was gone. You are missing some of the last opportunities you will have to see your Mom and maybe your daughter.

I know Kim Miller told you that he has replaced your earthly family with this pseudo family you call "Concerned Christians." I see that you have all age groups…I don't see any 17 year-old girls though.

If you come home, I will go to court with you to get your money back for you, I cannot do anything about the money you have spent on this extended vacation, but you still have some money left, waiting for your return to reality.

My actions have only been to protect you and to help your daughter handle the crazy world that Kim Miller gave her. I love you and John and wish that you would see that Kim Miller is very wrong.

I love you both. By the way, if you're going to route this letter around to all your so-called friends like you did Nicky's letter, I want to say that the grandma at the airport did not deserve the treatment she got. Your group persecuted the grandmother for her beliefs and she wasn't even allowed to hold her new grandbaby. At least she was able to kiss the baby. I hope you all come to your senses. Some may call this tough love but I need to make a point. I will pray for you until the end. God Bless you all and may the Lord protect your souls from the evil who lie.

Love,
Betty

Two days later, Nicky called me from the East Coast, "Aunt Betty, I just called to let you know that we parked the motor home on a beach in Georgia. Have you heard anything from mom?"

"No, I'm sorry I haven't. But I wrote to her a couple of days ago to tell her that Mom had a slight stroke."

"She did? Is Grandma okay?"

"Yes, she's okay but it really scared her. That's all that poor woman needs, it makes you wonder how much one person can take."

"Tell Grandma that I love her and hope that she feels better. Hey, do you think that I could call Aunt Carol?"

"Sure, if you want to. I know that Jan and Carol talk to each other. Maybe Carol can tell you something that I don't know, Nicky. I haven't talked to Carol for six months. You know Carol told me that she wouldn't speak to me if I petitioned for a conservator for Jan. I think Jan is using Carol to get even with me. The last email messages that I received from Carol scolded me for being cruel and persecuting Jan. Carol made a point of letting me know that it wasn't about the money and that Jan has insisted that the money was not important. I feel as if I lost both of my sisters, Nicky. I can't help thinking that Kim is behind Jan and Carol's efforts to ostracize me from their lives."

It was three days before Christmas. Mom called and told me that she talked to Carol. Apparently Jan told Carol what I said in the email. When asked if Mom was okay, Mom told Carol that it wasn't anything serious. I was disappointed that Mom didn't tell Carol how serious her condition really was. Then I realized the wisdom in Mom's judgment. Carol was taking chemotherapy and was very sick, she certainly didn't need to worry about Mom too. But, I did want Jan to know the seriousness of Mom's problem. Instead, I'm afraid that the whole situation reduced my credibility.

CHAPTER EIGHTY-ONE

▼

NEW YEAR 2000

December 31, 1999 proved to be uneventful. The world's attention turned away from the threat of Y2K, Kim didn't die on the streets of Jerusalem, and the Concerned Christian's did not commit mass suicide. Many Americans considered the predictions of the end of the world hype, although some cults remained focused on Armageddon.

I imagined that the Concerned Christians viewed the people of the world as being foolish...the sinners of the world didn't know that the world's calendar meant nothing in the realm of spiritual events...

CHAPTER EIGHTY-TWO

▼

NICKY'S HEALTH

In early February 2000, Nick and I were startled out of a sound sleep when the telephone rang in the middle of the night. Nick reached for the telephone by the bed. Nick and I immediately took a mental role call on everyone in our immediate family. Nick fumbled for the phone and said, "Kris is home right?"

"Yes Kristopher is home."

Nick picked up the telephone, "Hello?"

"This is the nurse at Virginia Medical Institute, may I speak to Betty?"

"Sure," Nick handed me the telephone and said, it's a nurse at VMI."

"Hello this is Betty, is there something wrong with Nicky?"

"I'm afraid she has a problem with her stomach and we're afraid she is dehydrated and could possibly have the flu. We are unable to reach her dad and I need permission before I can send her to the emergency room at the local hospital."

"Okay, please take care of her and let me know how she is."

"Thank you, we will take care of her. We'll have her call you when she can."

I hung up the telephone and felt helpless. Nicky is going off to some hospital and I am over a thousand miles away. I didn't even know what was wrong with Nicky or how serious her condition was. I worried about Nicky. It would be a couple of hours before I could track her down. I would call until I found her. There couldn't be too many hospitals in Lexington, Virginia.

The next morning, I wrote to Jan so that she knew that Nicky was sick. I wondered if Jan would come home if she knew her daughter was in the hospital. I could only write and keep her informed

Date: *February 2000*
To: *Jan and John*
From: *Betty*

Jan and John,

I thought I would let you know that I received a telephone call from Nicky's school last night around midnight. She was very ill and wanted permission to send her to the emergency room. I gave them permission to send her. Nicky was dehydrated and very weak. Apparently Nicky had a very bad case of the flu. I called the hospital around 5:00 am and found out she had been dismissed. The school nurse said that they would call me with the results of the emergency room visit. They did not call and I have not heard from Nicky. I hope she is doing ok.

Nicky will be spending her Spring Break with me. We are looking forward to her visit. If you are interested, I will keep you informed of such things in the future. Write back and let me know if I should bother you with this type of information.

While I'm on the subject of people who love you. Mom is losing weight and feeling better after her surgery. (She had a knee replaced and the other one scraped.) She walks with a walker some of the time. She is looking pretty good but is frail.

I love you both very much and hope that you come home soon. God bless you and keep you safe.

Love,
Betty

Nicky called as soon as she could. And I immediately wrote to Jan and John to tell them that she was okay. I was sure that they were as worried about her. I was determined to have Jan and John involved in Nicky's life, if not physically at least they could share her life cyberly. But then I wondered if Kim wasn't telling Jan and John that Nicky's illness was only the Lord's way of teaching Nicky a lesson.

Date: February 2000
To: Jan and John
From: Betty

Jan and John,

I know that you love your daughter, I wanted to let you know that Nicky left a message on our recorder last night to say that she had food poisoning and that she had to spend the day in the VMI hospital. She says she is feeling better now and is looking forward to coming home.

The only other thing Nicky said was that she is looking forward to visiting us and she told us that she loves us. I was disappointed that I missed her call. That's all the news I have for you. I hope you are both doing ok and we love you very much.

God Bless You Both and Keep You Safe.

Love,
Betty

CHAPTER EIGHTY-THREE

▼

KILLING ENEMIES

On Friday, February 25, 2000, John responded to my email by telling me that Nicky was not following the Lord's will because she was willing to kill her enemies and refused to join him and Jan in their Christian walk. He said that the Concerned Christian's opposed weapons and because Nicky chose a military life, Nicky could not be a part of Jan and John's lives. John ended his message with sincere wishes for Nicky's good health, particularly wishing Nicky a healthy Christian life.

Date: *February 2000*
To: *John*
From: *Betty*

John,

Nicky loves both of you unconditionally. I am not particularly fond of her choice in careers either but I feel that she has been backed into a corner. She was only 14 or 15 years old when a very large man, (Kim) standing over her telling her that her biological Daddy did not love her and at the same time telling her that the message was coming from the true Lord. The tall man told Nicky not to call her biological father on the phone ever again. This obviously upset her tremendously and she immediately called and asked him if he loved her. Her daddy responded by telling her that he DOES love her and that is when he came to pick her up from your house. (Of course, by her daddy telling Nicky that he loves her this invalidated what the large man had to say…Nicky naturally concluded that the tall man was lying.)

Nicky told me that she never thought she would be gone from both of you forever. By casting her out because of a decision she made under such "strange" circumstances and a decision she made as a child is not fair to her. She was and still is a child. As I learn more about Nicky's situation, I believe that much of what has been said to the media came from an outside source.

I love Nicky and want her healthy in every way too. Just as I do our Mothers. They do not deserve to be treated as they are. What happened to you and Jan's unconditional love for your own Mothers? They will be on this Earth only a very short time.

The only reason I am writing to both of you is to let you know how Nicky is. I love you both and wanted to keep you informed because she is still your child. I feel I am looking out for you and Jan's best interest as well as Nicky's. Nicky is in VMI because she was lied to. Unfortunately, it is through VMI that Nicky has found structure, order, and family. Nicky loves the Lord Jesus Christ and prays to Him. I believe, as Nicky does, that you do not need an earthly mortal to be a conduit to Jesus Christ. Jesus Christ knows Nicky's heart and it is not for us to judge.

I pray that you both are well and that you will accept and love Nicky unconditionally…just as we love both of you unconditionally. No matter what you ever say or do, we will always love you both. By the way, Nicky is feeling much better now and counting the days that she will be home with us. If you don't mind, I will send her your love. God bless you and Jan forever and keep you safe. I pray that you come home soon.

Unconditional Love,
Betty

On Saturday, February 26, 2000, John wrote back and said that Nicky had lied about what Kim Miller said to her. John said that he was there when Kim told her not to call her biological father, but instead, to have a loving relationship with him. Kim told Nicky that she was not to love her biological father more than God. Kim thought that Nicky loved her biological father more than she loved God, and threatened that she would reap spiritual devastation if she continued. Nicky is worshipping the VMI god of this world now. John told me that I have twisted the truth about Kim Miller and so have all my television friends. John told me that I have an opportunity to listen to the audiotapes and learn the truth.

Date: *February 2000*
To: *John*
From: *Betty*

John,

Please do not take this personally. I cannot worship tapes just as I can't worship the Jehovah Witness Watchtower publication. I can only worship the Bible and the true Lord Jesus Christ. There may be some truth in the tapes, but I see personal opinion and hypothetical foregone conclusions in the tapes. I am not convinced that the one speaking in the tapes is chosen by God to speak for Him, nor do I believe that this mortal man (who has sinned as any average mortal) is qualified to speak for the Lord Jesus Christ. I believe that only the Bible is Truth. Kim Miller may have the best intentions but I have concluded that Kim Miller is not representing God's Truth.

*Please don't judge Nicky, she is a wonderful young girl who had her home destroyed by a ministry who insisted on leaving her instead of fighting for her soul. I do not believe that Nicky has lied to me. I believe she has not understood all the events that have happened since she was young. Your ministry has decided to judge Nicky as an adult. **She is** still a child and I think that she believes what she told me about the large man. Can you honestly say that you were around Kim Miller every time Kim Miller said anything to Nicky? Even if you were, you are an adult and understand adult communication much more than a child would.*

*Also, have you seen Kim Miller's television interview? His spoken word and actions were questionable...at best. You know that I have heard Kim Miller for many years and that I have held on to **some** of his teachings, (the teachings that are backed by the Bible) but I do not believe in everything that he says as you apparently do. I am sorry that Kim Miller's teachings include the removal of yourself and Jan from your family. I cannot believe that the true Lord Jesus Christ would want you to turn away from people you believe are sinners only to leave them "unsaved" and eventually send them to Hell.*

*You have critical thinking skills, John. You know that Nicky has not killed anyone. You know that Nicky loves her Mom and both of her Daddies unconditionally. You know that Nicky is still a child. You know that Nicky left your home under duress, Nicky felt she was being pushed by Kim Miller (real or perceived) and at the same time pulled by her father. She left your home at an age where many teenagers are confused and impressionable. Understand that Nicky was a child when she heard her Mom talking to me about giving Jan's only child up to the Lord. Your ministry has painted Nicky as a terrible person who is destined to go to Hell. Nicky is still a child in the eyes of the Lord, she is not perfect, but then **none** of us (including those in your ministry) are perfect and certainly were not perfect at her age.*

*I believe that Jesus Christ is pure Truth. His Ten Commandments **were** written in stone and one of them said to "Honor Thy Mother and Father." Yet, I see my Mom without her daughter and your Mom without her son in their end days. Your ministry has basically sentenced our Mothers "to Hell." I do not believe that this is because you personally want our Mothers to go to hell, nor do you want your daughters to go to Hell. If you feel so strongly about your ministry, why are you only saving yourselves? I don't understand.*

I am not here to judge your walk with the Lord Jesus Christ nor am I here to judge Nicky's walk. That is the sole responsibility of Jesus.

I have only written to both you and Jan to let you know what is going on in Nicky's life because I know that Nicky loves both of you and I love you both too. If I were in your position, I would want to know the things that I am telling you. We have very ill relatives. Our relatives are hurt because your ministry keeps you from them. They do not deserve to be treated so badly. Also, I do not want you to wake up someday and realize that it's too late. Our Mothers, daughters, sisters, and brothers will not be with us forever. They will leave this Earth and go where? Can you save them? Or are you too busy saving your-selves? You cannot regain the time lost, but there is still time to come home and love them for the rest of their lives.

John, I pray that you and Jan and I will understand God's purpose for our existence. How are we making a difference in this sinful world? Are we mak-ing a difference in a way that honors our Lord Jesus Christ and His original Word? Are we leading our children to Hell? Are we setting an example that would glorify the Lord Jesus Christ? Do we spend time loving our Lord or con-demning people with self-righteous conviction?

God Bless You and Keep You from Harm.

Love,
Betty

On February 29, 2000 John wrote to tell me that I know that Kim Miller is teaching the true gospel and since I love my life, I am unwilling to join the Concerned Christians. Instead, John says, I have chosen to fight against them. John reminded me that the Concerned Christians were willing to lose their reputations and pick up their crosses for Jesus. He warned me that I would reap a severe punishment for leading others astray. He ended his message by telling me to step aside.

I simply responded:

Date: *February 29, 2000*
To: *John*
From: *Betty*

John,
I have questions that your ministry cannot answer. You condemn me for my questions. I, like you, believe that I know Jesus Christ. I feel that He blesses me everyday and I live a very happy, healthy life filled with love for Jesus. I am

sorry if I offended you. It's hard to understand what you are doing, John. I was only asking questions to understand (since you brought the subject up). The purpose of my original letter was to keep you informed about Nicky because I love you and Jan. If I were in your position I would want to know what is going on with my family. We simply love you and always will. My love for you really is out of your control.

Unconditional love is just that, unconditional. It doesn't matter what you ever say to me or about me or do to me. I will always love both you and Jan, unconditionally. I pray that you both stay safe and well.

By the way, Nicky will be here in just three days. We are looking forward to her visit. Mom wants to get together with Nicky when she's here. We will probably go to dinner on Tuesday or Wednesday of next week. I wish you both could join us. We seriously do love and miss you both.

Love,
Betty

On March 1, 2000, I received a message from John but I believed that the message was a consolidated response from all of the Concerned Christians. The message began by telling me that the Concerned Christians had the answer to any question about doctrine but that I chose not to listen to the answer. They said that I was very wicked and that Nicky and I were running from the messages on the audiotapes by claiming that the Concerned Christians were worshipping the tapes. The Concerned Christians claimed that I ran from the tapes because the tapes were right. They accused me of twisting the facts by claiming that the tapes were full of errors. The Concerned Christian's said that if there was something wrong with the tapes that I would have the news media involved in exposing them as proof of the Concerned Christian's error.

I considered the comment a challenge. I wondered if the Concerned Christians wanted me to present the world with the message on the audiotapes. I never before thought of making our communications public. But John's message challenged me.

The Concerned Christians made it clear that I could not possibly understand the things of God because I am only capable of a "natural man" understanding as evidenced by using the media and the courts to reach Jan and John. I intentionally destroyed Jan and his reputation through lies in an ungodly court and before judges that are of the world and not of God. John went on to tell me that I believe that life, liberty, and the pursuit of happiness are of God and that the Bible says "for who ever loses his life for the sake of the Lord and the gospel shall save it." According to the Concerned Christian's philosophy, if a person seeks to pursue life, liberty and happiness, the person cannot be saved through the gospel.

It saddened me to read the email. I understood John's message to mean that in order to please the Lord, a person must not be happy or have freedom. They referred to the verse "life, liberty, and the pursuit of happiness" as Thomas Jefferson's gospel. Like so many cults before the Concerned Christians cult leader used the Constitution to convince followers that in order to earn eternal life, they must not belong to America and they must endure suffering by "losing their life to the Lord."

The Concerned Christians continued by quoting a verse that proved that Jesus Christ is not loved by the world. "If the world hates you, then it hated me before it hated you." The world wants their freedom so the world believes in the gospel of Thomas Jefferson instead of the believing in the Bible. Nicky preaches the gospel of Thomas Jefferson as evidenced by her willingness to kill for America. Jan taught Nicky the truth and I was assisting Nicky in believing a lie. The Concerned Christians said that I lie when I say I love Nicky and that I am only using her to pursue my life. Nicky and I support each other and are both headed for Hell.

John closed the email by saying that I do not truly love but he does and that he was losing respect for me.

I really liked John. I had to remind myself that it was not John that was writing to me but an entire group of people, most of who did not know me. It seemed to me that Kim approached our correspondence like a game. I sensed that his game plan included targeting me as the villain. Obviously a master at spiritual blackmail, the Concerned Christian's seemed to believe that Kim knew the inner thoughts of the Lord. Like a jealous lover, Kim seemed to destroy the Concerned Christian's relationships with family and friends by turning all threatening relationships into enemies of the entire group. In the meantime, I presumed Kim's own wife and son had been elevated as extensions of the cult leader's connection to the Lord.

I played into Kim's game plan by criticizing the cult leader. My criticism was surely considered blasphemous and I became an easy patsy for anything that Kim could not control. I knew that Kim was using me as a scapegoat, blaming me for Jan and John's beloved daughters not joining the Concerned Christians. As a result, I was a major source of pain for both Jan and John. It displeased me greatly. I sent John a return email.

Date: March 2000
To: John
From: Betty

John,

I'm sorry you feel as you do. I really am not interested in starting this whole thing back up with you and your group, and no, I'm not running. I do not see that I will ever change your view, as I know that you will never change mine. Kim Miller's tapes are not truth…they are bizarre. You did not know the Lord before you fell into this situation. I guess it's hard to think critically when you have such a myopic view. Your ministry's anti-American view has gained your group much notoriety. Your natural man leader would like you to believe that your notoriety comes from righteous Christian persecution caused by me feeding the media information. I'm sorry but you have been deceived. You are captive, not for the Lord but because of a natural man.

Whether you respect me or not, it doesn't matter. John, if I were running, I would not give you the time of day. I only contact you to let you know what is going on in the family. I went to court to protect the money for you, because your family requested that I do so. You realize that they went to court first and could not protect all of your money, so they asked me to protect the rest. I had nothing to gain and theoretically everything to lose by trying to protect you. I know you don't like me for what I did, I'm sorry that you feel this way.

You avoid talking about our Mothers…how do you justify your treatment to them? I cannot believe that the Lord did not mean it when He said, "Honor thy Mother and Father" in the Ten Commandments. No, I do not believe what you believe. But I will always love both you and Jan.

By the way, I'm not a follower of Thomas Jefferson…but go ahead and accuse me if it helps you justify your actions. Only the Lord Jesus Christ's judgement of me has any value.

I pray that the Lord keep you both from harm. In Jesus Christ Our Lords Name, God Bless You Both.

Love Unconditionally,
Betty

John wrote a quick note back to me on Friday morning, March 3, 2000 to give me what he called a humble suggestion. John said that I would gain tremendous spiritual knowledge if I understood just one of the tapes and suggested that I start by listening to the radio messages. I wondered where I was suppose to find the radio messages. Were the tapes that they sent me originally radio messages? John referred to 400 prophecy tapes that were longer than the tapes that I had already received and John mentioned 10,000 teaching charts. All this information was suppose to sum up world history from God's perspective. John told me that he understands the tapes and charts so I am foolish to say that they are bizarre.

He signed the email, Love, John.

CHAPTER EIGHTY-FOUR

▼

TWISTED

I wanted Jan and John to really question they're reasoning because some of their doctrine just didn't add up in my mind. I wrote:

Date: *March 2000*
To: *John*
From: *Betty*

John,

I appreciate your humble suggestion and I will pray about what you have said.

*Still, I am perplexed about your avoidance about the Ten Commandments. Contrary to what you have said, I **do** know the Gospel and the Ten Commandments are Gospel. Few people will argue the fact that the Ten Commandments are Gospel. "Honor thy Father and thy Mother" How do you and the members of your group justify how they treat their Mothers? When you all returned from Greece, I witnessed a mother from New Jersey who was basically ignored and not allowed to hold the grandchild that she just met for the* *first time. As a grandma, I can imagine the pain of not being able to hold my grandchild. I talked to this woman and she was deeply hurt by this situation. She did not deserve to be treated like a stranger by her family. Will that mother ever see her children or her grandchild again? I also know that your own mother misses you, John, and loves you unconditionally. I understand that she feels betrayed because you will not see her in person. I know what has been said to my mother, and it does not resemble "Honor" in any way, shape, or form. I simply do not understand how your group is complying with the Lord Jesus Christ's command to "Honor thy Father and thy Mother." I don't want you to waste precious time that could be spent truly honoring our fathers and mothers.*

*Historically, the action by religious groups to remove themselves from family and society are consistent with cults. You'll have to help me out here John. I have to get over the fact that your group fits in this mold, before I can even consider to take the tapes or the radio messages seriously. I believe that the Bible is the **only** true Gospel. I understand that the charts that you speak of come from the philosophy of one man, is this true? If the Lord wanted us to have 10,000 charts, he would have provided them in the Bible. The Bible says exactly what the Bible means. The message is timeless.*

Let's start with the answer to two questions, 1) Why don't the Concerned Christians have to honor their Father and Mother and comply with the Gospel of the Bible's Ten Commandments? 2) Why do the Concerned Christians need tapes and charts as a supplement to the true Gospel of the Bible? Let's focus on these two issues first, John, then maybe we can get somewhere.

I love you and Jan unconditionally.

Love,
Betty

John's return email written on Saturday, March 4, 2000 was not signed in "love." Apparently my questions were unnerving to the Concerned Christians so they responded by telling me that the charts and tapes were meant to teach the non-believer. They wanted me to know that Kim has been given the truth about prophecy because he sought after the truth.

The message slapped me by saying that I was purposely teaching a false doctrine so that I could live my secular life, adding that Kim knows so much that it would make my head swim.

They referenced Daniel 2, 7, 8, and 9, and claimed that there were many more verses that Kim needed to explain to me. People who truly know Kim Miller would find my criticism of Kim Miller ridiculous and find it funny that I run from the radio messages so that I can lie about Kim Miller teaching false doctrine. The message said that I was wicked and asked me how I could teach the Bible when I am only a child in Christ.

As I read on, I realized that the Concerned Christians had turned the tables and accused me of what I accused Kim of doing. I'm sure it pleased Kim and I would have liked to see the expression on Kim's face when he read that I was arrogant and a master at twisting the obvious.

Then the Concerned Christians hit me with the first good counter argument that I had heard since I corresponded with any of them. They asked me how I could support Nicky's efforts after Nicky dishonored her own mother. But I realized that I never encouraged Nicky to dishonor her mother and besides, I never thought Nicky actually dishonored her mother. I could see that Kim was twisting everything. Nicky spoke out against Kim's teachings. Nicky wanted to save her mother from living Kim's lie.

The message explained to me how the Bible instructs the Christian to honor their father and mother as long as it does not prevent the Christian from doing what the Lord wants the Christian to do. If the Christian's relationship with his or her parents prevents them from serving God then the Christian must let the relationship go. The Concerned Christians praised God that some people are willing to follow through with this action in order to express the truth that America is Babylon the Great. They added that many people oppose this doctrine so that they may live their secular lives.

Satisfied that they made their point, they called me Mrs. Ten Commandments and told me that they were tired of me bearing false witness against John, Jan, and "a man who did absolutely nothing to harm me."

Date: March 2000
To: John
From: Betty

John, Dear John,

Your response to my questions has always ended up in negative accusations towards me to justify your treatment of your own mothers. You don't understand that I really don't care what you or your little group thinks of me. I've told you that before. I care for you and Jan and realize that you are not in a position to understand. I will continue to pray for you both.

Your ministry is a ministry of Daniel and Revelations and whatever serves your philosopher's agenda. Go ahead and ignore the Lord's Ten Commandments to serve your philosopher. Place a higher value on selected verses that your philosopher shows you and ignore the Ten Commandments, and the Lord will discipline you!

I, on the other hand, **do** honor my Mother and my Father. I **do** love the Lord and depend on the Lord Jesus Christ to show me the Truth. I do not need a natural man to show me how to serve the Lord. And Nicky's walk with the Lord is her walk and the Lord knows that Nicky is a child. No, I'm not taking credit for Nicky turning from her Mom but I am thankful that the Lord has shown Nicky the Truth.

This "man" who has done nothing to harm me, has taken my sister and brother and made them go against the Ten Commandments. This "man" who has done nothing to harm me…has taken my beautiful nieces mother and father away from her (yet this man can go to an "American" bankruptcy court and protect his good name and take his family with him. Maybe this is why he is Hell bent on America!). This "man" who has done nothing to harm me…has pitted sister against sister, brother against brother, father against daughter and son, mother against daughter, and daughter against mother. This "man" who has done nothing to harm me…has stolen the soul of two people that I love in the name of Our Most Holy Jesus Christ…which is a blasphemy in itself! This "man" has done **much** damage. Not to mention all the pain that this "man" has caused.

You, have chosen to follow Kim Miller and his teachings, I simply have not. I have chosen to take the Bible at face value. The Bible was written for sinners like you and I and there is no secret interpretation. I do not believe that God sent someone like Kim Miller to interpret His Word for him…God is not into trickery. Believe what you want about America and the rest of this crazy world…it is all God's plan and nothing your group can ever do will change God's plan. There have been martyrs throughout time; there have been people who dedicate their lives to their spiritual leader. You have made the choice to abandon your Mothers and dishonor the Ten Commandments.

Your inability to answer the questions from the last email without becoming hostile confirms what I already know. I will continue to pray for you and Jan.

*I Pray that God will Bless You Both and Keep You from Eternal Hell. I pray that He understands that you have good intentions and that you have been lead astray. Go NOW to your Mothers, Jan and John. Honor your mothers and praise them for the rest of their natural lives. When you have done so, I am **positive** that Nicky will go to her own Mother with the same intentions.*

Love,
Betty

While volleying back and forth the email of doctrine, John's natural charm was revealed as he titled the subject of the next email dated March 5, 2000, "Backhand return, your court." For a moment, I remembered how much I missed John. I read the first line and saw that my intentional paraphrase of the Bible was used against me. I knew then that I should not try to be clever when responding to their email. I messed up. My strategy backfired on me as the Concerned Christians criticized my level of understanding of the Bible.

The Concerned Christians recognized my words as corresponding to Matthew 10:34-38 and informed me that the verse meant the exact opposite from what I had "twisted" it to mean.

They continued to tell me that I was in serious spiritual trouble. Like many cults before them, the Concerned Christian's used Matthew 10:34-38 to convince people to leave their families.

The Concerned Christian's asked why I bothered playing the game of claiming to be a Christian. They accused me of liking to be the leader of people and that I have so much hatred in my heart that I would rather send everyone close to me to Hell.

The Concerned Christians reminded me that their God has given me letter after letter explaining the true Gospel and an opportunity to repent for masquerading as a Christian. They warned me to take advantage of their God's grace, while I still have a chance or someday real soon my cries will not be heard. They said they were not kidding around with me. John signed the message.

I paused for a moment and wondered if I had lost another email battle. I realized I had goofed, but I knew that the Ten Commandments presented them with a problem. I knew that each of them loved their mothers and would never want to hurt them. I decided that their answer about overriding other verses over the Ten Commandments was not good enough for me. I responded with a final email.

CHAPTER EIGHTY-FIVE

▼

FINAL E-MAIL

Date: March 6, 2000
To: John
From: Betty

John,

    I understand the Gospel and I know a loving God. You have not left your family for the Lord Jesus, but you have left your family for Kim Miller. If you were serving the Lord Jesus you would have tried to save their souls. You choose to save yourselves. You have decided that your mothers are non-believers and have chosen to forget them and leave them to find Truth themselves or send them to Hell. You are in a dark and hateful ministry. God, have mercy on your souls. This verse tells the Christian to honor the Ten Commandments, Matthew 5:19, "Anyone who breaks one of the least of these commandments and teaches others to do the same will be called least in the kingdom of heaven, but whoever practices and teaches these commands will be called great in the kingdom of heaven." John, read Matthew 7:15-29, it is a potent verse that warns of false prophets.

Tell me, where are your good fruits in you life? I see thistles in your words. Jesus Christ is Love, and Life through Jesus is filled with happiness. I'm not ashamed of my love of Jesus and the happiness in my heart placed there only because of my life through Jesus.

I continue to love you both unconditionally.

Love,
Betty

CHAPTER EIGHTY-SIX

▼

THE TEN COMMANDMENTS

A week later, I was cleaning the living room when I received a telephone call from Mom. Her slow speech and shaky voice gave me all the clues I needed. "What's wrong Mom?"

"Oh nothing really," Mom's somber voice cracked.

"Yeah, there is something wrong…what is it?"

"You always could tell when there was something wrong with me, Betty. I didn't want to tell you or upset you."

"You're not going to upset me Mom, what's wrong?"

"Well, Jan called me on the telephone."

"She did? What did Jan say? Was she nice to you or mean to you?"

"Well Betty, Jan just wanted to know if she was dishonoring me."

I paused and then realized that Mom didn't tell Jan how she *really* felt about what Jan was doing. Mom didn't want to upset Jan, I knew before I even asked, "Yeah, and what did you say, Mom?"

"Well, I told Jan that she wasn't dishonoring me. Betty, I don't want to add to the problem."

"You did? You told Jan that she wasn't dishonoring you? Okay, then what?"

"Jan accused me of loving you more than her. Jan said that I was going to go to hell with you. Jan was angry with me because I didn't go to court to prevent you from petitioning for a conservator. Jan really wasn't very nice, Betty, and all I want is to just leave Jan and John alone."

"Mom, I'm sorry Jan called and upset you. I guess I should have defined the word honor as treating an individual with respect. Jan's so insensitive that she doesn't even realize that the telephone call alone was disrespectful and dishonorable. Mom, you know Jan called because Kim allowed her too, Jan is so brainwashed. Kim has certainly inflicted pain in our lives."

"Betty, I just don't want anything to do with this stuff, I never did. Jan has made her choice and Jan chooses her new family over us. Let Jan be."

"Jan's heart is so cold mom. If I left my children, I would hope that one of my brothers or sisters would shock some sense into me. I tried to make Jan see that she was dishonoring you Mom, but instead my actions have caused you more pain. I'm sorry.

I figured that Kim knew that if Jan upset my Mother because of something I said or did, I would back off, so Mom wouldn't get hurt. Kim's a very calculated man. He has convinced Jan that you are involved in what I'm doing, Mom. You know as well as I do that I have acted totally on my own. I will do what I can to avoid hurting you. I'll back off, Mom."

CHAPTER EIGHTY-SEVEN

▼

HONORING MOM

Mom came to visit Nick and I before we all left for our vacation to Spain. I walked out to the car to meet her and help her carry in her luggage. Mom carried a plastic container full of home cooked noodles while I carried the small carry on luggage that Jan bought her years ago. "Mom, how have you been? Are your knees still bothering you?

"Yes Betty, they are very painful. Oh, I brought a letter to show you."

"Really? Who is the letter from?"

"Jan."

"Jan? Really, I don't imagine it's a nice letter."

"I'll let you read it, Betty." Mom said as she reached into her purse and pulled out a yellow envelope and handed it to me.

I sat down and opened the letter. It was dated March 8, 2000. Daddy would have been 82 that day. I continued to read, Jan accused Mom of not loving all her children the same and said that Mom had favorites.

I couldn't agree with Jan's comment, Mom always tried to treat each of us the same. Jan message sounded so childish. Then I realized that as a mother of two children I realize that it is possible to love two children the same. But Jan only had one child. From Jan's perspective maybe she really didn't think it was possible to love two or more children equally.

My frustration increased as I continued to read. I realized that the telephone call and the letter were still part of a well thought out plan to get me to back off of the Concerned Christians. I was making some progress with my messages to the Concerned Christians about honoring the Ten Commandments and Kim knew that I would not allow my mother to continue to be abused by them.

Jan demanded that Mom order me to stop saying she was dishonoring her. My eyes narrowed as I read Jan's mean words to Mom. Jan told Mom not to call her "Sweetheart" after silently endorsing my actions and publicly displaying Jan's life. Jan accused me of conspiring to create a division between her and Mom.

I put the letter down in disgust. He did it again, I thought, Kim twisted the truth. I was not trying to divide Mom and Jan, but instead, I was trying to bring Mom and Jan together.

Jan insulted Mom's intelligence by saying that she would explain it to Mom again as simply as she could; I have been discussing to John and Jan about breaking one of the Ten Commandments–Honor Thy Father and Mom. Jan badgered Mom to tell me to stop my spiritual blackmail. Jan said that Mom was my pawn in a wicked game, as long as Mom remains silent…I would lead Nicky to hell.

I thought for a moment. Isn't she using spiritual blackmail on Mom? It was obvious to me that Kim was doing everything that he accused me of doing.

Jan objected to being falsely accused of being a crazy person who could not control her finances, and that we have portrayed her as being an unloving Mom and a wife that led her husband astray. Jan mentioned the national morning talk show in New York and called Nicky and I liars, she said that Nicky and my display of emotion and affection was ridiculous and self-serving.

The last paragraph said that Jan wasn't going to give into my spiritual blackmail. I was infuriated as I read the last line, Jan was sorry that Mom didn't have a backbone to tell me that she wasn't going to play my wicked game.

I leaned back in my chair and realized that the Concerned Christians won again. I could not subject our Mother to any more rude telephone calls or letters. I prayed that Jan and John would realize the truth before it was too late.

CHAPTER EIGHTY-EIGHT

▼

KISS AND MAKE UP

I often called Carol's daughter, Bobbi to see how her mom was feeling. Bobbi sounded so much like her mother on the telephone that I had to remind myself who I was talking to. Bobbi said that her mother's health was deteriorating. Carol was making medical history. Bobbi said that the doctor told Carol she outlasted all recorded cases of her type of cancer. The doctor's were doing all that they could to make her well. The doctor's were trying a new radiation treatment. Although the situation looked grave, we couldn't underestimate the power of the Lord.

I felt a tremendous amount of sorrow for Carol. My heart ached knowing that she was just a telephone call away, but she didn't want to talk to me because of my actions with the conservator. Her failing health coupled with the fact that Carol was openly angry with me bothered me more than how Jan was treating me. I told Bobbi that I missed her mother very much and that I wanted to call her.

Bobbi suggested that I did not call.

I told Bobbi that I was worried about her mom and warned her that I feared Carol was being heavily recruited into the cult. Bobbi listened quietly and agreed to review an email that Carol sent to me to see how serious the situation had become.

Bobbi must have seen the seriousness in the email. Within a few weeks, Carol called me. "Betty, this is Carol."

Tears flowed from my eyes. "Carol! It's so good to hear from you. How are you feeling?"

"Oh, I'm okay. I know that mom is going to have an operation on her knees and I just don't want her to go into surgery thinking that we are not speaking to each other. She has enough problems, she doesn't need our strife added to everything else. I want mom to go into surgery knowing that we kissed and made up."

Choked up, I replied, "I think that's great Carol. I would like to see you."

"Well, I would appreciate it if you wouldn't tell Jan that we are speaking to one another."

"No problem, Carol. I won't tell Jan."

"I don't want Jan to stop writing to me, Betty. It would be nice to see you, maybe you can arrange to stop here on your next business trip."

"Well, I'm not traveling very much anymore. But I would like that Carol."

"I'm going to go lie down now, Betty, I'm not feeling well. Be sure to tell Mom that we are talking again. Okay? I love you."

"I love you, too. I'll call Mom right away."

As soon as I hung up the telephone, I called Mom. She was happy to hear the news and I felt elated. I had my sister Carol back and I was going to see her again.

▼

CHAPTER EIGHTY-NINE

LIFE BY THE MEDITERRANEAN SEA

Nick, Kristopher, and I left for vacation a few days later. We were spending one short week in Malaga, Spain and hoped to visit Gibraltar. Jan continued to be on my mind. Jan lived by the Mediterranean Sea during 1999 and I was looking forward to seeing first-hand the lifestyle of the Europeans and life by the Mediterranean.

We awoke early on March 11 anxious to get to the airport. As I put on my makeup I felt a rush of excitement. "You know the best part, Nick? Nicholas Shawn, Lynn, and baby Nicholas will meet us in New York."

Nick peeked around the door of the master bath, "What?"

"We're going to have that sweet baby with us. One whole week of holding and loving our baby grandchild!"

Nick smiled as he raised his thick eyebrows, "Yes Betty, having our family together and seeing the baby is best part of this vacation."

"We have to leave for the airport in twenty-five minutes. I'm going to wake up Kristopher so he can get ready."

I knocked on Kristopher's bedroom door. "Kristopher, you…"

"Mom, I'm already awake. I'm so excited!"

"I know, we are too. Get ready so we can get to the airport on time."

Thirty minutes later we were in the car and pulling out of the driveway. It didn't matter how much time we allotted ourselves...we were always late.

"We're in luck Nick. The traffic is light today. I don't think we're going to have any problem. I have all of our passports, we have our traveler's checks, our tickets, and our clothes. we are ready!"

Nick, Kristopher, and I boarded the airplane headed for JFK Airport in New York. We settled into our seats and listened to the safety review. I glanced at Kristopher and he was in the nap ready position. "That kid can sleep anywhere, Nick."

"He was out until 1:30 am last night. I know he's tired. Didn't you feel him come in our room and give you a kiss when he came home?"

"Yes but I didn't know what time it was. You know, Nick, the last time I was at JFK Airport was when I saw Jan. I wish things could have turned out better. Our meeting was not a pleasant experience.

"Nick looked at me and said sarcastically, "No kidding? When I saw you on *Dateline*, you were really giving her an ear full but she ignored you. You did all you could, Betty. Besides, I told you that you should have taken handcuffs with you. If you would have cuffed her to you, you might have pulled her away from the cult. You should just forget Jan and try to have a good time, okay?"

"Your right Nick, but where was I suppose to get handcuffs? I think it was divine intervention that put Jan and I in New York at the same time."

I placed my tray table up and my seat in the upright position minutes before the flight attendant strolled by. "The plane has landed."

Nick quipped, "You have a real eye for the obvious, Betty. Hey, as soon as we get settled at the next gate I'm going to go look for Nicholas Shawn, Lynn, and the baby. Their flight from Houston should have arrived ten minutes ago."

"Okay, I'll wait at the gate just in case you guys miss each other."

Nicholas Shawn and family arrived at our gate minutes after Nick left to find them. I didn't mind having the baby for myself and I couldn't wait to hold the baby. "My what a chunk! He's gotten so big! Your dad went to find you, Nicholas Shawn. He should be back here looking for you in a few minutes."

Nicholas pouted, "Well, aren't you happy to see me?"

"Of course Nicholas Shawn, I love you," I chuckled as I reached over to give him a kiss.

Nick and Kristopher returned to the gate. I tingled as I watched the commotion as everyone hugging each other. Nothing else mattered but our being together. The joy we felt when we were together meant more than any trip or any material thing. The trip was just an excuse to be together.

I carried the baby as Nick, Kristopher and I boarded the plane to Madrid. We searched for our seats and were pleasantly surprised to find that Nick, Kristopher, and I had seats in business class. Nicholas Shawn and Lynn looked above our heads at the seat numbers as they walked past our seats. After a while Nicholas walked back to our seats with another pout on his face. I babied him, "What's wrong Nicholas Shawn?"

Nicholas Shawn scowled playfully, "Lynn and I are in *zoo* class."

I jeered, "Poor Baby!" I wish you could have let me get your tickets. Then maybe you would have had seats next to us instead of "zoo" class.

I watched Nicholas disappear past the curtained area. I quietly stared out the window and wondered how many times Jan and John flew over the Atlantic during the past few years.

Hours later we landed in Madrid and changed planes. The baby traveled with his mom and dad. Nicholas Shawn and Lynn. Nick, Kristopher and I arrived in Malaga by mid-morning. After a thorough search of the airport, we couldn't find Nicholas Shawn, Lynn, and the baby and attempted to have them paged in both English and Spanish. We couldn't' understand what happened to them.

The next flight from Madrid did not produce our loved ones or our bags. Frazzled, Nick, Kristopher, and I asked airline personnel to page

Nick and Lynn. After forty-five minutes Kristopher said impatiently, "Maybe Nick and Lynn caught a taxi and went to the villa, Dad."

Nick laughed as he walked up to the rental car. "It looks like you got a big enough car, Betty, a nine-passenger Autobus."

Kristopher pleaded, "Oh no Dad, we're not going to drive around in that thing, are we. I thought that the Europeans drove around in BMW's and Mercedes. This thing is huge!"

The three of us climbed on the step next to the door and stepped into the roomy Autobus. "I hope we find Nicholas Shawn and Lynn pretty soon."

We drove away from the airport and caught our first glimpse of white Spanish villas landscaped by the deep blue Mediterranean Sea. "This could be paradise, Nick. Look at the villas, each one has a perfect view of the Sea. Wouldn't this be a wonderful place to live? No wonder the Concerned Christians decided to live by the Mediterranean Sea."

The nagging guilty feeling resurfaced. Once again I questioned whether I should have petitioned for a conservator to control Jan's finances. Although I have never been to Greece, Spain shared the same beautiful Sea and it was absolutely beautiful. I started to second-guess whether I should have petitioned for a conservator. I thought, if Jan thinks that America is Babylon, why should she have to live in America? I know that I would not have bothered Jan if Nicky were an adult, but Nicky was a minor and she needed support.

Suddenly we heard an alarm sound off in the Autobus. "What was that?" I asked.

"I don't know, Betty. This Autobus is brand new. Look! It only has fifty miles on the odometer! It doesn't sound good. Now what do we do?"

"Can you believe it? What a day we're having! We better turn around and go back to the airport, Nick."

"Can we get a BMW, Dad?"

"No, Kristopher," Nick and I said in unison.

We were on a one-way highway with no way to turn around. We would have to wait to find a cambio de sol to turn around and go the other way. Suddenly we heard a loud POP!

"Ah…oh, I guess this is as far as we go," Nick said in dismay.

Our second autobus, 500 pesetas, 150 miles, one duffel bag, and six hours later we found Nicholas Shawn, Lynn, and the baby. We were finally enjoying a long awaited vacation.

CHAPTER NINETY

▼

SO-LONG SPAIN

Our vacation seemed to be over before it began. Even though we didn't receive the rest of our luggage until the third day, we improvised without a problem. The sixth day, Nicholas Shawn, Lynn, and the baby had to catch their return flight. Nick, Kristopher, and I drove back to the airport and said our good-byes.

On the way back to the villa, the three of us decided to try to find a castle. "There's the Malaga turn off," declared Nick as he turned on his signal light. We'll just drive around and see what there is to see. I heard there are some castles in Malaga and also a beautiful cathedral."

We found a decrepit park with a fountain and a list of soldiers that died in a Spanish war. We parked and got out of our Autobus and walked over to the fountain to read the names on the monument. I looked around at all the vacant parking lots in the midst of a town swarming with people, "I think we should move the car, this doesn't look like a good place to park. If this area was a good place to park there wouldn't be any parking places." I reasoned.

Kristopher echoed my sentiments so Nick gave in and we all climbed back into the Autobus and proceeded to find a parking place. I don't know how he found it but he pulled into a parking garage and parked the car again.

We had exactly two hours. The parking attendant made sure that we knew we only had two hours and nothing more. We walked around the block and saw the Picasso birthplace and museum. We would have to go through it on our way back because Kristopher was hungry and there would be no peace until he was fed. We continued on until we found a restaurant.

As we left the restaurant Nick mentioned that he wanted to see the old cathedral. We could barely see one of the steeples at the top of the roofline. With our eyes glued to the steeple we started walking to find the cathedral. We approached the cathedral and noticed it was a 14th century catholic church. I recognized the stories in the Bible told by the magnificent paintings, sculptures, and beautiful architecture. I could not help but notice the saints, and I thought of Jan. The saints, angels, and figurines of church authorities made me think of how different my own beliefs were.

I sank deeper into thought and began to justify my conflict with Jan. I am not so self-righteous to believe that everyone must think as I do. Each person is responsible for his or her salvation. I have enough to do without involving myself with their business. Then I reasoned, unless, of course, children are involved. After all, it is important to lead children to the Lord. Unfortunately there are people who will mislead children and adults alike for personal gain. There it is! I feel justified in what I have done.

We walked deeper into the cathedral and immediately the ohhhhhh's and the ahhhhhh's started flowing with our mouths wide open in amazement from the rich and beautiful architecture. We stepped in the doorway entering the chapel and our breath was taken away as we gazed at the three story high organ. Next to it was another just like it. Every inch of the chapel was strikingly beautiful. The cathedral was filled with riches.

As we left the church a band of gypsies approached us. They grabbed our hands and started to read our fortunes, in Spanish. I looked around and saw that Nick and Kristopher were busy with their own fortuneteller and noticed that there were more gypsies waiting for us if we broke away from this group. I could hear Nick as he tried to convince his gypsy that he had to leave. We all kept interrupting our fortuneteller to say that we did not understand Spanish. It was easy to see that the gypsies were professionals, they started their well-rehearsed lines by effectively using sign language. They wrapped up their speeches and said, "Five hundred pesetas."

"Five hundred pesetas?" Nick echoed.

"Yes, five hundred pesetas," his fortune-teller repeated as she pointed to his wallet.

Meanwhile I grabbed my fanny pack. It occurred to me that it is easy to tell where people keep their money because when people are threatened they immediately reach for their wallet. My fortuneteller pointed at my wallet and told me, "five hundred pesetas!"

All of the sudden I panicked at the thought of our rental car getting towed from the parking space. We promised the parking attendant that we would be back in two hours and after stopping for breakfast, the cathedral, and Picasso's home the time had expired. Unfortunately, we wandered around enough to get lost and now we had to find the parking garage in an unfamiliar city, in a foreign country. I turned and grabbed Nick's arm in a theatrical display of anguish and said, "They're going to tow away our car!"

He looked at me with equal panic and grabbed Kristopher's arm and pulled him away from his fortune-teller. We blazed past the army of gypsies and starting scurrying through the maze of tall buildings to find the garage. We must have looked crazy to the locals in Malaga. As we reached each corner we reenacted a dramatic triage decision process. Nick has a better sense of direction so we followed his lead. I really didn't have confidence in his direction, or his infamous shortcuts.

I saw a nice Spanish lady walking down the road. I started to ask her in broken English where the Picasso home was. Kristopher shook his head at me as if to tell me that I should even attempt to communicate with anyone who doesn't speak English. He said a few words in Spanish to tell her that the parking garage was close to Picasso's home. Naturally, she didn't speak English and she wasn't familiar with Spanish Pig Latin. But she was able to communicate to let us that we needed to stop a taxi and ask the driver if he could help us.

We flagged down a taxi driver. At this point, we would have given him all the money in our wallet to get us to the car. He looked at Nick's parking receipt and nodded his head to get in. We turned the corner and there was the first parking place we had in the decrepit park and all the parking spaces were filled. I guess the area wasn't as bad as I thought. Nick gave me a look letting me know that he noticed it too. When we saw the parking garage we cheered. The parking attendant looked at us complacently. We got into our nine-person autobus and drove down the busy narrow streets of Malaga.

We now had time to take a breath. We laughed at the adventure we just experienced. Nick sighed, "This is our last day in Spain. I wish Nicholas Shawn, Lynn, and the baby could have stayed one more day. Our breakfast was the best that we have had so far. Since Nicholas Shawn owns a Picasso lithograph he would have especially enjoyed the Picasso Museum, but I think they would have enjoyed the cathedral the most."

Kristopher said, "I think that taxi driver just drove us around a while so that we would pay him more money. We really were not that far from the parking garage."

"I think you're right," Nick added, "he drove us around the block a couple of times."

We laughed at how funny we must have looked frantically searching for our car. I turned to look at Kristopher's face, "Don't you wish you would have studied your Spanish more Kristopher?"

Kristopher scowled.

"I wish I would have learned Spanish growing up. I'm determined to learn it! We're coming back here." Nick said.

I grinned and said, "Yeah, it's funny, Lynn is the only Irish Pollock in the group and she is the one who speaks fluent Spanish. Boy, did we miss her today!"

We were silent for a few minutes when Kristopher commented, "People may complain about giving money to the government in the form of taxes, but historically people have given freely to their church. And throughout history there have been people who have stolen from the church. Did you see where Malaga cathedral was robbed of gold and priceless art during one of the wars?"

I said, "Yes, I saw that. There have always been people who will take advantage of deep religious beliefs of people, either by stealing from the church or by stealing from them directly. They prey on their religious convictions." I added, "This is morbid, but it reminds me of the morticians who prey on people who lose loved ones. They're professionals in getting to the core of a person's soul, using grief, guilt, and desperation as their emotional sales tools to sell the biggest and best funeral program to the grieving survivor."

Nick was maneuvering in and out of traffic. We loved the city of Malaga but the traffic was getting to us. We just wanted to be in open spaces again. Finally, we were on the highway back to Estepona. I reflected back on our discussion about con artists preying on people's emotional convictions, "Think about it, if a husband and wife both buy into a religious doctrine they are at the mercy of their spiritual leader. That's what has happened you know, Kim Miller needed Jan and John to both believe his doctrine because Jan would not spend John's money without John's consent. Kim Miller knew that so Kim worked on getting John to buy into his plan."

"The inheritance laws are definitely in the cult leader's favor. I guess that's why cult leader's try to include the children," Nick added, "That way, no one is left to petition to protect the estate."

"But if the spiritual leader does not let the cult victim go to court to fight for their assets, what's the motivation? If the assets are protected, then the cult leader cannot gain monetarily. So, is the motivation power? Or is the motivation madness? Maybe it's both," I commented.

"But, if Jan and John would come and get their money, wouldn't the court make them prove their competence?" Kristopher asked.

"I guess you're right, if they came back to get their money the courts would probably make them go through counseling in order to prove that they would not give their money up to Kim Miller," I responded. "So, Kim Miller will never allow them to return for their money. Besides he has convinced them that Satan rules the governmental systems in which the courts are naturally a part of."

"But didn't Kim Miller go to court to claim bankruptcy? Nick asked.

"Yes, that's what I understand. It was about the same time that he prevented Jan from fighting for custody for Nicky. Jan has lost precious teenage years with Nicky, that age is here and gone so fast never to return."

"Hey Dad, there's a BMW dealership. Can we stop and look at the new BMW's?"

"Okay Kristopher, but then we better get back to the villa so we can get our bags packed for tomorrow, we're leaving pretty early in the morning."

PART V

▼

FIVE AUDIOTAPES

CHAPTER NINETY-ONE

▼

ACCEPTING THE CHALLENGE

In April 2000, I finally gave in to John's persistent plea to listen to all of the five audiotapes that contained the basis of the Concerned Christian's beliefs. My plan was to weed out all the redundant messages and concentrate on identifying idiosyncrasies.

It was 2:30 am in the morning and I couldn't sleep. The early morning hours allowed my mind to see illustrated parables that were appropriately hidden during the day. I saw Jan as if she were a prisoner of war, brainwashed and unaware of her captivity. I wanted to rescue Jan and bring her back to reality. But religious captivity was different than being a prisoner of a political war. The religious prisoner's state of mind resembled that of a kamikaze and no strategy could save them from conforming to their abductor's commands.

I walked downstairs and sat on the white couch in the dark living room, surrounded by research material and I began typing. The light from my laptop computer illuminated the room. I was determined to hear the so-called hidden wisdom in the audiotapes and to discover the reason why

Jan and John traded their fairy-tale lives for a life of suffering. I wanted to compare the Concerned Christians beliefs to my own. Ironically, I couldn't help but question my own sanity. Did it make sense for me to be preoccupied with analyzing the obsession of a cult leader without a social conscience?

I pulled out the first tape and read the cover, "Foundation Series #1, 3-03-93, All Nations Under God, Tape 1." I bet Jan typed each label herself, I thought as I remembered that I never spent the time to completely listen to any of the other tapes that Jan sent me over the past ten years. I put on the headphones and turned the recorder on. I heard a soft-spoken voice of the speaker; a voice that I was certain was Kim Miller's. He talked with compassion to his listeners. He began by consoling the listener and asking them not to become frustrated with the message. The message, he warned, would be difficult to understand. His compassionate voice turned condescending as he reminded his attentive listeners that he possessed divine knowledge that the "natural" man would have difficulty understanding.

It dawned on me while typing each word that it would be more difficult than I had previously thought. I paused and took a deep breath. I knew that it would be very hard to remain objective but I continued to type.

In the beginning, Kim promised to explain in great detail the United States role in Bible prophecy. He mentioned that the United States was referenced in the Bible in great detail and especially during the end times.

I paused from typing for a moment and noticed that the tapes were recorded in a quiet room. Occasionally, a sound of a baby in the background, religious music, or classical music could be heard. After listening to three hours of the first tape I concluded that it was difficult to understand Kim's message. Not because of his profound wisdom but because of the Kim's tendency to repeat salient points he called "understandings" and jump from the Bible to charts with continual promises for a better understanding in the future.

I typed every "er, uh, and um" in order to see if Kim was struggling with the words. Although there appeared to be some interruptions in

Kim's thinking, he appeared to be a seasoned speaker and stumbled very little over his words. As the theology of the Concerned Christians resonated in my ears I noticed a spackling of truth from the Bible.

I recognized something that I instinctively knew. In that in spite of the fact that the Bible tells us not to add or subtract from the Commandments, Kim chose to elevate other verses in the Bible over the Ten Commandments. Kim convinced his victims that they only have to "Honor thy Father and Mother" if their parents believe the philosophy of the Concerned Christians.

The audiotapes were Kim's way of planting seeds of understanding. Kim stressed in the tapes that the most important aspect of the listener's knowledge of prophecy was the Christian's walk with God and to understand how the Christian is to live during this age.

Unfortunately, my creativity peaked in the early morning hours and was interfering with my ability to muster up any objectivity. I tried to get back on tract and forced myself to continue typing. I stopped the tape. I remembered that I heard Kim once worked in marketing, the cynical side of me paraphrased Kim's message…the audiotapes are a promotional tool that I use to prey on good Christian's and to obtain their assets. In the process of my obtaining wealth and elevating my ego, I will convince the Christian that I have divine knowledge and that the Christian must remain by my side. In order to reinforce the Christian's commitment to be faithful to god through me, I will destroy the good Christian's world, as they know it. The good Christian will not be able to return to any country or any loved one out of fear from the Lord and embarrassment of ridicule.

Kim promised that he would tell the Christian how to live to please the Lord and told them that they would have to die to themselves like Jesus died to Himself. Kim added that eventually the Concerned Christians would become like saints and live and reign with Jesus Christ. To reinforce his message, Kim immediately posed a threat of judgement summarizing Revelation 19:15 and 19:19.

I thought it was interesting as I heard Kim emphasize that when Jesus Christ returns, one of the objectives was to destroy the enemies of God. Kim quoted Zechariah 14:3 and Jude 14 to support his teachings by saying thousands of saints will execute the Lord's judgment against all the ungodly who have committed sins and spoken against him. Umm, In other words, Kim Miller's church consists of a body of saints called the Concerned Christians who will execute judgement against His enemies when the time comes. I realized that the Concerned Christian's probably considered me an enemy of God. With an "us verses them" message, Kim Miller tells the listener that they can run away from the message but that the listener will not be able to hide from the Truth. I remembered, again, the files found in Israel containing Charles Manson quotes. No wonder the Concerned Christians are afraid to defect, I thought.

Kim warned the listener that they could not go to another country to escape America the Babylon. He said that eventually there will be a literal destruction of all the governmental systems of the world. Kim said that every governmental system in the world is rooted in evil. Kim quoted Isaiah 2:2-4 to demonstrate the religious political system of theocracy and wars would end leaving one religion, resulting in peace and prosperity on Earth.

I saw a familiar trend as I typed Kim's words. Like many cults, the believing victims were left with no alternative but to stay in an environment that they believed was pure and focused on the Lord. Once they committed to Kim's truth, they turned from friends and family, their community, and ultimately their country. With no possessions to call their own, the cult victims became dependent upon the cult.

I heard harsh descriptive words like "crushing the world" and "destruction," words that could be construed as terrorist threats by someone who was unfamiliar with the Bible. But I believed that the threats were not terrorist threats against any country but were meant to terrorize the victims in the cult and re-enforce that they had no place to go. The words served Kim's hidden agenda.

I worried as I thought about the lunacy in Kim's mind. The tapes were from 1993 and this was year 2000, was his madness escalating? I paused to pray for the innocent victims of the Concerned Christian cult.

At a point in the tapes, where the listener is shocked into realizing that they have no other place to go, Kim spoke of the rewards of joining the Concerned Christian sainthood and referenced Revelation 20:4. Kim created an allusion of promises that the Concerned Christians would become saints and reign with Jesus Christ during a thousand-year period of time. To reinforce the Concerned Christian's security and wellbeing, Kim promised that Satan would be bound during their reign with Jesus Christ.

With descriptive words, Kim painted pictures of destruction on earth and serenity with the Concerned Christian's Heavenly Kingdom Church in the listener's mind that made them believe that the Concerned Christians had an insight to eternal salvation.

CHAPTER NINETY-TWO

▼

THE PROMISE

It was the last week in April and my third week typing what I had nick-named, "Kim's promotional tapes." The redundancy of the message nau-seated me. In typical marketing fashion, Kim continued to reinforce to the prospective Concerned Christian that the saints were destined to rule the Earth during the millennium. Obviously, this was the part of the audiotapes that told the listener what was in the ministry for them, the "sales" hook. Of course, Kim let the listener know that they needed the ministry, because the whole world was corrupt and bound for Hell.

I shook my head in disbelief as I typed Kim's promises as he told the hopeful listeners that he would eventually discuss the details about how and when the saints would rule the earth. To prevent his listener from being too disappointed, Kim enticed them with another verse confirming the Bible's promise to the saints by quoting Daniel 7:18.

Kim told the Concerned Christian saints that they would judge the world, but warned them that they were not to go to the courts of the gov-ernment. Each of the Concerned Christians, as saints, were being prepared to judge the world in the millennium and beyond and to reign with Jesus Christ.

I cringed at the thought of such a hypocritical man.

CHAPTER NINETY-THREE

▼

REWARDS OF PEACE

The next portion of the tape was intended to provide the cult victims with motivation and courage to endure a life of suffering. Kim promised that if the Christian served God the way he taught, the Christian would receive the reward of eternal peace. His sales pitch was followed by threats of experiencing the perils of Hell for refusing to join the Concerned Christians. To deny Kim, was equivalent to becoming part of the destruction of the worldly governmental systems. Kim chose select verses in the Bible to twist the message to conform to his plan. I looked up each verse in the Bible to be sure that the speaker quoted the Bible as it was written. I found that the verses were sometimes quoted without full explanation and often without reading the rest of the chapter to grasp the intended meaning.

I listened to Kim as he quoted 2 Timothy 2:12, "If we endure, we will also reign with him, If we disown him, he will also disown us."

It made me sad as I realized the true suffering that the delusional man was inflicting on all of his victims.

CHAPTER NINETY-FOUR

▼

THE OVERALL PLAN

After more than four weeks of listening to the speaker's words and rewinding the tape to be sure that I understood what he was saying, I had long abandoned my attempt to be objective. I could not listen any more without thinking that Kim's calculated motives brought him undeserved wealth and status. In my mind, I envisioned a vampire sucking the life out of innocent victims and the tapes and audiotapes were just a tool to perpetuate Kim's livelihood. I continued typing each word verbatim, this time, to hear if Jan and John were in imminent danger.

The topic was a familiar one. Kim reiterated his previous message about the saints reigning as priests and kings with Israel, the nation over all nations. He promised the listener a long life for those who serve Jesus and a death penalty for anyone sinning against God during Christ's reign.

Kim threatened the listener that if they chose not to join the Concerned Christians and chose to remain in a world ruled by Satan, that the listener would not be found in the Book of Life and would be judged before God as the wicked dead and cast into the Lake of Fire. Kim reinforced that

America was not a nation under God but instead a nation under Satan and strengthened his position by repeating to the listener that they had no place to go because every nation was under Satan. He told them that the rest of the world was deceived but the listener must act on their new knowledge and reap the benefits of eternal salvation or be condemned to Hell.

Five hours later, I took off the headphones and moved from my laptop computer, I was becoming irritable from force-feeding Kim's redundant message through my mind and out my fingers. It was time that I walked away from the tapes for a few days. I didn't want to hear anything more about the Concerned Christian's closed society of saints in which they are the only chosen ones who will sit on the right hand of the Father.

▼

CHAPTER NINETY-FIVE

CUP OF COFFEE

It was 8:00 in the morning and I wanted to call Carol before I started work. I used to like to sit with her and visit over a cup of coffee. When Carol moved away, we had our visit and cup of coffee over the telephone. I was unaware that Carol had given up drinking coffee. I dialed Carol's number. I knew Carol was awake during the morning hours. She liked to visit with Jack before he went to work "Hi Carol, I just wanted to call you and visit over a cup of coffee."

Carol sounded weak, "I'm not doing very well, Betty. I have a tremendous amount of discomfort from chemotherapy. I'm going to go to bed. Before I go, have you heard anything from Jan?"

"No Carol, I'm sorry you're not doing very well today. I have not heard from Jan in over six weeks. I don't know what's going on with her. I'll let you go and get some rest. I'll talk to you later when you feel better."

As I hung up the telephone I realized that I must remind Carol of Jan. Carol always mentioned Jan every time I talked to her. For a moment, I resented Jan. Carol was suffering and wanted nothing more than to hear from Jan, the Jan we used to know. But Jan could not hear Carol's crying plea. Kim surrounded Jan's mind and emotions with an incredibly strong, but invisible fortress.

I thought about Carol's situation, Kim's evil plot, and Jan's insensitivity…I lost my composure and cried.

Chapter Ninety-six

▼

Carrying Your Cross

Although I did not get back to the tapes for three days, Jan was on my mind every day. Would I be able to uncover any information that would give me peace of mind about Jan's absence? I had to find out. I sat down on the white couch and placed the headphones over my ears. With a speck of renewed energy, I placed my hands on the keyboard and began typing.

I listened to a few words…more of the same, I thought. Kim began to close his "sell" by talking about picking up your cross to follow Jesus through the Concerned Christian's ministry. It was obvious to me that Kim wanted to portray his ministry as a loving and giving body of Christians. He told the listener that God wants them to have love in their hearts for those people who hate them. He spoke in great length about the heavenly kingdom church and how God would make the people prove their love by submitting to Him and by carrying their crosses.

Kim reminded the listeners that they were honored to be among unique people who could abide by the principles that the Lord demanded. He quoted 1 Peter 2:9, "But you are a chosen people, a royal priesthood, a holy nation, a people belonging to God, that you may declare the praises of him who called you out of darkness into his wonderful light." The verse about peculiar people was another reinforcement of why the Concerned Christians had to remain "different" from ordinary people. It was the peculiar people who would gain the rewards in Heaven. Again Kim encouraged the listener to leave everything behind quoting a verse from Luke 9:23. Kim added that the Concerned Christians were not to love possessions or their country.

For listeners who were wondering why the Lord tested them, he said that the Lord wanted to refine the saints. The difference between the Concerned Christian's and the rest of the world was that it was an honor for the Concerned Christian to experience fiery trials, their suffering was a way to partake in Christ's suffering and be rewarded by reigning with God.

CHAPTER NINETY-SEVEN

▼

RESISTING EVIL

I found the next tape interesting because my perspective of the audience was not that of a newcomer, but an existing follower within the Concerned Christians. The topic was not new of course. I heard the same redundant message that I had heard since I started the journey for truth. As usual, the speaker's argument and scripture selection had a vague relationship with one another. But he continued to speak as if his message were profound and enlightening.

Kim reminded the Christians not to go to court and judge people. Although Kim quoted the same scriptures again and again, I sensed an ulterior motive for the discussion. Kim did not want the listener to go to the secular courts of the world and he did not want the Concerned Christian to talk outside the group. He promised that the listener would judge the world at a later time.

To protect his domain, Kim lectured that each member of the Concerned Christians were tasked with the responsibility to judge inside of the church to make sure that the church remained pure. Kim instructed his followers to walk humbly among the Concerned Christians and to help each other work through their trials and tribulations, to confess their sins to each other and to walk in love for the Lord.

I turned off the tape and remembered that Jan once told me that each member of her Bible study shared intimate details about their lives as testimony to the Lord and to cleanse their souls. I reflected back on my own experience with groups that gathered and shared their deepest and darkest secrets and experiences. The secrets bonded the relationships of the members through trust, realizing that each of their vulnerabilities could be subject to exploitation. The common intimacy pulled the group together, created longer lasting friendships, and minimized the possibility of separation. The shared secrets virtually consummated the relationship. I realized that this practice was critical to the success of the cult.

To enforce loyalty, Kim warned that wicked people who cause division among the group would be excommunicated. Kim reinforced the severity of causing division by calling it a wicked act of treason punishable as if it were one of the Ten Commandments.

I remembered how Jan looked at John when we were in JFK Airport in New York when they were deported from Greece in December 1999. She would look over her shoulder at John as John was talking to Dave. As Jan shielded herself from me, she glanced back at John as if to say, 'John, you better get away from those people and stop talking to them.' Until I heard this part of the tape, I didn't understand why Jan was so concerned about John. I wondered if Jan was worried that others in the church would try to excommunicate John from the church? I thought how silly it would be to excommunicate the primary financier of the group. Then again, I didn't know if John had any control over his money anymore. Maybe John already gave Kim all the money he had. Regardless, I was sure that Jan did not want John to lose favor with the rest of the group. Maybe Jan was just concerned that someone at the airport would try to abduct him.

The reports that the Concerned Christians were a doomsday cult came vividly to my mind as I listened to Kim quote Luke 12 and Matthew

10:28. "Do not be afraid of those who kill the body but cannot kill the soul. Rather, be afraid of the One who can destroy both soul and body in hell."

I wondered if Kim was desensitizing the Concerned Christians about death. Although the message was referring to war and evil men, I wondered if the message was intended to dull the victim's fear of destruction so that the Concerned Christians could become perfect vessels in the eyes of the Lord.

I hoped my fears wouldn't come to pass.

CHAPTER NINETY-EIGHT

▼

LOVING THE WORLD

Finally I was listening to the last audiotape. I didn't expect anything new but I remained hopeful that I would acquire additional insight to the Concerned Christians beliefs. Unfortunately, what I heard was more of the same message with emphasis on self. Actually, I thought it was ironic that Kim was giving a sermon on *self.*

Kim babbled on about self and how the fallen world system encompassed not only self but also the collective political system of man. In light of the promotional appeal to his message, I only heard the message that Kim wanted the listener to give up everything. And of course, I couldn't help but think of whom he was really thinking about. It wasn't our mothers, our fathers, our sons, or daughters. It wasn't the employer, the mortgage lender, or all the friends of the listener. My spirit told me that it certainly wasn't God. The God I knew wanted love and souls. No, It appeared to me that Kim's whole focus was on **self.** It was his ministry that would reap the rewards of the victim's sacrifice.

I sighed long and heavy and I typed the very last words of the audio-tapes. My exposure to Jan's life of subservience to Kim over the years had already prepared me for what the tapes said. Unfortunately, I couldn't present my counter-argument because Jan and John stopped responding to my email messages. In fact, everyone that I knew lost contact with the Concerned Christians.

The worst part was Jan was not calling Carol anymore. I couldn't imagine anyone suffering from the loss of Jan's communication more than Carol, except maybe Nicky.

PART VI

GIVING UP LIFE

CHAPTER NINETY-NINE

▼

CRACKED FOUNDATION

It was Friday, and I was finally finished listening to the dreaded voice on the tapes. Only one more month before summer, all plant life seemed to have turned green overnight. I felt uplifted with the weight of the tapes off my shoulders. The entire world was beautiful and I was thankful to God for everything, even for the exercise in perseverance in typing out the words on the Concerned Christian's tapes. Typing the tapes verbatim actually brought me closer to God, not because of Kim's divine knowledge but because his words compelled me to research the Bible for Truth and ask for God's guidance. I needed Him to show me where to go in the Bible, and He never disappointed me. I simply prayed before I opened the Bible and when I needed to research something that didn't quite sound right to me, the answers were there as if someone was pointing at the words. I was thankful that He gave me the gift of discernment and for showing me that He is a forgiving and loving God.

I walked into the kitchen and sat at the desk counter. I rummaged through the top drawer searching for some upbeat music. Ah, there it is, just the right one to change the mood. I placed *The Best of the Who* in the tape player and drifted in my mind to a better place. The last song was playing on the tape when I heard keys jingling outside the front door and quickly the door opened.

Nick walked in, took two steps and set his briefcase down. Unaccustomed to hearing music when he walked in the door his face brightened as he said to me with a toothy smile, "No more tapes of your favorite cult leader, huh?"

"No, praise the Lord, I'm done with them. I've always heard that the Lord only gives you what you can handle. In a way, I feel that I wasted valuable time away from Kristopher. He's only going to be with us two more months before he heads off for college. I'll miss him when he's gone. Kristopher's is my favorite distraction. I can't believe that I allowed Kim to rob *me* of six weeks of life as a mother. But I had to find out for myself if Kim had a profound message or if his words were just senseless rhetoric."

"At least Kim didn't rob you of spending the last two school years with your only child like he did Jan."

"Nick, You're right but that's the melody of life." I bent my back to try to relieve my discomfort. "My lower back is killing me from sitting all day and night."

"What do you mean the *melody of life?*"

"Well, a beautiful melody has high notes and low notes, long and short notes, and periods of no sound at all. Beautiful paintings have dark colors with contrasting light colors, bright and dull colors. I think that life is the same way, Nick. There are happy times. We all like happy times. But if people don't experience sadness and pain they never realize how happy they are. That's what I mean when I say *the melody of life*. The bad things that happen in a person's life make them appreciate the good things. That's why I praise the Lord for the bad things in my life as well as the good. Besides, the bad could always be worse. That's something to be thankful for, right?"

"Okay, Betty. You need to get some fresh air. I think we should celebrate by walking down to the lake. Why don't you grab a couple of cold bottles of water and we'll drink them when we get to the bench overlooking the lake."

"Sounds good to me. I don't feel like walking though, the little girl in me wants to run! I need to change my sedentary lifestyle."

"Well, tell that little girl to get her running shoes on so we can go!"

"No problem!" I ran up the stairs and searched through a mountain of shoes until I found a pair of old tennis shoes suitable for a muddy climb. I walked out of the bedroom and sat in the middle of the stairs in the hallway, "I feel good that I finished listening to the tapes. Now I need to move on. I need to piece all of this together and see if there is something I can do, something that will entice Jan and John to listen to me or at least talk to Carol. To the Concerned Christians I'm the antichrist or something. They are convinced that they are saints that will rule as priests and kings on the right hand of God. I just pray that the Lord graces them with that honor when they get to heaven. In the Concerned Christian's minds, they have suffered in His name."

I crossed my leg and tied my running shoes slightly off-center. "You would think that by now I could tie my shoes so that they wouldn't come undone."

Nick gazed back at the mountains toward Boulder as we walked toward the lake, "It's a shame that Kim put Jan and John through the unnecessary pain and suffering to earn their way to heaven.

We walked out of our yard and into Jefferson County Open Space, "I guess it was foolish to try to think that I could talk them out of Kim's clutches, maybe I should never have tried."

"First of all, you had to find out for yourself, Betty. If you didn't try to do everything you possibly could to reach them, this whole thing would have eaten at you for the rest of your life. In the Concerned Christian's minds and in their hearts, all of Kim's victims are suffering for God. I can't help but think that the Lord will hold them in high esteem, but Kim on the other hand…well, let's put it this way, the Lord isn't going to be pleased."

"I hope you're right, Nick. You know, I can't figure out if Kim has a personality disorder or if he is a crook. Of course I'm just guessing here Nick, but I don't think the Lord will be harsh on him if he's demented. But if Kim is intentionally deceiving people by taking their money and robbing each of them from a happy life with their families, the Lord's wrath will be horrendous."

"Here's the bench, hand me one of those bottles of water." Nick twisted off the cap and placed the cap in his pocket. "So, now what do you plan to do?"

I swallowed and shrugged at the same time, "I don't know, I guess I'll still try to reach Jan and John as long as I can. I don't want them to think that I've given up on them. I think that they have an undeniable flaw in their doctrine. We'll see what happens."

Surprised that I didn't tell him before, Nick looked at me with genuine interest, "What do you mean? What kind of flaw?"

"It's actually one that I realized before the tapes. The tapes didn't tell me anything that I either already knew or suspected. It bothers me that the Concerned Christian's pick and choose which commandments to honor. In so many words, they say that they do not have to honor their parents if their parents keep them from the Lord. You know that the Bible says that no one should add or subtract from the Ten Commandments in Deuteronomy 4:2, "Do not add to what I command you and do not subtract from it, but keep the commands of the Lord your God that I give you." I believe that the Bible says exactly what it means. The idea that the Concerned Christians do not have to honor their parents because of some little known verse that is taken out of context is unbiblical. Anyway, we'll see what happens from here, but I'm ready to accept that I've done everything in my power to reach them. I will leave their fate to the Lord."

"I think you've done enough, Betty, it's a spiritual war anyway.

CHAPTER ONE HUNDRED

▼

A SILENT CRY

Early the next morning, I was wakened by a telephone call from Mom. "Carol's not doing very well, she says she is bloated and uncomfortable. Carol cannot get in to see her doctor until next week. She's apparently going to get a "CAT scan" at that time but we will not know the results for about two weeks."

I sat up in bed as I heard each depressing word, "I'm so sorry, Mom. I wish I could do something."

"She doesn't want me to visit though. Carol insists that she will be just fine."

"I'm afraid that if I visited her, I would just remind her of Jan and the fact that Jan isn't around anymore." I paused as I thought of how badly Carol wanted to speak to Jan. "Carol always asks me if I've heard from Jan. You know Mom, of all the people in the family, Carol is the one who stays the closest to her roots. She keeps in contact with relatives that I haven't seen for thirty-five years. One phone call from Jan would put Carol in better spirits. Think of the peace of mind Carol would have if Jan would just visit Carol, Mom." I imagined Carol and Jan embracing and talking about one of their favorite past-times cooking. "It's sad, Jan is in bondage and although she loves Carol, she cannot leave Kim's clutches."

"I know, Betty. There's nothing we can do about Jan. She chose her path in life."

"Mom, It occurred to me that this is probably the first time that an alleged "cult" has been in contact with family members on a regular basis. Due to technology and to John's vast knowledge about computers, the Concerned Christians communicate with each other from all around the world. Imagine that, the electronic age of e-mail even changed the way "cults" do business. I don't know how I could have handled Jan's disappearance if I wouldn't have been able to communicate with her. I just wish Jan would e-mail Carol…it would mean so much to her."

"Well Betty, why don't you give Carol a call in a few days to see how she is doing? Let me know if there is anything that I can do."

Mom's voice cracked and my eyes filled with tears as I heard Mom struggle to say good-bye. Although I was sixty miles from Mom, we were strangely comforted with each other's words of kindness, but our sorrow seemed to be never-ending.

CHAPTER ONE HUNDRED-ONE

▼

DISTANT COMFORT

It was May 23, 2000 and I had been trying to reach Carol all week on the telephone but no one answered. I called at 10:30 am thinking that Carol would be awake after a full night's rest.

Sounding very weak and groggy Carol picked up the telephone, "Hello?"

"Oh Carol, I'm so sorry did I wake you up?" I said knowingly, as I rolled my eyes, gritted my teeth, and slammed my fist into the cushion on the couch.

"Yes, I haven't been feeling very well."

"You sound really tired, Carol, I'll let you go to bed, I just thought this would be a good time to call since you usually nap in the afternoon."

"No, I sleep all the time anymore. I'm not doing very well. If you wouldn't mind, I would like to go back to bed."

"I'll just talk to you another time. You have a good rest. Love you, Carol."

"I'm sorry, Betty. I love you."

I hung up the telephone. I felt bad that I disturbed Carol. I knew that Carol had bad days in the past, but the new chemo that she was taking was draining her energy. She was usually into the swing of things within a day or so after her treatment, but she wasn't rebounding back like she used to.

   After hanging up the telephone, I felt the urgency to make a trip to visit Carol...I needed to see her and soon.

CHAPTER ONE HUNDRED-TWO

▼

SUMMER STORM

The rain was pouring and lightning illuminated the sky. I ran outside to let the dogs in the house. Our youngest dog was psychotic and habitually freaked out every time dark clouds gathered in the sky. The lights in the house were flickering and the telephone lines were down. I sat a safe distance from the window and looked out at the misty shades of gray hovering over the lake's boundaries.

My mind drifted as I thought of Carol and I was thankful that I had my loving sister back in my life. But Carol was very ill and taking Tylenol with codeine, Percoset, and many other pills to counteract the symptoms of her cancer. I admired Carol's strength as I observed her struggle to maintain a positive outlook on life. Carol wanted to visit Jan again, she needed the comfort of her little sister Janet more than anything in the world.

As soon as the electrical storm was over I wrote to Jan. Jan needed to know that her big sister needed her. I suspected that Kim would read my email and convince Jan that my message was some sort of "spiritual blackmail," but I could not give up, I felt that Jan and Carol needed my intervention.

Date: Tuesday, May 23, 2000 3:50PM
To: Jan
From: Betty

Jan,

I thought you would want to know that Carol is very sick, her stomach is bloated and Mom tells me that she is getting a CAT scan today to find out what is causing her bloating. Carol told Mom that her stomach sticks out so far that she looks pregnant. We will not know the results of the CAT scan for at least another week. I asked Mom if grandma bloated before she passed on. Mom said that Grandma did, but it took a while.

I know that you must feel as bad as I do about Carol's condition. We need to pray for her. This is a time when she needs her family…together.

You will not be able to email Carol any longer because she discontinued her service, it was too expensive and I understand that you have stopped communicating with her anyway. I know that you could make a difference in Carol's life if you would just come home.

We love you very much, Jan. Do yourself a favor and get in touch with Carol if you can. I understand that most days Carol is so sick that she will not answer the telephone. Mom says she tries to sound cheery and upbeat in spite of her illness.

That's Carol…a true earthbound angel.

Love,
Betty

I felt good about writing to Jan and I prayed that she could contact Carol. All day long I wondered how Carol was feeling. I called Carol at 7:00 p.m. on March 25th to see if she was feeling any better. Jack answered the telephone, "Hello."

"Hi Jack, How's Carol doing?"

"Well, she's sleeping right now."

"Has she been sleeping all day?"

"Yep, I sure hope that she kicks this thing."

"I do too, she sure is having a rough time. I'll just call Carol another time, Jack, don't bother her."

"Carol will call you back Betty, she has a phone card you sent her. She has to use the phone card sometime, she might as well use it to call you."

"Or I can call Carol back later, Jack. I hope she feels better. You take care and I'll talk to you later."

"Okay, I'll tell Carol to call you. Good-bye."

My stomach churned, I could feel the tears swell in my eyes. God, I wish Carol didn't have to suffer. If only there was some way I could help her. I've got to go be with her for a while. I decided that I would drive out to see Carol during a long weekend…and soon.

The sun shone through the window reflecting on our Honduras mahogany dining table as I walked over to the telephone to try to call Mom for the seventh time in two days. "Did Mom tell me where she was going? As I grew older I realized that Mom frequently repeated herself. When Mom told me anything, I figured I would listen the next time she told me, I wondered if Mom repeated herself because she knew I wasn't listening. I searched my memory for the answer to where Mom was. Maybe I should drive to Greeley and see what's going on.

Two hours later I remembered that Mom was helping Aunt Betty while she recovered from surgery. Relieved, I left a message for Mom to call me when she came home.

Finally, the telephone rang at 8:00 p.m. "Betty? Didn't you remember I was staying at Aunt Betty's house?"

"Yeah Mom, I forgot, how is Aunt Betty anyway?"

"She's having some trouble with her legs, and she has fallen a couple of times. But I have some good news! I talked to Carol and she's doing good!"

Mom's voice was upbeat and happy. I always believed that Mom's happiness was directly proportional to how healthy and happy her children were. I paused for a moment then asked, "When did you talk to Carol?"

"I just talked to her early yesterday morning and she said she was just doing fine."

Sighing I said, "Mom, I talked to Carol this morning and to Jack this evening. Carol never got out of bed. I don't think she's doing very well. I think that I should go a see Carol real soon. I'm worried."

I heard Mom's voice gradually getting lower and slower as she was obviously disappointed that Carol was again feeling poorly, "Oh r e a l l y? I'm sorry to hear that. she sounded so good yesterday when I talked to her."

"Mom, I'm so worried about Carol."

"I know, I feel the same way."

I always felt bad when I told Mom bad news. I rationalized that I needed to tell Mom so she could make the decision whether or not to travel to see Carol. I became angry with myself for upsetting Mom. Why did I tell Mom anyway? She was enjoying her day. Feeling guilty for destroying Mom's good mood I said, "Well Mom, I didn't want to tell you but I thought you would like to know."

"Betty, I'm glad you keep me informed. I don't think Carol always tells me how she's feeling. I know she doesn't want me to worry."

I searched for something to say that would relieve the helplessness that Mom and I felt, I said, "All we can do is pray for Carol, the Lord will take care of her." I felt that I needed to change the subject, "So, you're leaving again to go to Aunt Betty's house?"

"Yes, and you have a good trip to Houston over Memorial weekend. Give that grandbaby a kiss for me."

"I will, Mom. I leave tomorrow. Nick and Kristopher left for Arizona today so Kristopher could compete in discus throwing at the Nationals. Kristopher's pretty excited. I hope he does well. Nick and Kristopher will be back on Sunday and I'll be back on Monday night."

"Good, maybe I'll see that baby when you come back then."

"Good! We'll plan on it, Mom. Take care.

CHAPTER ONE HUNDRED-THREE

▼

NOT TOO LATE

On May 26, 2000, my attorney called to let me know that there was a scheduled court hearing to review a petition to have Jan pay for some *past* expenses for Nicky. Every member of my family reacted like a junkyard dog to protect the remaining dab of money in Jan's conservatorship. My wound was freshly opened as each family member informed me that they did not approve of anyone but Nicky touching Jan's money, and only if the expense was legitimate. They reminded me that Jan and John's money was supposed to be held for them to renew their lives…if they ever returned.

Since the first petition notice, Carol was very protective about Jan's money. Carol wanted to make sure that the money in the conservatorship would go to Jan and not be squandered away by lawyers and relatives who did not have Jan and John's best interest in mind.

Since Carol was obviously too sick to travel, and the rest of the family either too ill or too far away to go to court, I had to represent all of them. I had to fight to protect Jan's remaining money. I faxed letters to Boulder District Court requesting that a court hearing not be granted. Why should

Jan have to pay for any court costs, particularly when the issue should have been settled years ago when Jan was in Boulder? I argued that the funds must be available for Jan upon her return…

Unfortunately, Nicky was in the middle of a feud over money. I became angry at the thought of the courts giving away money that I risked my valued relationships to save. For the first time I regretted petitioning for conservatorship. Maybe I should have let Jan have her money, then at least, Jan could have given her own money away instead of having the courts do it for her.

I took a deep breath. "Surely the courts will do the right thing. They wouldn't deplete Jan's funds for something that she was adamantly against!" Angry, I clinched my fists and squeezed until my knuckles turned white and my fingernails forged small crescent bruises in my palm. "If the court gives Jan's money away, I don't know how I will be able to cope. Why do I complicate my life? Why did Jan have to fall for Kim's lies?"

I knew that if Jan could see what I was going through, she would laugh. Jan would laugh at my humanistic, petty efforts to persuade Satan's court to protect her money.

The sound of the telephone broke the room's silence.

Jeez, the phones never stop ringing at this house! I search for the portable phone. Finally, I saw the telephone half hidden under the dust cover on the chair. I picked up the phone and pushed the "talk" button, "Hello?"

A weak voice responded, "Hello Betty? This is Carol."

"Hi Carol, how are you feeling today?"

I heard Carol crying on the other end and I couldn't quite make out what she was saying. I struggled to get rid of the static on the telephone. "I'm sorry, let me grab a hard-wired phone." I ran up the stairs and switched telephones. All I could hear was soft whimpering on the other end. "Carol? What's going on?"

"Oh Betty, I finally got that letter for the petition. I've signed the letter and I sent it off today. I'm afraid that it's too late."

"No, it isn't too late, Carol, I will send it overnight when I get it. Don't worry."

"I'm in a lot of pain, my doctor has prescribed some more medicine. I have diarrhea so bad today, and I've had it really bad for four days now. I am really weak. I called the doctor's office and the nurse scared me!"

"How did she scare you, Carol?"

"She asked me if I was weak and I told her I was. The nurse quickly told me that I should go to the hospital."

I heard a strange sound on the other end, like Carol was struggling to chuckle, as if she was about to say something funny, "I'm drinking everything in sight so that I can replenish my fluids. I didn't drink yesterday and I paid for it."

"That's a good thing to do, Carol. You should drink lots of fluids. How are you doing with the chemo? Are you still bloated?"

"They've got me on some good chemo, it's some stuff that has a proven tract record for breast cancer. There are five of us girls on it now. They think it will work for my kind of cancer too."

"That sounds promising, I hope it works," I could feel the lump in my throat growing so I quickly changed the subject. "Hey, do you think it would be okay for Nick and I to come visit you during Fourth of July? I thought we could drive down there. You wouldn't have to do anything. We'll stay somewhere else. Nick and I just want to visit you and Jack."

"I don't know what condition I'll be in by then."

"Well, I could help you. I could take you to chemo in St. Louis or something Carol. I want to help. Nick and I will just stay at a Bed and Breakfast or something."

"Jack doesn't mind taking me to chemo, Betty. There is a Bed & Breakfast near by."

"I'm sure Jack loves to be with you, Carol, no matter what you're doing together. About that petition to keep anyone from getting Jan's money, we'll pull together as a family and protect Jan, since Kim will not allow her to protect herself.

I could hear Carol sobbing again. Maybe I should just be quiet. Carol doesn't need to hear this from me.

"Well Betty, I wish I could do more to help Jan. Lord knows you have enough to do. You always have a lot on your plate."

"Everything will work out fine and if the courts award the money, then that's the way it will be."

Carol reflected back when Jan was deported from Greece and said, "When Jan got to the hotel in New York, she called me. Jan let it slip that John stopped taking his heart medicine when they came to America."

"Oh Carol, you're kidding me?"

"Yeah, I understand that the Concerned Christians are leaving their medical concerns for the Lord."

"Oh no! I'm sorry to hear that. I just wish Jan and John would come home. I sent Jan an e-mail the other day and told her that she needed to call you because you need to hear from her."

I could hear Carol sniff back her tears on the other end of the telephone, "I don't know why that dirty Kim won't let Jan talk to me."

An incredible wave of sadness filled my heart, I knew that Carol needed to hear from Jan. "I haven't heard back from Jan either. I understand that no one has received any messages from any of the cult members since April."

"Well Betty, I need to lie down again. It was good talking to you and I'll talk to you later."

"Okay Carol, you get some rest. I love you."

"I love you too. Bye."

I walked downstairs to check my email. As I watched the screen say "no messages" My anger turned toward Kim. Jan did not respond to my plea to contact Carol. The last time Jan contacted Carol was when she was in New York, relief of Carol's pain meant more to me than saving Jan from her pain. I hit "new messages" and began to type.

Date: *Friday, May 26, 2000 6:15 PM*
To: *John and Jan*
From: *Betty*
Subject: Carol

John and Jan,

Come home. You are missing opportunities to see your loved one alive. I know that Kim has told you that I am the devil's advocate. He has deceived you long enough.

*John, you need to take your medicine for your heart. Do not believe Kim any more. He doesn't care if you **die**, he will have everything that was once yours and will have robbed you of your loved ones. Come home before it's too late! Jesus Christ does not want you to do this to yourselves. **You are in a cult!***

I love you unconditionally,
Love,
Betty

I knew that Jan and I were at a stalemate and that we would never agree on doctrine. At least when we didn't agree before she left Denver we could agree to disagree.

I waited for a reply.

CHAPTER ONE HUNDRED-FOUR

▼

SEEING CAROL

By mid-July, our family lost the court battle to protect a portion of Jan's money from being awarded to a distant relative. It appeared that the courts saw Jan as a mother who deserted her only daughter and not as a person who was brainwashed. I noticed an alarming difference between how the two judges viewed Jan's predicament. The judge involved in awarding a conservator for Jan seemed to see Jan as a victim of her circumstance and the judge involved in distributing some of Jan's protected money seemed to view Jan as an undeserving mother who deserted her only child. I stood in front of the courtroom to defend Jan and to tell the judge that Jan was a good mother. But, the judge figured that Jan's bank account had enough funds to award the money and still leave Jan some money to live on…if and when she returns. Our family was disappointed that we lost our court battle, especially Carol.

Three months had passed since Carol last heard from Jan. Bobbi realized how important Jan's correspondence was to her mom so Bobbi set

Carol up with a new email account. Bobbi and I sent separate emails to Jan to let her know Carol's new email account.

On my subsequent telephone visits with Carol, she let me know that she checked her email and was waiting for Jan to write. She was disappointed each day that went by without a message from Jan.

Carol insisted that Jack needed to get away and take a little vacation. Carol talked to her doctors and arranged to make a trip to Colorado to visit the family. Carol and Jack drove from Licking, Missouri to Ft. Collins, Colorado and stayed at Bobbi and her husband, Dale's house. It was a difficult trip for Carol. She was accustomed to having her stomach pumped every week. Bobbi arranged for Carol to go to a hospital in Ft. Collins to have her stomach pumped and relieves her discomfort.

Carol made a special point to call and invite me to come to Bobbi's house and visit her. I was elated to have an opportunity to see Carol again since she didn't want anything to do with me the last time she was in town. Carol warned me that she did not look the same as she did before, she said that her hair was gone and that she lost a lot of weight. I tried to make Carol feel comfortable about her appearance and told her that I didn't look the same either. I told her that my hair was short and I had gained some weight since she last saw me. I told her that it didn't matter what we looked like, I couldn't wait to visit with her.

On the day of our scheduled visit, I drove sixty miles to see Carol. I gave myself a little pep talk and couldn't believe how nervous I was about seeing her. I decided to wear sunglasses into Bobbi's house because I didn't want Carol to detect my uneasiness. I didn't have any idea how I would react to Carol's appearance. I knew that I loved her no matter what she looked like but I feared that I would unintentionally hurt Carol's feelings through an involuntary look, or uncontrolled tears. Since she lost her hair, Carol had experienced a multitude of strange responses from people. Carol told me numerous times that she couldn't handle sympathy. She hated anyone displaying that kind of compassion toward her.

I walked up to Bobbi's house, and admired the pond that overlooked Horsetooth Reservoir. I decided that I could always change the subject and talk about the waterfall in the pond. Before I knocked on the door I heard someone tell me to come in. As I stepped in the door I smiled at Carol as she walked toward me. I was counting on the sunglasses to hide the tears in my eyes. I could never have prepared myself for this meeting. Carol was bald, frail, and very, very thin. Although dulled by illness, I recognized her dancing blue eyes and sweet smile. Carol wrapped her arms around me and said, "Oh Betty! You look just like Jan!"

I hugged her skeletal frame for an extended amount of time. I was happy that I looked like Jan to Carol. I wondered if my presence brought Jan a little closer to her, at least for the day. I regained my composure knowing that I could not wear the sunglasses much longer. "It's so good to see you, Carol. It's been a long time…too long."

"Yes it has. Come over her and sit so we can talk."

I said a few words to Bobbi and Jack but I mostly talked to Carol. We talked about the quilts that she made and how her children and grandchildren were doing. Carol said that she was hoping to move back to Colorado in March 2001 after Jack retired.

Carol made an extra effort to look like she was full of energy, even though she was obviously ill. I watched as Carol walked from the couch to the sink, and then to the bathroom, then finally back into the living room to rest in the chair next to me. She stayed only a few minutes before she stood up and walked over to the couch to lie down. I knew that Carol was trying hard to make me believe that she was doing fine. She seemed upbeat and energetic. If I didn't know better, I would have thought that she was fine…it almost seemed like old times.

I couldn't stay long, Carol took frequent naps and I didn't want to overtire her. I hated to tell her goodbye but I knew that I had to go. We promised that we would see each other again as we hugged each other and said that we loved one another.

I cried on the way home wondering if this visit was our last.

CHAPTER ONE HUNDRED-FIVE

▼

SENTENCE

It was 11:00 a.m. during the first week in August, and I had a strong urge to call Carol. No, I thought, Carol is probably sleeping. I'll wait and give her a quick call around 4:00, she usually makes supper at that time.

The telephone rang at 12:30. "Betty? It's Carol," she said softly.

I was naturally concerned about Carol's health, I could sense that something was wrong. I silently prayed that Carol did not have bad news for me. "Hi Carol, I was going to call you earlier, but I thought you would be sleeping."

"Well, I was probably on the telephone anyway, trying to settle a few things. How is that grandbaby?"

"Carol, Baby Nicholas is so cute, he's eleven months old now. He loves music, he waves his index fingers in the air when he dances as if he was conducting an orchestra. I just love that baby so much."

"Babies are really a joy. I wish I could see him. I bet he's cute."

"He really is. Hey, I tried to call you yesterday, were you at the doctor's office?"

"Yeah, I was. And I suppose some people already expect...that...uh...you know Betty, I can't bring myself to tell Mom..." Carol sobbed.

She didn't have to say anything more. I knew what she was going to say. I started to cry...trying not to let her hear my sniffling. I listened quietly so that I could learn what she found out from the doctor. "Okay," I choked.

"The doctor says that chemo will not help anymore. The doctor said there are two things he can do...oh, Betty. I'm not ready to go...." Carol took a deep breath as if to hold back the tears, "You know how I've been falling down lately and how my stomach as been filling with liquid? Well, the doctor says that the reason I'm having all this trouble is because of the cancer, not because of the chemo. The doctor says that he can continue to give me chemo...but it wouldn't help me, or he can just make me as comfortable as possible. The doctor says I'm terminal."

Overdosed on adrenaline, my natural fight or flight instinct made me want to run away from the news. I couldn't stand it. But, I knew that I had to be strong, so I mustered up all the strength that I could to prevent her from hearing the sorrow in my voice, "Oh Carol...I'm so sorry. Is there anything I can do?"

"I can't tell Mom. Would you mind? I suppose she already suspects it. You know how bad I looked when you saw me? Well, I guess it's as good as I'm ever going to look," as Carol broke down in tears.

I searched for an encouraging word. The silence was unsettling. I searched for a positive word, finally I sobbed, "Are you taking vitamins?"

"Yes, but they are really hard to get down. I've been drinking one of those full meals in a can and its seems to help, I hate the taste though."

Relieved at the sound of a hint of hope in Carol's voice, I added, "I'll look for you some stuff at the vitamin store. I bet I could find a liquid food supplement that would be good for you, Carol."

"The doctor said that there's a liquid medicine that I might be able to try."

"You know Carol, the doctors were wrong when they first told you that you had cancer. You've lived a lot longer than they suspected. This might be the same thing, maybe they're wrong. Maybe chemo isn't the answer, maybe there's something new, or who knows? Maybe the cancer will just take a long time. You just have to make sure you get your nutrients, Carol."

Carol agreed hesitantly, "Maybe you're right, Betty. Who knows?"

"Take care of yourself and we'll pray to God that you'll get better, Carol."

"Well Betty, that's all the news I have."

"I'll call you in a day or so. In the meantime take your vitamins. I love you Carol."

I could hear her crying harder as she said I love you and hung up the telephone. I couldn't stand to hold back the tears anymore so I let them flow as I walked upstairs. Moments later I realized that I subconsciously walked straight to the spare bedroom that displayed a beautiful heart covered quilt. As I lay on the quilt I realized the real reason why the quilt was called a "comforter." Carol must have known that I would find comfort in this quilt someday. It was the most beautiful quilt in the world, a special work of art in Carol's favorite color. Suddenly I felt like I was feeling all the love Carol intended as she hand-quilted the comforter for me…stitch by stitch.

I felt the overwhelming need to write Jan one more email and to plead with her to contact Carol. A loving word from Jan would mean so much to Carol. I had to let Jan know…

Date: *September 6, 2000*
To: *Jan and John*
From: *Betty*
Subject: *Carol*

Dear Jan,

   Please call Carol and tell her that you love her. You may never get another chance.

Love you forever,
Betty

CHAPTER ONE HUNDRED-SIX

▼

TERMINAL

It was September 14, 2000, I just finished work when the telephone rang…it was Mom, she struggled back the tears, "Betty, I just checked my messages, Jack called a few hours ago. Things look grim. Jack sounded very distraught and asked me if I would come and visit them for a while."

"He did? Oh Mom!"

"Apparently, Carol is falling down a lot and she is having a hard time taking care of herself while Jack is at work. She fell the other day and thought that she would have to yell out at the mailman to come in the house to help her get back up. Jack considered getting some help from the hospice, but Carol is afraid that they will take away her pills, without the pills, her pain would be unbearable."

Tears rolled down my cheeks, "The doctor told Carol that he could just keep her comfortable with pain pills. Mom, I think that you should be with her."

"Okay Betty, you know that we have to brace ourselves," Mom said quietly.

"I know. A person is never prepared for this kind of news. I'll call the airlines and see how much a ticket will cost, last minute travel is usually pretty expensive."

"Jack said that he has some air-miles that I can use, Betty."

"Let me see what I can do, Mom."

I thought about what the doctor told Carol. "You know, mom, I don't think the doctor should have told Carol that she was going to die. I think he robbed Carol of some quality time. Twelve years ago, her cancer was diagnosed as terminal. She survived then, she can survive now."

"Carol needed to know, Betty."

"It's obvious that she is struggling to fight the cancer. She has lost a tremendous amount of weight and her stomach is bloating. I just don't think the doctor should have told her. Now Carol will be depressed all the time, her quality of life is gone."

"Well there are arrangements to be made, Betty. Carol needs to finalize some business." Mom reasoned.

"I know. I just think the bad news adds to Carol's problem. Anyway, I'll call you after I call the airlines."

After hanging up the telephone, I searched to find the best airfare, but I could not find an affordable flight on short notice. Finally, I made up my mind to drive Mom to Missouri. I needed to see Carol too. Driving was a lot cheaper than flying and I took off the next two days from work. I decided that I could drive down to Missouri, spend the night, and drive back to Colorado the next day to avoid missing any more work. I sighed as I wished that I had not used up my vacation earlier in the year. I wanted to spend more time with Carol.

Mom drove to Arvada that evening and spent the night at my house so we could leave early the next morning. I enjoyed visiting with Mom especially through eastern Colorado and western Kansas.

When we pulled in Carol and Jack's driveway at 10:30 p.m., it was obvious that Carol and Jack were appreciative that Mom was staying with them. They were both awake and waiting for us to arrive. Carol was standing with her walker when we entered the front door. I was sure that she was making a valiant attempt to prove to us that she was feeling fine, but we knew better. Carol had lost a significant amount of weight since the last time I saw her. She smiled and welcomed Mom and I into her warm home. I wished that we could have arrived earlier so that we could visit, but we were beat from the drive and Carol and Jack needed to rest.

A few minutes after everyone was in bed, I overheard Carol tell Jack, "I'm glad Betty is here, I could just talk to her all night. I don't see enough of her."

There was a long pause, then I heard Jack say, "If we can just get by until next March, then I can retire and we can take care of each other for the rest of our lives."

I smiled as I thought of how wonderful it was to be with Carol again. I prayed that the good Lord would bless her, take away her pain, and give Jack and Carol more wonderful years together.

I fell asleep praying.

CHAPTER ONE HUNDRED-SEVEN

▼

WRONG PRIORITIES

When I woke up the next morning, Carol insisted on cooking. She positioned her walker directly in front of the stove as I stood by her side and assisted her by giving her spices and utensils on demand. Cooking was one of Carol's favorite ways of showing her family that she loved them. I bowed my head and quietly thanked the Lord for giving me the opportunity to participate in an activity that we both enjoyed and could share with everyone.

Carol, Mom, and I gathered in the living room after we ate. Carol had something on her mind and I could tell that she was struggling with whether to share her thoughts with me. She gradually gave me information about Jan and the Concerned Christians. She said that Jan and John came to Missouri to try to get her and Jack to join the Concerned Christians. All four of them met at a RV camp. The events that happened during the meeting were vague, but it was clear that Jack wasn't interested in leaving everything behind to join Jan and John and the Concerned Christians.

Carol paused for a few minutes and seemed to be agonizing over whether to tell me more information about Jan. Finally, Carol said that Jan called one day and said that it was common practice for the Concerned Christians to confide in one person when they had problems or felt conflicted. Although many of the Concerned Christians talked to Jan about their issues, Jan was disturbed that she did not have anyone to confide in. Jan asked Carol to be her confidante.

Carol mentioned something about Kim's son elevated status in the church. I had a hard time figuring out what it was that Carol really wanted me to know. Carol paused. I noticed her expression change. She looked troubled. It was then that I suspected that Carol knew important information about Jan. I watched for a few minutes as Carol agonized over whether or not to tell me. I wondered if Carol was conflicted because she feared that if she were to die, the message she had about Jan would never be heard, or worse yet, the information would be discovered too late. The mysterious facts aroused my curiosity and I wondered if I could protect Jan if the truth were known. But, as Carol became increasingly uncomfortable about breaching Jan's confidence, I couldn't watch Carol's anguish any longer.

At least I could take away this discomfort, I thought as I said, "Carol, we can talk later, you should get some rest."

After a while, Carol relaxed and drifted off to sleep. When she awoke, we visited for only a short time before I mentioned that I had to head home. Carol seemed surprised that I was leaving so soon. I stayed a few short minutes longer. As I said farewell, I wondered if I would regret my decision to leave my beautiful sister.

I pulled Mom to the side and said, "Be sure to take care of yourself, Mom. I'll call when I get home and everyday to see how things are going. Please let me know if you need anything. You know, maybe you and Carol can play cards, listen to some soft music, or something. It's too quiet here, there's too much time to think of death and dying. Maybe you can try to lighten Carol's spirits a little and get her mind off her illness."

I detected a little doubt in Mom's eyes as I watched her nod her head in agreement. Maybe I was living in a fantasy world. I was used to Carol living life to the fullest. She enjoyed her farm animals, her family, and everything life had to offer her. All her joy was replaced by the cold silence of her impending doom.

I kissed Mom good-bye and walked over to Carol and said, "Listen, I'll be back here for your birthday, Carol. Do me a favor and keep those quilts coming. I know you are having a tough time seeing your stitches, I'll buy you a lamp so that you can sew without straining your eyes. You make such beautiful quilts. I'll be sure to get you the lamp by Wednesday."

Carol gave me a weak nod. I didn't know if my suggestion to her to keep sewing was something that she knew was physically impossible or if she was just tired. I looked forward to seeing her again and prayed that she would feel better when I returned. We had to make up for valuable lost time…time lost when I petitioned for a conservator for Jan…time that I felt Kim indirectly stole from us.

I loaded my luggage in my car and glanced back at the house and I noticed that I could see Carol through the window busily working on the final touches to a quilt designed especially for a dear friend. The image of Carol was etched into my memory.

CHAPTER ONE HUNDRED-EIGHT

▼

STRANGE PHENOMENON

I wanted to be close to Carol, but the best I could do was to call her every day. In the beginning, Carol talked to me, always mentioning how much she missed Jan and wished that she could talk to her again. I wondered if Carol needed to talk to Jan because of what Jan told her in confidence. But, Carol was so weak that I couldn't risk traumatizing her over a discussion about Jan. I felt helpless. I couldn't take away Carol's physical pain caused by her cancer, or her emotional pain caused by the loss of contact with her sister.

It was the beginning of October when Mom called. I was surprised to hear Mom's upbeat voice on the other end of the telephone. "There is something happening to Carol, we think it might be a good thing. Let me get Carol on the telephone so that she can tell you the news."

With uncertain promise in her voice, Carol said, "Betty, I'm not as bloated as I was before. A strange thing is happening."

"What's that, Carol?"

"Well, I don't feel as uncomfortable as before because my stomach is not filling up with liquid as fast. It's weird though, I have fluid coming out of my feet."

"You've got fluid coming out of your feet? How can that happen?"

"I don't know, my skin is really dry and the liquid just comes out of my feet, I guess through my cracked skin. But I'm not as bloated as I was before."

"That's a good sign then, huh?"

"I think so, Betty. I pray it is."

"Me too, Carol."

"I'm very tired, Betty. I have to get some rest now. I'll talk to you tomorrow. I love you."

"I love you too. I hope you have a good rest."

Carol's feet continued to excrete liquid and it became obvious that she was deteriorating. After a short while, Carol and my telephone conversations became shorter and shorter and eventually, Mom relayed my messages to Carol because she was too weak to talk. Every day I left a variation of the same message, "Tell Carol that I am thinking of her, and that I love her very much. I'm praying that her pain goes away and that she feels better soon."

Each day Mom tried to tell me that Carol was getting worse, but I was in denial. Carol wanted to live and I believed that through the power of God, Carol would conquer cancer.

CHAPTER ONE HUNDRED-NINE

▼

HEAVEN'S NEW ANGEL

At 5:30 a.m. on Monday, October 16th, Mom called and said that Carol had passed on. Tears shot out of my eyes and streamed down my face as my heart ripped in two. Although, I was thankful that the Lord relieved Carol from her suffering, I knew that I would miss Carol for the rest of my life. My heart ached for her devoted husband, and beautiful sons, daughter, and mother.

CHAPTER ONE HUNDRED-TEN

▼

ETERNAL SISTER

Whether physical or through cult practices, death is the greatest felon…robbing individuals of the zest of love and precious time on earth with God ordained loved ones. It dawned on me that toward the end of Carol's life, my sister's lives paralleled. I listened to both Carol and Jan struggle with giving up their lives, their loved ones, and everything that they held dear in this world.

I vowed to continue my quest to penetrate through the invisible fortress that shielded Jan and John from enjoying their mothers, their daughters, their son, and family and friends who loved them. I prayed that I could reach Jan and John so that they could honor their mothers before it was too late, to celebrate life, and cherish their fleeting time on earth.

CHAPTER ONE HUNDRED-ELEVEN

▼

HEAVEN BOUND

Mom said that Carol is in Heaven playing with baby Nancy.

Sometimes when I'm alone and missing my sisters, I picture them with God, healthy and fully restored. I imagine Jan reaching up into the air to touch Carol and Nancy's glowing hands. The three of them cup their hands together while Daddy looks on and laughs. He watches Jan, Carol, and Nancy toss their heads back and giggle as they twirl around in a circle and dance…looking forward to the day when the rest of us will join them in Heaven.

It's the best way I know how, to be close to them.

About the Author

▼

A Colorado native, Betty J. R. Chavez has two sons and a grandson, and resides with her husband in Arvada, Colorado. Betty is the youngest daughter in a family of six children. She is an advocate of family values and enjoys biking, reading, snow skiing and fishing with her husband. She is a nationally recognized career professional in areas of management and nondestructive testing and is an accomplished technical writer.

Printed in the United States
1010500003B